Christianity and Neo-Liberalism

Christianity and Neo-Liberalism

The Spiritual Crisis in the
Orthodox Presbyterian Church and Beyond

Paul M. Elliott

The Trinity Foundation

Christianity and Neo-Liberalism
The Spiritual Crisis in the
Orthodox Presbyterian Church and Beyond
Copyright © 2005 Paul M. Elliott
All rights reserved.

The author can be contacted by e-mail at
pelliott@teachingtheword.org

Published by
The Trinity Foundation
Post Office Box 68
Unicoi, Tennessee 37692
www.trinityfoundation.org
ISBN: 0-940931-68-0

Contents

Part Three: The Growth of Neo-Liberalism

CONTENTS

CONTENTS

Appendices

Chapter 1

A Little Leaven

You ran well. Who hindered you from obeying the truth?
This persuasion does not come from Him who calls you.
A little leaven leavens the whole lump.
Galatians 5:7-9

Members of the medical profession will tell anyone willing to listen that cancer is a silent enemy. It begins undetected and unrecognized. Physicians have learned that much of their success in treating cancer depends on early diagnosis. Otherwise, treatment is usually a losing battle.

Doctors say that cancer's three great allies are ignorance of the nature of the disease, complacency when warning signs are present, and denial when it is clear that something is wrong. Often, people are simply not willing to listen. As one Canadian health care report put it, "We need hard-hitting information to break through ignorance, complacency, and denial."[1]

Like cancer in the human body, liberalism in the body of the church begins undetected and unrecognized. By the time Christians who are still true to the Word of God recognize the cancer of liberalism and are stirred to action, often it is too late to stop its deadly progress. The damage has been done, and a spiritual crisis is upon the church.

1. Division of Aging and Seniors, Health Canada, *Workshop on Healthy Aging: Aging and Health Practices* (Ottawa: Minister of Public Works and Government Services Canada, 2002), 32.

The Orthodox Presbyterian Church is now in such a spiritual crisis, and the crisis has spread well beyond it. The crisis centers on the conflict between authentic Biblical Christianity and an Antichristian counterfeit. The church needs to understand the nature of the crisis, how it came about, its deadly effects, and what Scripture says must be done. That is the purpose of this book.

Neo-Liberalism Defined

The cancer of liberalism – or to put it in 21st century terms, neo-liberalism – has grown and spread, slowly and subtly, for at least three decades in the OPC. *Neo-liberalism is the denial of fundamentals of authentic Biblical Christianity by reputedly conservative churchmen, who simultaneously claim that they remain completely faithful to Scripture and to the doctrinal standards of their churches.* Neo-liberals pretend to be what they are not, and profess to believe what they do not.

Neo-liberalism principally manifests itself in the denial of the full inerrancy, infallibility, and authority of Scripture, and denial of the Gospel doctrine of justification by faith (mere belief) in Christ alone. But from those two fundamental errors, the cancer of neo-liberalism spreads to corrupt sound teaching on other foundational truths. We shall define the marks of neo-liberalism in more detail in the next chapter.

This is not to say that neo-liberals shout their denials of authentic Biblical Christianity from the housetops. Speaking of the neo-liberal attack on the doctrine of justification by faith alone, Dr. E. Calvin Beisner told students at Knox Theological Seminary:

Today, that doctrine is under attack even within Reformed circles. My saying so should not prompt you to look for articles in Reformed theological journals or popular magazines or at Reformed websites bearing titles like "Four Reasons Why I Renounce *Sola Fide*" or "A Biblical Critique of the Doctrine of Justification By Faith Alone." No, error cloaks itself in the language of orthodoxy. Those who are the greatest threat to *sola fide* do not explicitly reject the doctrine by name, as Roman Catholics do, but affirm it while redefining its terms.[2]

The Apostle Paul had this kind of insidious apostasy in mind when he warned the elders at Ephesus:

> Therefore take heed to yourselves and to all the flock, among which the Holy Spirit has made you overseers, to shepherd the church of God which He purchased with His own blood. For I know this, that after my departure savage wolves will come in among you, not sparing the flock. Also from among yourselves men will rise up, speaking perverse things, to draw away disciples after themselves [*Acts* 20:28-30].

Most pastors and elders of the OPC have not heeded this warning. Their ignorance of the nature of the crisis, complacency despite many warning signs, and denial even when confronted with clear evidence of serious departures from Biblical truth have facilitated neo-liberalism's quiet advance. Conditions in the present-day OPC parallel those that existed in the Presbyterian Church in the U. S. A. in the

2. E. Calvin Beisner, "Norman Shepherd and the Faith that Justifies," www.knoxseminary.org/Prospective/Faculty/KnoxPulpit/cbeisner_faith .html.

13

1920s and 1930s. The PCUSA was then being consumed by the cancer of the old liberalism, often referred to as modernism. In 1936, after a long struggle, a remnant committed to the truths of authentic Biblical Christianity separated from the PCUSA to form the OPC. But today the OPC has become corrupted by the same sins as the PCUSA of three generations ago. The mistakes of history are being repeated.

The OPC and Westminster Seminary

The OPC and its quasi-official ministerial training ground, Westminster Theological Seminary (WTS) in Philadelphia,[3] exert an influence in the Christian community far greater than numbers would suggest. The OPC is a small denomination comprising just over 300 congregations and approximately 28,000 members, but it has been highly influential because of its reputation for conservatism and scholarship. Westminster in Philadelphia is not the largest Reformed seminary, but it has become known as "the Harvard of conservative seminaries."

Over 200 WTS graduates currently serve in the pulpits of the Orthodox Presbyterian Church. Many others are ministers in the Presbyterian Church in America (PCA) and other denominations and independent churches. Ordained OPC ministers and WTS graduates hold dozens of faculty and key administrative positions in seminaries and Christian colleges throughout North America and on other continents, through which they have influenced thousands of students over the past several decades. WTS faculty and

3. Not to be confused with Westminster Seminary California (WSC), which has its roots in WTS Philadelphia but has become separate and independent.

14

alumni have produced a sizable share of the Reformed theological literature of the past several decades, as well as many books for the general Christian audience.

Over seventy percent of the faculty of Westminster itself are men who were trained at the seminary. Nearly half of the faculty members also have degrees from "mainstream" liberal seminaries and universities such as Cambridge, Chicago Theological Seminary, Columbia, Dartmouth, Harvard, Princeton, Rutgers, and Yale that are openly (and often aggressively) hostile to authentic Biblical Christianity.

Most people in the Christian community at large, as well as in the OPC itself, mistakenly believe that the OPC and WTS remain bulwarks of conservative theology. They assume that both still follow the path charted by their leading founder, J. Gresham Machen, who was guided by the principle that "the Bible forbids a man to substitute any human authority for the Word of God."[4] Few in the OPC, or in the Christian church at large, understand that the OPC and WTS have long since taken a different path, the path of neo-liberalism, and that this has led the OPC to its spiritual crisis. In some cases, this misunderstanding results from lack of information; in other cases, from misinformation. But in still other cases, as we shall see, it stems from disinformation – that is, misinformation deliberately disseminated by church leaders to conceal the facts and history of the crisis.

In chapter two we shall examine Machen's description of the distinguishing characteristics of liberalism in the 1920s and 1930s. We shall see how present-day neo-liberalism strikingly parallels the old liberalism, but with contem-

4. J. Gresham Machen, "Statement to the Presbytery of New Brunswick" in *J. Gresham Machen: Selected Shorter Writings*, D. G. Hart, editor. (Phillipsburg, New Jersey: P&R Publishing Company, 2004), 340.

porary points of emphasis and new subtleties. In later chapters, we shall examine neo-liberalism's corrupting influence on the OPC and other denominations.

Principal Facts of the Crisis

One needs to understand just three principal facts of the situation in order to comprehend the crisis in broad terms. These are facts that neo-liberals do not wish Christians in the OPC to recognize, much less act upon.

The first principal fact is that the Orthodox Presbyterian Church has permitted two ways of salvation to be taught for over thirty years. During the past three decades, "another gospel" of justification by faith in Christ plus works has moved from quiet protection to open endorsement within the OPC. Because the OPC, despite repeated opportunities, has not dealt with this error, its corrupting influence has spread beyond its boundaries into other churches and denominations. The OPC bears grave responsibility for the spread of this heresy which has come to be known by various names – among them Shepherdism, covenantal nomism, and Federal Vision theology.

The so-called New Perspective on Paul (NPP) is another current in the same river of error regarding the doctrine of justification. Although its roots in mainstream academia go back to the 1960s and its intellectual antecedents go back into the nineteenth century, James Dunn of the University of Durham (Britain) coined the term "New Perspective on Paul" in 1982. Professor E. P. Sanders of Duke University has contributed much to the development of New Perspective theology. N. T. Wright, Anglican Bishop of Durham, has done a great deal to popularize it, even among American evangelicals. Some neo-liberals who endorse the teachings of Norman Shepherd have also embraced the NPP. But other Shepherd supporters, such as Richard B. Gaffin, Jr., of Westminster Seminary in Philadelphia, have sought to distance themselves from the New Perspective.[5] However, as far as the doctrine of justification is concerned, this is a distinction without a difference. Although they begin from different starting points, both Shepherdism and the New Perspective on Paul arrive at the same wrong destination on the doctrine of justification and all other elements of the Gospel. Furthermore, as we shall see in chapter six, Richard Gaffin has his own "new perspective on Paul" which is not so different from that of Dunn, Sanders, and Wright.

Shepherdism and the New Perspective on Paul equally qualify as "another gospel" on the most basic grounds: both teach justification by faith plus works. By permitting both brands of error to be taught and tolerated, the OPC has compromised the foundational doctrine of justification by faith alone. This is the doctrine by which Martin Luther rightly said the church either stands or falls. We shall discuss this development in more detail in chapters five through seven.

The second important fact is that the OPC has imperiled the teaching of sound doctrine across the board, by abandoning sound principles for interpreting the Scriptures in favor of what it calls "a hermeneutic of trust." This development helped pave the way for the encroachment of another gospel. But neo-liberalism is far wider in scope than the justification controversy. Under the influence of the "hermeneutic of trust," an ever-broadening range of doctrines has become fair game for un-Biblical revision in the OPC. In addition to justification by faith alone, the doctrines under attack in-

5. Richard B. Gaffin, Jr, "Paul the Theologian," *Westminster Theological Journal* 62 (2000), 121-141.

clude creation, the covenants, the church, election, baptism, imputed righteousness, sanctification, glorification, and the Last Judgment. These doctrines are all forever settled in the Word of God, and long affirmed in the plain meaning of the confessional standards of the church. But those plain meanings are under attack. We shall discuss this development in more detail in chapter eight.

The third important fact is that the spread of another gospel and the abandonment of Scriptural authority in the OPC are dividing the church. Neo-liberals (and even some conservatives) have become increasingly outspoken in labeling the opponents of neo-liberalism as the ones causing division. But this allegation perverts the Scriptural definition of schism. It is the neo-liberals, not conservatives, who have brought division to the church. They have overthrown the peace and unity of the church by destroying its doctrinal purity. Martyn Lloyd-Jones noted that the Apostle Paul had

> no hesitation in condemning those who "preach another
> gospel" or in commanding separation from those who
> do not follow the apostolic teaching. (See, for example,
> 2 *Thess.* 3:6; 2 *Cor.* 6:14-18; 2 *John* 10-11, and, indeed, the
> whole of John's *First Epistle.*)[6]

Elsewhere in his writings, Dr. Lloyd-Jones directs the church's attention to *Romans* 16:17-18:

> Now I urge you, brethren, note those who cause divi-
> sions and offenses, contrary to the doctrine which you

6. D. M. Lloyd-Jones, "Maintaining the Evangelical Faith Today" in *Knowing the Times: Addresses Delivered on Various Occasions 1942-1977* (Edinburgh: Banner of Truth Trust, www.banneroftruth.co.uk, 1989), 47. Though they were delivered many years ago, several of these addresses are highly relevant to the present crisis.

learned, and avoid them. For those who are such do not serve our Lord Jesus Christ, but their own belly, and by smooth words and flattering speech deceive the hearts of the simple.

J. Gresham Machen understood that separation from apostasy is not schism. Rather, Machen said that remaining in a church that has departed from the faith is itself an act of schism, because it separates the believer from his fellow believers within true churches of Jesus Christ.[7] Schismatics are those who teach things contrary to sound doctrine, not those who mark them and avoid them.

Despite the efforts of conservatives committed to the one true Gospel, the full authority of Scripture, and the unity and peace of the body of Christ, neo-liberalism has come to dominate the theology of the OPC and has spread beyond it. There are still churches within the OPC that stand without compromise for authentic Biblical Christianity. But they exist in an overall environment of deepening error on foundational doctrine, an environment devoid of any sign of denominational repentance. These local churches are like still-healthy organs in a body increasingly ravaged by cancer. Once the body is overwhelmed, even still-healthy organs are deprived of life.

To call the situation a crisis is no overstatement. This is not a situation involving minor matters, or disagreements on issues where faithful men within the body of Christ may legitimately differ. As we shall see in later chapters, the OPC is now on record with its departures from both the Gospel and the full authority of Scripture. On such matters, there can be no differences within Christ's church.

7. Ned B. Stonehouse, *J. Gresham Machen: A Biographical Memoir* (Grand Rapids, Michigan: Wm. B. Eerdmans Publishing Company, 1954), 494.

CHRISTIANITY & NEO-LIBERALISM

Neo-Liberalism's Strategies

Until recently, Ronald Reagan's description of Communism's tactics in the political realm[8] also applied to neo-liberalism's tactics in the church. Like the Communists in the political arena, neo-liberals in the church have historically made each advance just small enough so that the opposition would say, "This one isn't worth fighting over." Neo-liberals have long taken advantage of their opponents' timidity to further their objectives bit by bit. While making much of "preserving the peace and unity of the church" they have all the while been systematically destroying the foundations of its doctrinal purity.

In this way, the malignancy of neo-liberal thinking has spread gradually, over a period of decades. It began in seminary classrooms, principally at Westminster in Philadelphia, where neo-liberal professors have now taught generations of students. It has moved from there to the pulpits of the OPC and other churches, as those students have entered the ministry or gone to the mission field. It has spread from pulpits to pews, Sunday after Sunday, month by month, year by year, as those ministers have preached to their people based on the patterns of neo-liberal thinking that formed the foundation of their seminary training. It has spread to other seminaries as men trained in neo-liberal thought have taken teaching positions in them. In the course of time, the cancer has spread to the committees and agencies of the church as neo-liberals and their sympathizers have gained positions of leadership and authority.

Christians in the OPC need to understand that the main

8. Peter Schweizer, *Reagan's War* (New York: Anchor Books, 2002), 35.

dangers to their church are not external, but internal. Martyn Lloyd-Jones asked,

> What have we to say to those who argue that in view of the urgency of the times and the [external] dangers threatening the church, we must all get together and minimize our differences, no matter what they may be? Our answer is that the Bible warns us against this very thing. In *Acts* 20:17-35 we have a clear outline of the duty of the overseers in the church of Christ. St. Paul warns the elders of the church in Ephesus that "grievous wolves" would come, and men would arise from among the number of their own church "speaking perverse things, to draw away disciples after them." Such warnings run right through the New Testament, from the words of our Lord in the *Gospels* to the last pages of the *Revelation*, where almost the last words of the book warn the reader not to add to, or to subtract from its words. The Christian has been told to expect false prophets within the church and he is clearly told to contend for the true faith, to fight for it. He is to beware of all that leads the church astray.[9]

In recent years, some in the OPC have once more heeded the Holy Spirit's call to "contend earnestly for the faith which was once for all delivered to the saints. For certain men have crept in unnoticed..." (*Jude* 3-4). They have begun to publicly withstand the neo-liberals. In response, neo-liberals have shifted their tactics from subtle advancement to open aggression. They are more openly promoting their heresies through public conferences, guest lectures at colleges and seminaries, books and magazines, radio and tele-

9. D. M. Lloyd-Jones, "Maintaining the Evangelical Faith Today," in *Knowing the Times*, 42.

vision, and the Internet. Neo-liberals have long used parliamentary maneuvers in church sessions, presbyteries, and general assemblies to impede and silence conservative opposition, but in recent years they have done this more frequently and with open belligerence.

They have labeled men who have called for a return to authentic Biblical Christianity in the OPC as unethical, intolerant, mean-spirited, unfaithful to their ordination vows, spiritual adulterers, and worse. When conservatives have done nothing more than to expose neo-liberalism by naming names, and accurately stating facts associated with those names that are on the public record, neo-liberals have loudly (but un-Biblically) protested that this somehow violates the ninth commandment or *Matthew* 18:15-17. Neo-liberals have accused the conservative opposition of "fierceness" and of having "made it a virtue not to listen to others."[10] Neo-liberals have said that those who oppose their false teachings are "stupid, irresponsible, and divisive" and "do not have the intellectual, theological, or spiritual maturity to prepare students for gospel ministry."[11] Neo-liberals have attempted to have presbyteries declare that faithful pastors, whose only "sin" is to stand for the truth of the Gospel, are no longer ministers of the Gospel. Neo-liberals have told those who have separated from the denomination in obedience to Scripture that they have not merely left the OPC, but have left the Church of Jesus Christ.

10. James S. Gidley, "Quick to Hear, Slow to Speak, Slow to Anger," *New Horizons in the Orthodox Presbyterian Church*, Vol. 25, No. 6 (June 2004), 8.

11. John M. Frame, Foreword titled "A Note on Norman Shepherd, Covenant and Justification" in *Backbone of the Bible: Covenant in Contemporary Perspective* (Nacogdoches, Texas: Covenant Media Press, 2004), xii.

In Which Group Are You?

Various groups of people inside and outside the OPC will respond in differing ways to the crisis. Pastors, elders, and the general membership of the OPC fall into four broad groups in relation to the crisis. This book is a call to action for each of them.

First, this book is addressed to those in the OPC who have been truly unaware of the rise of neo-liberalism in their denomination.

In this group are a few pastors, many elders, and perhaps most members of OPC congregations. How is it that so many are so uninformed? There are numerous reasons, among them the following.

In the larger picture, the denominational leadership of the OPC bears much of the responsibility for keeping many of its elders and members in the dark. Official histories of the OPC are largely devoid of any discussion of some of the deepest controversies that have occurred along the path to the present crisis. When those chapters of the story are dealt with at all, the treatment all too often takes the form of propaganda favorable to the neo-liberal cause, rather than factual history recounted in the light of Scripture.[12]

In the local church setting, many pastors and sessions have simply wished to avoid controversy. Some of those pastors have known the facts of the crisis but have hesitated to discuss them with their sessions. In other cases, pastors have informed their elders, but the sessions have chosen not to make the facts known to their congregations.

12. See John W. Robbins, *Can the Orthodox Presbyterian Church Be Saved?* (Unicoi, Tennessee: The Trinity Foundation, 2004), which includes an extensive critique of the writings of official OPC historians.

Some pastors and sessions have kept quiet because they actually fear that their people will awaken to action. Some say that their cover-up – and that is the accurate term for it – is motivated by a desire to maintain peace and unity in the church. But keeping God's people in ignorance actually undermines the doctrinal purity without which true peace and unity cannot exist.

Some other pastors and sessions have remained silent because of a misconception about Presbyterian polity. Practically speaking, they have adopted the posture that "good churchmanship" requires them to keep silent in the face of evil, not only in their local churches but even in their presbyteries and general assemblies. That only plays into the hands of neo-liberals who stand ready to manipulate church law and the rules of parliamentary procedure to further their ends.

Machen addressed these and several related points in remarks to the Bible League of Great Britain in 1932. I quote him at length because his statement is so very pertinent to the present crisis in the OPC:

> In the first place, [our defense of the faith] should be directed not only against the opponents outside the church but also against the opponents within. The opponents of Holy Scripture do not become less dangerous, but they become far more dangerous, when they are within ecclesiastical walls.
>
> At that point, I am well aware that widespread objection arises at the present time. Let us above all, men say, have no controversy in the church; let us forget our small theological differences and all repeat together Paul's hymn to Christian love. As I listen to such pleas, my Christian friends, I think I can detect in them rather

plainly the voice of Satan. That voice is heard, sometimes, on the lips of good and truly Christian men, as at Caesarea Philippi it was heard on the lips of the greatest of the Twelve. But Satan's voice it is, all the same.

Sometimes it comes to us in rather deceptive ways.

I remember, for example, what was said in my hearing on one occasion.... "If you go heresy-hunting for the sin in your own wicked hearts," said the speaker, as nearly as I can remember his words, "you will have no time for heresy-hunting for the heretics outside."

Thus did temptation come through the mouth of a well-meaning man. The "heretics," to use the term that was used by that speaker, are, with their helpers, the indifferentists, in control of the church within the bounds of which that utterance was made.... A man hardly needs to "hunt" them very long if he is to oppose them. All that he needs to do is to be faithful to the Lord Jesus Christ, and his opposition to those men will follow soon enough.

But is it true, as this speaker seemed to imply, that there is a conflict between faithfulness to Christ in the ecclesiastical world and the cultivation of holiness in one's own inner life? My friends, it is not true, but false. A man cannot successfully go heresy-hunting against the sin in his own life if he is willing to deny his Lord in the presence of the enemies outside. The two battles are intimately connected. A man cannot fight successfully in one unless he fights also in the other.

Again, we are told that our theological differences will disappear if we will just get down on our knees together in prayer. Well, I can only say about that kind of prayer, which is indifferent to the question whether the gospel is true or false, that it is not Christian prayer; it is bowing down in the house of Rimmon.[13] God save us from it!...

Again, men say that instead of engaging in controversy in the church, we ought to pray to God for a revival; instead of polemics, we ought to have evangelism. Well, what kind of revival do you think that will be? What sort of evangelism is it that is indifferent to the question, "What evangel is it that is to be preached?" Not a revival in the New Testament sense, not the evangelism that Paul meant when he said, "Woe is unto me, if I preach not the gospel." No, my friends, there can be no true evangelism which makes common cause with the enemies of the cross of Christ. Souls will hardly be saved unless the evangelists can say with Paul: "If we or an angel from heaven preach any other gospel than that which we preached unto you, let him be accursed!" Every true revival is born in controversy, and leads to more controversy. That has been true ever since our Lord said that he came not to bring peace upon the earth but a sword. And do you know what I think will happen when God sends a new reformation upon the church? We cannot tell when that blessed day will come. But when the blessed day does come, I think we can say at least one result that it will bring. We shall hear nothing on that day about the evils of controversy in the church. All that will be swept away as with a mighty flood. A man who is on fire with a message never talks in that wretched, feeble way, but proclaims the truth joyously and fearlessly, in the presence of every high thing that is lifted up against the gospel of Christ.

13. Rimmon was the Syrian god of storms. See 2 *Kings* 5:18.

But men tell us that instead of engaging in controversy about doctrine, we ought to seek the power of the living Holy Spirit.... A man can hardly receive the power of the Holy Spirit if he seeks to evade the question whether the blessed book that the Spirit has given us is true or false.

Again, men tell us that our preaching should be positive and not negative, that we can preach the truth without attacking error. But if we follow that advice, we shall have to close our Bible and desert its teachings. The New Testament is a polemic book almost from beginning to end. Some years ago I was in a company of teachers of the Bible in the colleges and other educational institutions of America. One of the most eminent theological professors in the country made an address. In it he admitted that there are unfortunate controversies about doctrine in the epistles of Paul; but, said he in effect, the real essence of Paul's teaching is found in the hymn to Christian love in the thirteenth chapter of 1 *Corinthians*, and we can avoid controversy today if we will only devote the chief attention to that inspiring hymn. In reply, I am bound to say that the example was singularly ill-chosen. That hymn to Christian love is in the midst of a great polemic passage; it would never have been written if Paul had been opposed to controversy with error in the church. It was because his soul was stirred within him by a wrong use of the spiritual gifts that he was able to write that glorious hymn. So it is always in the church. Every really great Christian utterance, it may almost be said, is born in controversy. It is when men have felt compelled to take a stand against error that they have risen to the really great heights in the celebration of truth.[14]

For those who have until now been uninformed or misinformed, whatever the reason, this book is a call to become fully acquainted with the spiritual crisis in the OPC, and to understand the Biblical course of action. For those who have hesitated to sound the alarm as faithful watchmen should, this book is a call to fulfill your God-given responsibility (*Ezekiel* 3:16-21 and 33:1-9).

Secondly, this book is addressed to faithful pastors, elders, and church members who have recognized the growth of neo-liberalism in the OPC (though perhaps not by that name) and have actively opposed it.

In some cases congregations have stood shoulder to shoulder with their pastors and elders. But some of these ordained men have taken their stand without congregational or even sessional support. Within some sleeping congregations, individuals and small groups have arisen to oppose the growing error, and to alert others. For those of this faithful remnant, this book is a call to recognize the dangers of remaining in the OPC, and to acknowledge that the time has come to separate from it.

Thirdly, this book is addressed to those that Machen called the "doctrinally indifferent" – pastors, ruling elders, and members of congregations who have been aware of developments but have ignored, denied, or tolerated the growing apostasy.

Those individuals cannot plead ignorance. For them, this book is a call to recognize that neutrality regarding truth

14. J. Gresham Machen, "The Defense of the Faith" in *J. Gresham Machen: Selected Shorter Writings*, D. G. Hart, editor (Phillipsburg, New Jersey: P&R Publishing Company, 2004), 146-149.

and error is impossible. It is a call to take an unambiguous stand for the truth.

Lastly, this book is addressed to neo-liberals in the OPC, and to those who have openly aided and abetted their cause.

We who continue to stand for the truth fear for your souls. That burning concern is one of the things motivating conservatives to oppose you, and to stand for the one true Gospel, the authority and inerrancy of Scripture, and the unity and peace of the body of Christ. We fear that you have sold your birthright. We fear that you, like Esau, having fallen short of the grace of God, will find "no place for repentance, though he sought it diligently with tears" (*Hebrews* 12:17).

We pray that the Holy Spirit will awaken godly sorrow producing repentance in the hearts of those who have been deceived by the evil one. May it be said of you what Paul said to the church at Corinth:

> Now I rejoice, not that you were made sorry, but that your sorrow led to repentance.... For godly sorrow produces repentance leading to salvation, not to be regretted; but the sorrow of the world produces death. For observe this very thing, that you sorrowed in a godly manner: What diligence it produced in you, what clearing of yourselves, what indignation, what fear, what vehement desire, what zeal, what vindication! In all things you proved yourselves to be clear in this matter [2 *Corinthians* 7:9-11].

There is also a fifth group, outside the OPC, for whom we hope this book will be helpful and challenging. Some of the things that will be said about the Orthodox Presbyterian Church in these pages could also be said of other churches and denominations. This is partly because the cancer of neo-liberalism, which began in the OPC and in particular at Westminster Seminary in Philadelphia, has spread to other congregations, denominations, and seminaries. Faithful pastors, elders, and church members in other places may recognize the crisis in the OPC as their own crisis as well.

How Will You Respond to the Crisis?

Some, both in the OPC and elsewhere, will choose to remain in ignorance, complacency, or denial. Some will claim that there is no crisis. They will insist that conservatives paint an exaggerated picture, and the situation is not that serious. Some will allege that men and documents have been quoted out of context or incompletely. Some will insist that the differences between conservatives and neo-liberals do not cross the divide between truth and error, but are merely misunderstandings resulting from poor communication or problems of semantics. The evidence we present will show these to be specious arguments.

Others will object to this book *per se*. Some will reject the theological positions this book affirms, and the actions it advocates, as un-nuanced and simplistic. Some will say that the opponents of neo-liberalism are intolerant, unloving, or mean-spirited. Some will accuse them of being unethical, schismatic, spiritual adulterers, and worse.

The author, and others who have taken a clear stand for authentic Biblical Christianity in the OPC, have heard all these things directly from our opponents. But we are unmoved, because the facts support our position – and more than that, because Scripture supports our position. These objections and accusations are the stock in trade of neo-liberalism when someone has the audacity to expose it. We invite neo-liberals to defend, if they can, their efforts to replace the Gospel with a counterfeit, to debase the authority of Scripture, and to cause division in the church – rather than relying upon abusive *ad hominem* attacks, red herrings, and *non sequiturs* to divert attention from their actual words and deeds. The truth of the matter is that neo-liberals cannot defend the indefensible.

Some will say that the proper place for such an invitation is in the courts of the church. That would be the proper place, if the courts of the church were still capable of rendering Scriptural judgments. But in every instance over the past thirty years where the courts of the OPC have had the opportunity to deal with the cancer of neo-liberalism – and there have been many – those courts have failed to excise it from the body.[15] Their failure to deal with it in the only manner Scripture will allow, and the lack of denominational repentance for this unfaithful stewardship, disqualifies the courts of the OPC as a place of recourse for those who stand for the truth.

Those who actively oppose neo-liberalism in the OPC encourage readers of this book to look at the evidence for themselves. It is ample and growing. Most of the material we cite is readily accessible in contemporary books and periodicals, on audio recordings, and in reliable sources on the Internet. Some documents, especially recent General Assembly records, are in print but have limited distribution. But every OPC pastor receives a bound copy of the General Assembly Minutes and appendices each year, and should be

15. In 2003 the provisional session of Bethany OPC, Oxford, Pennsylvania, found ruling elder John O. Kinnaird guilty of heresy. This was the one time in OPC history that a court of the church condemned Shepherdism. But that judgment proved to be an anomaly, and was quickly struck down under neo-liberal pressure. See chapter seven for a more detailed discussion of the Kinnaird case.

willing to make them available for review. These yearbooks are also on the shelves of some seminary libraries.[16]

In the present crisis, Christians who remain true to the Word of God must arm themselves with the truths of Scripture and the facts of the situation. Then they must rally unreservedly to the position stated so well by Charles Spurgeon, who wrote the following when he separated from the compromising London Baptist Association in 1888 during the "Down-Grade Controversy":

> Numbers of good brethren in different ways remain in fellowship with those who are undermining the Gospel; and they talk of their conduct as though it were a loving course which the Lord will approve in the day of His appearing. The bounden duty of a true believer towards men who profess to be Christians, and yet deny the Word of the Lord, and reject the fundamentals of the Gospel, is to come out from among them (*II Cor*. 6:14-18)....
>
> Complicity with error will take from the best of men the power to enter any successful protest against it. If any body of believers had errorists among them, but were resolute to deal with them in the Name of the Lord, all might come right, but confederacies founded upon the principle that all may enter, whatever views they hold, are based upon disloyalty to the truth of God. If truth is optional, error is justifiable....
>
> It is hard to get leaven out of dough, and easy to put it in. This leaven is already working. Our daring to

16. The Minutes of all OPC General Assemblies from 1936 to 2004 are now available on CD-ROM from the OPC Committee for the Historian, 607 N. Easton Road, Building E, Willow Grove, Pennsylvania 19090.

unveil this deep design [that is, this deep-laid scheme] is inconvenient, and of course it brings upon our devoted head all manner of abuse. But that matters nothing so long as the plague is stayed. Oh, that those who are spiritually alive in the churches may look to this thing, and may the Lord himself baffle the adversary![17]

At any rate, cost what it may, to separate ourselves from those who separate themselves from the truth of God is not alone our liberty, but our duty. I have raised my protest in the only complete way by coming forth, and I shall be content to abide alone until the day when the Lord shall judge the secrets of all hearts; but it will not seem to me a strange thing if others are found faithful, and if others judge that for them also there is no path but that which is painfully apart from the beaten track.[18]

Jesus warned His disciples to "beware of the leaven of the Pharisees and Sadducees." By this, He meant their heretical doctrine (*Matthew* 16:5-12). Their doctrine, like today's neo-liberalism, was founded primarily on two false principles: preaching a counterfeit salvation by adding works of the law to faith, and debasing the authority of Scripture by subordinating it to un-Biblical methods of interpretation.

Why was it necessary for even these men, the twelve who were closest to Christ, to "beware"? It was because they were men of sinful flesh, as we are. It is easy to be deceived.

The word that perhaps best describes neo-liberalism is one seldom used today: It is *pernicious. Webster's Dictionary*

17. Charles Spurgeon, in "Notes," *Sword and Trowel*, October 1888. Reproduced at www.spurgeon.org/s_and_t/1088nts.htm.

18. Charles Spurgeon, "Attempts at the Impossible," *Sword and Trowel*, December 1888. Reproduced at www.spurgeon.org/s_and_t/dg12.htm.

defines *pernicious* as "causing irreparable harm through insidious corrupting influence." Nineteenth-century theologian Robert Lewis Dabney wrote that "false principles once firmly fixed are very apt to bring after them their appropriate corollaries in the course of time, however distasteful to the promulgators of the parent errors."[19] Once error is accepted in one area of foundational doctrine, departure from the truth in other areas becomes probable. This is true even when such an outcome is repugnant to those who allowed the original error to be propagated.

It is like the breaching of a great dam. The breach may begin as a fingertip-sized hole allowing only a trickle to pass. But left to itself, the breach opens ever wider. The trickle eventually becomes a flood, and those responsible for the original breach are powerless to stop it. They themselves are often swept away, and others with them. Or, the flood of error may not come until after those who were originally responsible pass from the scene. But the damage will be done to succeeding generations.

The false principles of the Pharisees and Sadducees concerning the Gospel and Scripture are the underlying principles of neo-liberalism today. In the epistle to the *Galatians*, the Apostle Paul warned the believers against the same things. As the teachings of the Judaizers in Galatia were pernicious, so is the spread of neo-liberalism today in the OPC and beyond. Paul warned the church:

19. Robert Lewis Dabney, "The Public Preaching of Women," *Southern Presbyterian Review*, October 1879. Reproduced by Foundation for Biblical Studies, Lumberton, Mississippi, 1998.

You ran well. Who hindered you from obeying the truth? This persuasion does not come from Him who calls you. A little leaven leavens the whole lump. I have confidence in you, in the Lord, that you will have no other mind; but he who troubles you shall bear his judgment, whoever he is [*Galatians* 5:7-10].

Chapter 2

The Marks of Neo-Liberalism

I fear, lest somehow, as the serpent deceived Eve by his craftiness,
so your minds may be corrupted from the simplicity that is in Christ.
For if he who comes
preaches another Jesus whom we have not preached,
or if you receive a different spirit which you have not received,
or a different gospel which you have not accepted
— you may well put up with it!
2 Corinthians 11:3-4

Using the word "neo-liberalism" in the same sentence with the name "Orthodox Presbyterian Church" violates a widely accepted but false paradigm held by the vast majority in the OPC.[1] They believe that their denomination remains a bastion of conservative theology. They reject the idea that liberalism of any description could have gained a foothold in the OPC, much less have come to seriously corrupt it.

In this paradigm, liberalism by definition exists only outside the denomination – among "them," but certainly not among "us." Other denominations, including the PCUSA, from which the OPC emerged, deserve to be called liberal, but there are no liberals in the OPC. So, by definition, this paradigm says that there can be no liberal-

1. This is also true in the Presbyterian Church in America (PCA).

conservative struggle within the Orthodox Presbyterian Church.

Despite the evidence to the contrary, those who are bound by this paradigm insist that any controversies that exist within the OPC are nothing more than intramural disagreements among conservatives. And, therefore, they must be about "things on which sound men may differ." Three generations ago many people in the PCUSA held tenaciously to the same kind of paradigm. But subsequent events proved that their spiritual vision was seriously defective.

Skeptics have said to me, "Alright then, prove your case. Where are the marks of liberalism in the OPC? We don't see any. The OPC hasn't changed its confessional standards. The OPC isn't ordaining women or homosexuals to the ministry. The OPC isn't tolerating New Age paganism. The OPC is not even seriously discussing things like admitting women to the office of deacon."

All of this is true, of course. But the presence of such evils does not define liberalism. Churches that we would identify as liberal by those marks did not one day "flip an apostasy switch." They did not suddenly write entirely new confessions of faith, place women and homosexuals in their pulpits, and begin holding pagan ceremonies honoring the goddess Sophia – all of which happened in the PCUSA decades *after* conservatives separated to form the OPC. Those evils are the manifestations of final apostasy, when the cancer of liberalism has completed its work, and there are few if any living cells in the body of a "church" consumed by spiritual disease.

Nor does the *absence* of these evils in the OPC mean the absence of neo-liberalism's spiritual corruption. Satan, the adversary of the true Church of Jesus Christ, is much subtler in his strategies than Christians often imagine. He is far too cunning to invade the church in a single frontal attack bringing sudden and widespread devastation. Rather, *Ephesians* 6:11 speaks of "the wiles of the devil" – in the original, his *methodias*. The adversary of the church uses cunning and deceit to bring about a gradual downgrade.

The history of the church tells us that a church's descent toward full apostasy usually begins subtly and gains momentum gradually. It can occur over the course of decades or even generations. It may consist of many small downward steps, sometimes punctuated by temporary recoveries. The events of the incremental decline, even if recognized as such, may seem isolated and insignificant, and the issues not worth fighting over, until the larger pattern emerges. By then, it is often too late to overcome the momentum of the downward slide. The downgrade always has a beginning, it always has root causes, and it almost always reaches a point of crisis where true believers in Christ must face a test of their loyalties.

The Marks of the Old Liberalism

To debunk the no-liberals-here paradigm in the PCUSA, in 1923 J. Gresham Machen publicly identified the marks of the liberalism of that time. Machen said that liberalism is chiefly characterized by "its attack upon the fundamentals of the Christian faith."[2] These fundamentals include the Biblical doctrine of God, and the Biblical doctrine of man.[3]

2. J. Gresham Machen, *Christianity and Liberalism* (Grand Rapids, Michigan: Wm. B. Eerdmans Co., 1923), 17.

3. Machen, 54-68.

He said that liberalism is at first equivocal about the authority and inerrancy of Scripture, and that such equivocation begins the downward spiral to open denial.[4] He said that "in their attitude toward Jesus, Christianity and liberalism are sharply opposed."[5] He said that "with regard to the gospel itself, modern liberalism is diametrically opposed to Christianity."[6] Machen observed that liberalism

> differs from Christianity with regard to the presuppositions of the gospel (the view of God and the view of man), with regard to the Book in which the gospel is contained, and with regard to the Person whose work the gospel sets forth. It is not surprising then that it differs from Christianity in its account of the gospel itself; it is not surprising that it presents an entirely different view of the way of salvation. Liberalism finds salvation (so far as it is willing to speak at all of "salvation") in man; Christianity finds it in an act of God. [7]

Machen also noted that liberalism discards the distinction between the visible church – all who *call* themselves "Christians" – and the invisible church, those whom *God* has truly called to salvation.[8]

Machen rightly viewed the crisis in the PCUSA as not merely an intramural dispute among conservatives. Thus, he defined the conflict in its proper terms – the warfare between authentic Biblical Christianity and liberalism's

4. Machen, 69-79.

5. Machen, 80.

6. Machen, 54.

7. Machen, 117.

8. Machen, 158-159.

counterfeit. He saw Christianity and liberalism as we must see them today: not two different brands of Christianity, but two different and irreconcilable sets of beliefs, one leading to Heaven, the other to Hell. The two may often use the same vocabulary, but one is true, while the other is false. There is no middle ground. Counterfeits often look exactly like the genuine article, except on careful examination. Machen wrote:

> Clear-cut definition of terms in religious matters, bold facing of the logical implications of religious views, is by many persons regarded as an impious proceeding. May it not discourage contribution to mission boards? May it not hinder the progress of consolidation, and produce a poor showing in the columns of Church statistics? But with such persons we cannot possibly bring ourselves to agree. Light may seem at times to be an impertinent intruder, but it is always beneficial in the end. The type of religion which rejoices in the pious sound of traditional phrases, regardless of their meanings, or shrinks from "controversial" matters, will never stand amid the shocks of life. In the sphere of religion, as in other spheres, the things about which men are agreed are apt to be the things that are least worth holding; the really important things are the things about which men will fight.
>
> In the sphere of religion, in particular, the present time is a time of conflict; the great redemptive religion which has always been known as Christianity is battling against a totally diverse type of religious belief, which is only the more destructive of the Christian faith because it makes use of traditional Christian

terminology. This modern non-redemptive religion is called "modernism" or "liberalism."[9]

We are not dealing here with delicate personal questions; we are not presuming to say whether such and such an individual man is a Christian or not. God only can decide such questions; no man can say with assurance whether the attitude of certain individual "liberals" toward Christ is saving faith or not. But one thing is perfectly plain – whether or [not] liberals are Christians, it is at any rate perfectly clear that liberalism is not Christianity.[10]

The OPC's neo-liberalism today shares the core characteristics of the PCUSA's old liberalism in the 1920s and 1930s. The OPC is repeating the mistakes of history. Satan has not corrupted the OPC with precisely the same forms of error that he employed three generations ago. The church would perhaps be on its guard for that. Today the error is expressed in different words and with contemporary points of emphasis. But it has the same destructive force, and confronting it requires the same spiritual alertness and resolve.

What then are the marks of neo-liberalism, and how do they parallel the old liberalism of the past? We present here six key characteristics in abbreviated form. We shall develop them more fully in later chapters, as we examine their deadly effects on the OPC and beyond.

---

9. Machen, 1-2.
10. Machen, 160.

Neo-Liberalism's False Conception of God

The old liberalism and today's neo-liberalism both begin with an un-Biblical conception of God.

The old liberalism championed a form of mysticism – a God who is unknowable and need not be known. Machen observed that liberalism "is opposed to Christianity, in the first place, in its conception of God.... It is unnecessary, we are told, to have a 'conception' of God; theology, or the knowledge of God, it is said, is the death of religion; we should not seek to know God, but should merely feel His presence."[11]

The old liberals made God the mystical and universal father of all men. Thus they made all men brothers, and placed man in the same relationship to God as Jesus because He was man's "brother." The relationship of "father" and "son" was, in the old liberal view, merely an analogy of something mystical and incomprehensible.

But the old liberalism's "Father God" was not "the God and Father of our Lord Jesus Christ" revealed in Scripture. Machen countered that Jesus' relationship to His heavenly Father was not a relationship to something vague and impersonal, a mystical relationship that was merely put in human terms in Scripture by the analogy of Father and Son. This was the relationship between two real persons of the Trinity, God the Father and God the Son, whose existence and relationship is just as definite and knowable as "the existence of the lilies of the field that God has clothed." The very basis of Jesus' teaching "was a triumphant belief in the real existence of a personal God."[12]

Like the old liberalism, today's neo-liberalism is also

11. Machen, 54.

12. Machen, 57.

founded on a mystical conception of God. Herman Bavinck,[13] a philosophical hero of neo-liberal theologians such as Norman Shepherd, Richard B. Gaffin, Jr., and John M. Frame, asserted the following in the second volume of his *Gereformeerde Dogmatiek* (*Reformed Dogmatics*):

> Mystery is the vital element of Dogmatics. It is true that the term "mystery" in Scripture does not indicate abstract-supernatural truth in the Romish sense; nevertheless, the idea that the believer would be able to understand and comprehend intellectually the revealed mysteries is equally unscriptural. On the contrary, the truth which God has revealed concerning himself in nature and in Scripture far surpasses human conception and comprehension. In that sense Dogmatics is concerned with nothing but mystery.[14]

Bavinck thus begins an entire volume on the doctrine of God by telling believers that we "cannot understand and comprehend intellectually" the God of the Bible – not even after He has clearly revealed Himself in Scripture. Bavinck uses the term "mystery" in an un-Scriptural sense, and one that is far more "Romish" than he admits. Mysteries in the Word of God are not that which remains inscrutable, but rather divine secrets that have been revealed and explained in the Scriptures for human understanding through the enlightenment of the Holy Spirit.

Bavinck continues his discourse by acknowledging that God has revealed Himself. This seems encouraging until the

13. 1854-1921; Professor of Systematic Theology, Free University of Amsterdam, 1902-1921.

14. Herman Bavinck, *The Doctrine of God*, translated and edited by William Hendriksen (Edinburgh: The Banner of Truth Trust, 1977), 13.

reader sees the kind of God that Bavinck says has been revealed. He claims that "Christian theology made the idea of God's incomprehensibility and unknowability its point of departure.... God's revelation in creation and redemption fails to reveal him adequately."[15] He seeks to support this viewpoint by approvingly quoting a number of early and medieval theologians:[16]

> Accordingly, adequate knowledge of God does not exist. There is no name that makes known to us his being.... *Father, God, Lord*, are not real names but "appellations derived from his good deeds and functions."[17]

> The fact that God exists is evident, but "what he is in his essence and nature is entirely incomprehensible and unknowable." When we say that God is unborn, immutable, without beginning, etc., we are only saying what he is *not*. To say what he is, is impossible. He is nothing of all that which exists....[18]

> ...[T]here is no concept, expression, or word, by which God's being can be indicated. Accordingly, whenever we wish to designate God, we use metaphorical language. He is "supersubstantial infinity, supermental unity," etc. We cannot form a conception of that unitary, unknown being, transcendent above all being, above goodness, above every name and word and thought. We can only name him in accordance with his works, because he is the cause and principle of everything. Hence,

15. Bavinck, 21.

16. The words in quotation marks are from early and medieval theologians; the rest are Bavinck's own words.

17. Bavinck, 21.

18. Bavinck, 22. Emphasis in the original.

on the one hand he is "without name," on the other hand he "has many names." But those positive names which we ascribe to God because of his works do not disclose his essential being to us, for they pertain to him in an entirely different manner than to creatures. Hence, negative theology is better than positive, for the former teaches us God's transcendence above the creature. Nevertheless, even negative theology fails to give us any knowledge of God's being, for in reality God is exalted above both "negation and affirmation." [19]

Whatever is said concerning God is not God....[20]

Bavinck wrongly claims that "Reformed theologians were in agreement with this view" from the time of the Reformation. "Gradually, however," he says, "the significance of the doctrine of God's incomprehensibility was lost sight of also in those circles where the principles of the Reformation once flourished." Bavinck considers this an error that must be reversed.[21] And from this starting point, he builds an entire systematic theology. Commenting on these statements, John W. Robbins observes that

> any informed Christian, actually any sane person, reading these pages in Bavinck, would stop and lay his book aside. The reader has just been told, repeatedly and emphatically, that no thought or language adequately and accurately describes God, that we have and can have no knowledge of God. If that is so, there is obviously no point in reading further, unless it is to

19. Bavinck, 22-23.
20. Bavinck, 25.
21. Bavinck, 26.

45

attain a clinical understanding of how a mind can become so disordered as to write a book on a subject about which he can know and say nothing.

This is the Antichristian irrationalism that passes for Christian theology in both Protestant and Catholic, "conservative" and "liberal" seminaries. It explains a great deal about the "dialectical," that is, contradictory, pronouncements that issue forth from every modern school of theology. In such a turbid atmosphere, anything goes, including the simultaneous affirmations that justification is by faith alone and also by faith and works. No Christian doctrine, none whatsoever, can be maintained in such a mystical, skeptical, and irrational framework. It is a black hole that swallows and extinguishes all light and all rational thought. It is the medieval mother of all heresies, for the rejection of propositional revelation is the root of all error. Bavinck was a conduit carrying this rubbish into Reformed theology in the twentieth century.[22]

Bavinck was not the only such conduit. Cornelius Van Til, professor of apologetics at Westminster Seminary in Philadelphia from 1929 to 1972, and the leading philosophical influence on WTS and on three generations of OPC ministers, held that "we dare not maintain that [God's] knowledge and [human] knowledge coincide at any single point."[23] This position leads, as we shall see, to a completely defective view of the nature and authority of the Scriptures.

22. John W. Robbins, *A Companion to The Current Justification Controversy* (Unicoi, Tennessee: The Trinity Foundation, 2003), 41.

23. *Minutes of the 12th General Assembly of the Orthodox Presbyterian Church*, 1945, 15.

Neo-Liberalism's False Conception of Man

The old liberalism and today's neo-liberalism share an un-Scriptural conception of man and his fallen state.

Liberalism, said Machen, adopted a view of man that produced confidence in human goodness, a loss of consciousness of sin, and a defective conception of the law of God.[24] Liberalism denied the enormity of sin. It viewed man as essentially capable of improvement by imitating the ethical example of Christ. The old liberalism thus taught people to live by the Ten Commandments and the Sermon on the Mount. Liberalism's view of man, Machen observed, is diametrically opposed to the Bible's. Scripture portrays the law as the schoolmaster that brings men to Christ, causing them to recognize their inability to keep it and their resulting condemnation before God, in order "that we may be justified by faith" (*Galatians* 3:24).

Machen described the old liberalism's preaching thus:

> The fundamental fault of the modern Church is that she is busily engaged in an absolutely impossible task – she is busy calling the righteous to repentance. Modern preachers are trying to bring men into the Church without requiring them to relinquish their pride; they are trying to help men avoid the conviction of sin. The preacher gets up in the pulpit, opens the Bible, and addresses the congregation somewhat as follows: "You people are very good," he says; "you respond to every appeal that looks to the welfare of the community. Now we have in the Bible – especially in

24. Machen, *Christianity and Liberalism*, 64-68.

the life of Jesus – something so good that we believe it is good enough even for you good people."[25]

Neo-liberalism's view of man echoes old liberalism's preaching. In the OPC this thinking has been propagated for three decades through the teachings of Norman Shepherd[26] and his supporters. Shepherd writes:

> Because the evangelistic methodology prescribed for Abraham and his descendants was to result in world-wide blessing, Jesus prescribed precisely the same methodology for his church when he said that all nations of the earth were to be discipled by "teaching them to observe everything I have commanded you" (*Matt.* 28:20). Just as the gospel of the Abrahamic covenant taught God's people to do what is right and just (*Gen.* 18:19), so the gospel of the new covenant teaches us to seek first the righteousness of the kingdom of God (*Matt.* 6:33). The gospel of the kingdom (*Matt.* 4:23) is the Sermon on the Mount (*Matt.* 5-7).[27]

Shepherd asserts that "the Lord God deals with the power and corruption of sin by teaching his people how to live happy and productive lives."[28]

Shepherd's "gospel" is not the good news of redemption for helpless sinners who stand under God's condemnation

25. Machen, *Christianity and Liberalism*, 68.

26. Born 1933; former OPC and currently Christian Reformed minister; Professor of Systematic Theology at Westminster Theological Seminary, 1963 to 1981; highly influential neo-liberal speaker and writer.

27. Norman Shepherd, *The Call of Grace* (Phillipsburg, New Jersey: P&R Publishing, 2000), 75-76.

28. Norman Shepherd, *Law and Gospel in Covenant Perspective* (privately published, 2004); reproduced by permission at www.christianculture.com.

and wrath, who have no righteousness of their own, and who need their sins imputed to Christ and the righteousness of Christ's active obedience imputed to them. On the contrary, Shepherd rejects what he at least correctly calls the "evangelical view" that Jesus "fulfilled all the requirements of the law, and his law keeping is imputed to believers for their justification." He claims that the Apostle Paul did not teach this, despite his clear presentation of it in passages such as *2 Corinthians* 5:21 ("For He made Him who knew no sin to be sin for us, that we might become the righteousness of God in Him"). Rather, Shepherd teaches that the doctrine of the imputed righteousness of Christ was a later corruption of Reformed theology.[29]

In its place, Shepherd teaches a pseudo-gospel of salvation through good works done by people who have been made capable of doing good works because they have been baptized:

> For Abraham, the sign of both covenant privilege and covenant responsibility was circumcision. Paul calls circumcision "a seal of the righteousness that he had by faith" (*Rom.* 4:11), and is therefore simultaneously covenant privilege and responsibility.
>
> Corresponding to circumcision in the Great Commission is baptism, indicative at once of the grace of God and the response of faith, repentance, and obedience. As the Israel of the old covenant becomes the church of the new covenant, the circumcised people of God must be baptized, as they were on the Day of Pentecost. At the

29. Norman Shepherd, "Justification by Faith in Pauline Theology" in *Backbone of the Bible: Covenant in Contemporary Perspective*, Andrew Sandlin, editor (Nacogdoches, Texas: Covenant Media Foundation, 2004), 85-86.

same time, the circumcision of the nations is accomplished in and through their baptism into Christ.[30]

And what is the significance of baptism in Shepherd's false gospel?

> ...[B]aptism, the sign and seal of the covenant, marks the point of conversion. Baptism is the moment when we see the transition from death to life and a person is saved.[31]

Shepherd teaches that evangelism should focus on baptism, and not on regeneration:

> In contrast to regeneration-evangelism, a methodology oriented to the covenant structure of Scripture and to the Great Commission presents baptism as the transition point from death to life. The specific terms of the Great Commission describe the process of making disciples in terms of baptism and instruction in the commands of Christ. This means that evangelism does not end with regeneration, but continues as long as a person lives. Baptism marks the entrance into the kingdom of God and the beginning of life-long training as kingdom subjects. According to the Great Commission, conversion without baptism is an anomaly. A sinner is not "really converted" until he is baptized.
>
> ...The Philippian jailer and the members of his household are not said to have been regenerated or converted, but to have been baptized. Paul's experience on the road to Damascus is usually thought of as the

30. Shepherd, 76.
31. Shepherd, 94.

time of his conversion. The Bible does not say when he was regenerated, but it does say when he was baptized (*Acts* 9:18). His baptism marks the time when his sins were washed away (*Acts* 22:16).[32] When Paul exhorts the Romans to obey God, he does not remind them that they were regenerated or suggest that they might not be regenerate. Rather, he points to their baptism, and calls them to live out of that experience (*Rom.* 6:1-11).

...Christians are those who have been baptized. Unbelievers are those who have not been baptized.[33]

Tom Trouwborst, graduate of neo-liberal Bahnsen Theological Seminary, pastor of Calvary Orthodox Presbyterian Church in Schenectady, New York, and proponent of Federal Vision theology, concurs with Shepherd. Trouwborst states that baptized "children of believers, even from infancy, have regeneration, salvation, and the forgiveness of sins."[34]

Shepherd's teachings are also echoed in so-called "covenant succession" theology that is gaining increasing acceptance in the OPC, PCA, and elsewhere. Typical of its tenets are these affirmations and denials by Dr. Robert S. Rayburn:

32. Protestant exegetes (employing the principles that Scripture is its own interpreter and that less clear passages must be understood in the light of those that are more clear) have long recognized that *Acts* 22:16 does not support the doctrine of the remission of sins through the waters of baptism. And in *Acts* 22:13, Paul recalls that Ananias addressed the recently-converted and newly-commissioned apostle as "Brother Saul" *before* baptizing him. Also, Paul himself distinguishes baptism from the Gospel: "For Christ did not send me to baptize, but to preach the Gospel" (*1 Corinthians* 1:17).

33. Shepherd, *The Call of Grace*, 100-101.

34. Tom Trouwborst, "A Response to 'The Reformed Doctrine of Regeneration'" in *The Auburn Avenue Theology: Pros and Cons* (Fort Lauderdale, Florida: Knox Theological Seminary, 2004), 193.

It is affirmed.... The [baptized] children of Christian parents are to be considered Christians...until and unless they prove the contrary. Their situation, in other words, is the same as any other church member. It is denied: Covenant children are to be evangelized like every other lost sinner.

...It is denied: The spiritual history of covenant children will be marked by an experience of conversion....

...It is denied: Christian children, before reaching an age at which they are able to make a profession of faith, can, at best, only be considered as "Christians to be." [It is also denied that] in general they are to be regarded as unsaved until they show evidence of true faith in Christ.

...It is denied: The teaching of covenant succession is likely to produce nominalism and a crippling self-confidence.[35]

But that is exactly what it does produce. To say that someone may simply look to his baptism and to a lack of evidence of outright apostasy in his life as the proof of his salvation is not the Scriptural standard. There are millions of baptized people who live moral lives but are on their way to Hell. They are still in their sins.

To believe on the Lord Jesus Christ – to confess with the mouth, and believe with the heart – is the standard. Any

35. Robert Rayburn in "Quotations on Covenant Succession," *Credenda Agenda*, Volume 13, No. 2. Rayburn is pastor of Faith Presbyterian Church (PCA), Tacoma, Washington; President of the Board of Trustees of Covenant College; and a frequent theological consultant to numerous PCA committees.

other standard is nominalism by definition, and produces a self-confidence that is not merely crippling but soul-damning. Covenant succession is another error of the Pharisees that both John the Baptist and Jesus Christ denounced (*Matthew* 3:7-12, *John* 8:31-47). Our confidence must be in the blood of Jesus Christ, and that alone. And to say that we do not need to evangelize our children is to disobey God's command: "Go into all the world and preach the Gospel to every creature" (*Mark* 16:15). We are to bear witness to the salvation that is in Christ just as Israel was instructed to bear witness to it in a figure: "And it shall be, when your children say to you, 'What do you mean by this service?' that you shall say, 'It is the Passover sacrifice of the Lord, who passed over the houses of the children of Israel in Egypt when He struck the Egyptians and delivered our households'" (*Exodus* 12:26-27).

Despite these clear teachings of Scripture, in May 2005 the OPC's *New Horizons* magazine published a glowing review of a book promoting the covenant succession error. This book includes chapters by Trouwborst, Rayburn, and Federal Visionist Douglas Wilson, among others.[36]

Norman Shepherd and those who follow his errors substitute the waters of baptism for the blood of Christ. They teach, in effect, that God's covenant is a covenant in water, not blood. But our Lord says, "This is My blood of the new covenant, which is shed for many for the remission of sins" (*Matthew* 26:28). "Without shedding of blood, there is no remission" (*Hebrews* 9:22). "With His own blood He

36. Jack Bradley, review of *To You and Your Children: Examining the Biblical Doctrine of Covenant Succession* (Moscow, Idaho: Canon Press, 2005) in *New Horizons*, May 2005, 23. Bradley is pastor of Emmanuel OPC, Colville, Washington.

entered the Most Holy Place once for all, having obtained eternal redemption" (*Hebrews* 9:12).

Shepherd and other neo-liberals teach that man's salvation depends on a combination of God's grace and personal obedience beginning with water baptism, with the clear implication that man is capable of doing his part in effecting his salvation. Shepherd asserts that "abiding in Christ by keeping his commandments" (*John* 15:5, 10; *1 John* 3:13, 24) [is] necessary for continuing in the state of justification" and "the personal godliness of the believer is also necessary for his justification in the judgment of the last day."[37] This is also the teaching of Roman Catholicism.

While constantly claiming to reject what he calls a "works-merit paradigm," the bottom line of Shepherd's theology is justification by faith plus *faithfulness* – that is, justification by human works. He teaches that "the Pauline affirmation in *Romans* 2:13, 'the doers of the Law will be justified,' is not to be understood hypothetically in the sense that there are no persons who fall into that class, but in the sense that faithful disciples of the Lord Jesus Christ will be justified."[38]

In an article misleadingly titled "Justification by Faith Alone," Shepherd asserts that "saving faith has to be the same as justifying faith."[39] For his purposes, he makes it clear, the two terms are interchangeable. On this basis, he

37. Norman Shepherd, *Thirty-four Theses on Justification in Relation to Faith, Repentance, and Good Works*, theses 22 and 23; privately published by the author, 1978; reproduced by permission at www.hornes.org/theologia/content/norman_shepherd/the_34_theses.htm.

38. Shepherd, Thesis 20.

39. Norman Shepherd, "Justification by Faith Alone" in *Reformation & Revival Journal*, Volume 11, Number 2, Spring 2002, 82.

overthrows the Biblical distinction between the empty-handed faith by which a sinner is justified – declared not guilty based on the life, death, and imputed righteousness of Christ alone — and the *evidences* of saving faith manifesting themselves in a changed life through the grace of sanctification. Contrary to Shepherd's false gospel, Scripture plainly teaches that there is no such thing as justification by "faith plus works" (*Galatians* 2:16, 3:1-3, 3:12; *Romans* 4:4-5). In God's economy, faith and works are mutually exclusive in justification; mingling the two is impossible. Add one iota of works to faith, and it is no longer faith (*Romans* 11:6). But Shepherd says that the impossible is not only possible, but *necessary*. He redefines faith to be "faith-plus." He erects a false doctrine of justification that un-Scripturally packs all sorts of works into the "saving faith" which he equates with "justifying faith":

> Saving faith is described not only as believing whatsoever is revealed in the word of God but also as obeying its commands, trembling at its threatenings, and embracing the promises of God....[40]

This is simply not true. Here Shepherd misquotes the *Westminster Confession of Faith,* chapter 14, section 2, which actually says the opposite. It says that saving faith *results in* a Christian believing whatsoever the Word says so be true, as well as

> obedience to the commands, trembling at the threatenings, and embracing the promises of God for this life, and that which is to come. *But the principal acts of saving faith* are accepting, receiving, and resting upon Christ

40. Shepherd, 82.

alone for justification, sanctification, and eternal life, by virtue of the covenant of grace [emphasis added].

Shepherd frequently ignores the plain teaching of Scripture, summarized in the Westminster Standards, on cause and effect in relation to saving faith.

Shepherd calls his false doctrine a "covenantal understanding of the way of salvation." He believes it provides the basis "for a common understanding between Romanism and evangelical Protestantism."[41] And so it would, since it repeals the Reformation, capitulating to the Roman Catholic view of man as able to cooperate with divine grace in salvation through good works.

Like the old liberal "gospel" that Machen described, Shepherd's neo-liberal "gospel" is only good news for good people. It is a call not to sinners, but to those who think they are righteous. Jesus told the "good" people of His day, the Pharisees who boasted in their covenantal position and law-keeping, "Those who are well have no need of a physician, but those who are sick. I have not come to call the righteous, but sinners, to repentance" (Luke 5:31-32).

Shepherd finds his man-centered, works-centered gospel superior to "methodologies oriented to the doctrines of election and regeneration."[42] Thus Shepherd rejects the methodology of Jesus himself in John 6, which caused many who had professed to be disciples, but were actually relying on their own goodness, to go back and follow Him no more (verse 66).

Richard B. Gaffin, Jr., ordained OPC minister and Chairman of the Department of Systematic Theology at West-

41. Shepherd, The Call of Grace, 59.

42. Shepherd, 77.

minster Theological Seminary, glowingly endorses Shepherd's presentation of a false gospel on the back cover of *The Call of Grace*:

> This lucid and highly readable study provides valuable instruction on what it means to live in covenant with God. God's covenant is the only way of life that fully honors both the absolute, all-embracing sovereignty of his saving grace and the full, uninhibited activity of his people. *The Call of Grace* should benefit anyone concerned about biblical growth in Christian life and witness.

Gaffin and Shepherd were faculty colleagues at Westminster Theological Seminary for over fifteen years. Gaffin is a long-time staunch defender of Norman Shepherd and his teachings. Richard Gaffin has for over four decades been responsible for shaping the theological mindset of most of the men now occupying OPC pulpits, as well as many in the PCA and elsewhere, and most members of the Westminster Seminary faculty.[43]

Neo-Liberalism's Defective View of Scripture

The old liberalism and today's neo-liberalism both jettison sound principles of interpreting Scripture, and thus ultimately reject its authority.

Defective hermeneutics are erected on the foundation of defective doctrines of God and man. Like the serpent tempt-

---

43. For a more detailed discussion of Richard Gaffin's role, see Mark W. Karlberg, *The Changing of the Guard* (Unicoi, Tennessee: The Trinity Foundation, 2001); O. Palmer Robertson, *The Current Justification Controversy* (The Trinity Foundation, 2003); and John W. Robbins, *A Companion to The Current Justification Controversy* (The Trinity Foundation, 2003).

ing Eve in the garden, liberalism's opening moves are to plant doubt about the clear meaning of God's Word ("Has God indeed said...?") and to elevate human interpretive wisdom ("Your eyes will be opened, and you will be like God...").

The old liberalism's infamous *Auburn Affirmation* held that PCUSA ministers could believe that the Scriptures were inspired by the Holy Spirit, but without believing that they were inerrant.[44] Accordingly, the old liberalism characterized key doctrines of authentic Biblical Christianity as "not the only theories allowed by the Scriptures and our standards as explanations of [the] facts and doctrines of our religion." Liberalism insisted that other theories were admissible – theories rooted not in the plain sense of Scripture as revealed by its Author, but in anti-Biblical secular scholarship.

The old liberalism said that those who hold such un-Biblical views, "whatever theories they may employ to explain them, are worthy of all confidence and trust." In liberalism's view, such men should be accepted in the minis try without reservation so long as they continue to profess, whether through disingenuousness or delusion, that they subscribe to the doctrinal standards of the church when in fact they do not.

In chillingly similar words, today's neo-liberalism in the OPC asserts that we must "cultivate a hermeneutic of trust," even when men disagree on foundational doctrines. The church must, neo-liberalism says, cultivate a "community of interpretation" that sustains "confessional inte-

44. The *Auburn Affirmation* appears in full in Appendix A.

grity among its ministerial membership" without requiring agreement on foundational doctrines or on sound
methods of Biblical interpretation. [45]

In this vein, neo-liberalism entertains strange views of
what it means to interpret Scripture "literally" or "history-
ically." The 2004 General Assembly of the OPC approved
and commended to its churches a study committee *Report*
which states that widely divergent teachings on the nature
and length of the days of creation in *Genesis* 1 all fall into
the category of "literal" and "historical" interpretations. In
neo-liberalism's interpretive world of no fixed rules, a
"literal" and "historical" day can be virtually anything one
wishes it to be – an ordinary day, an ambiguous literary
figure, or a day-age comprising billions of years.[46] The
Report further says that, despite the unmistakable order in
the text, *Genesis* 1 "need not be [viewed as] chronological"
in order to be viewed as "historical."[47]

If Christians apply neo-liberalism's no-rules method of
interpretation to the Bible as a whole – and why shouldn't
they if seminary professors and ministers in the OPC lead
the way? – then no doctrine is safe from radical revision.

None of this is surprising given the fact that neo-liberalism has its philosophical basis in the thinking of men
such as Herman Bavinck and Cornelius Van Til. In his

45. "Report of the Committee to Study the Views of Creation"
(*Commissioners' Workbook for the 71ˢᵗ General Assembly of the Orthodox
Presbyterian Church*, 2004), 1607. Available online at www.opc.org/
GA/CreationReport.pdf. Members of the committee were Leonard J.
Coppes, Bryan D. Estelle, C. Lee Irons, John R. Muether, Alan R.
Pontier, Alan D. Strange (Chairman), and Peter J. Wallace.

46. *Report*, 1604.

47. *Report*, 1603-1604, 1631-1634, 1637, 1642-1643.

introduction to an edition of Benjamin B. Warfield's *The Inspiration and Authority of the Bible*, Van Til asserted,

> When the Christian restates the content of Scriptural revelation in the form of a "system," such a system is based upon and therefore analogous to the "existential system" that God himself possesses. Being based upon God's revelation it is on the one hand, fully true and, on the other hand, *at no point identical* with the content of the divine mind.[48]

Van Til also says elsewhere that both theology and apologetics must be based on the principle that Scripture contains only an "analogical system of truth." [49]

Van Til looks backward to Bavinck for support, asserting that Bavinck was "insistent...that the Scriptures are the Word of God and that its system of truth is an analogical system."[50] In other words, the Scriptures contain a system of "truth" that is "at no point identical with" but somehow resembles the unknowable truth in God's mind. The statements of Scripture are not God's truth itself.

Robert L. Reymond observes that Van Til's depiction of God's self-interpreting revelation in Scripture

> is no longer analogy at all but a form of equivocality, which God, according to Van Til, chooses to call true although it coincides at no point with the truth. This

---

48. Cornelius Van Til, Introduction to B. B. Warfield, *The Inspiration and Authority of the Bible* (Philadelphia: Presbyterian and Reformed, 1948), 33. Emphasis in the original.

49. Cornelius Van Til, *The Defense of the Faith* (Phillipsburg, New Jersey: Presbyterian and Reformed Publishing Company, 1955), 298.

50. *Defense of the Faith*, 296. Here Van Til also asserts, wrongly, that the Old Princeton theologians subscribed to his analogical view of Scripture.

contention ultimately ascribes irrationality to God and ignorance to man....[51]

In answer to this key principle in Van Tilian thought, Gordon H. Clark maintained that if God possesses the truth, and man possesses in Scripture only an analogy of God's truth – containing only that which is, in Van Til's words, *"at no point identical* with the content of the divine mind" – then it follows that man does not have the truth at all.[52] (And, I would quickly add, the Bible cannot be inspired, inerrant, or fully authoritative.) Clark contends that:

> To avoid this irrationalism, which of course is a denial of the divine image, we must insist that truth is the same for God and man. Naturally, we may not know the truth about some matters. But if we know anything at all, what we must know must be identical with what God knows. God knows all truth, and unless we know something God knows, our ideas are untrue. It is absolutely essential, therefore, to insist that there is an area of coincidence between God's mind and our mind. One example, as good as any, is the one already used, namely, David was King of Israel.[53]

And God's truth – communicated directly and not in analogical form – is precisely what God the Holy Spirit has given us in the pages of Scripture. It is true that in numer-

---

51. Robert L. Reymond, *A New Systematic Theology of the Christian Faith* (Nashville: Thomas Nelson Publishers, 1998), 103.

52. Gordon H. Clark, "The Bible as Truth," in *God's Hammer: The Bible and Its Critics*, John W. Robbins, editor (Unicoi, Tennessee: The Trinity Foundation [1982] 1995), 24-38.

53. Gordon H. Clark, *An Introduction to Christian Philosophy* (Unicoi, Tennessee: The Trinity Foundation, 1993), 76-77.

ous passages the Word of God employs analogies – comparisons based on resemblance – as in the types and symbols of Christ in the Old Testament. But Scripture is not, as Van Til plainly asserted, nothing but an analogy *in toto* of things of which human beings have – and can have – no knowledge. Van Til's assertion eliminates the concept of analogy as God uses it in the Scriptures.

Tellingly, Van Til himself admitted a key defect of his writings on theology and apologetics: "The lack of detailed scriptural exegesis is a lack in all of my writings. I have no excuse for this...."[54] Yet Van Tilian philosophy – taught by Van Til himself to generations of OPC ministers and future seminary professors, and still championed today by his followers at Westminster and many other schools – is the foundation on which much of neo-liberal thought has been erected.

Neo-Liberalism's Hijacking of Biblical Terminology

The old liberalism and today's neo-liberalism both hijack the terminology of authentic Biblical Christianity to formulate counterfeit doctrines.

This is not surprising when men of seminaries and pulpits abandon sound principles of interpretation. Liberalism's operating principle was that the church need not – indeed *cannot* and *must not* – take dogmatic positions on the meanings of words that define essential doctrine. Doctrine becomes nothing more than a wax nose that can be twisted and shaped at will. New doctrines can be devised

54. Cornelius Van Til, "Response by C. Van Til (to G. C. Berkouwer, 'The Authority of Scripture, A Responsible Confession')" in *Jerusalem and Athens, Critical Discussions on the Philosophy and Apologetics of Cornelius Van Til*, ed. E. R. Geehan (Phillipsburg, New Jersey: Presbyterian and Reformed, 1980), 203-204.

to fit any agenda. As we shall see in chapter three, they are usually old heresies in contemporary garb. The old liberalism, for example, held widely varying interpretations of critically important doctrinal words such as "atonement" and "resurrection" in order to widen its circle of fellowship to include men who preached another gospel.[55]

Today's neo-liberalism operates on the same principle. It says that we cannot insist upon a clear definition of the word "day" in *Genesis* 1, or the words "grace," "justify," "believe," "faith," or "righteousness" in Paul's epistles and in *James* – despite the fact that the only valid meaning of each of those terms in context can be readily discerned using sound principles of interpretation. Many neo-liberals still say that they believe in justification by faith alone. But like an American president infamously dodging responsibility by quibbling over the meaning of the word "is," neo-liberals then proceed to un-Biblically redefine all the terms of that foundational doctrine – "justification" – "by" – "faith" – and – "alone."[56]

Neo-Liberalism's Denial of the Authentic Gospel

The old liberalism and today's neo-liberalism both deny the one true Gospel of salvation by grace alone, through faith alone, in Christ alone. In the process, they diminish the person and work of Christ, and elevate the works of men.

The liberalism of the early twentieth century denied Biblical teaching concerning Christ's atonement. It suppressed Biblical teaching concerning the Lamb who,

55. As in the *Auburn Affirmation*, Appendix A.

56. As, for example, Norman Shepherd in "Justification by Faith Alone" (*Reformation & Revival Journal*, Vol. 11, No. 2, Spring 2002), 75-91.

through His sinless life and vicarious atonement, propitiated the wrath of a holy God on sinners' behalf. Instead, liberalism reduced Jesus, His perfect life, and atoning death to the status of a great moral and ethical example, and taught that man is able to save himself by following the example of Christ in good works.[57]

Today's neo-liberalism likewise attacks the gracious work of Christ on behalf of helpless sinners. It denies the sufficiency of the imputed righteousness of Jesus Christ to justify sinners, and says that men must add their own works of righteousness in order to be justified before God. Neo-liberalism still speaks approvingly, at least in some circles, of the doctrine of the passive obedience of Christ, principally His death on the cross. But it attacks the doctrine of His active obedience, especially His keeping the law perfectly on sinners' behalf, and the imputation of His law-keeping righteousness to sinners for their justification, because they have no righteousness of their own.

Neo-liberalism says that men must add a righteousness of their own in order to be justified before God.[58] And therefore, like the old liberalism, it holds out law observance – emulation of Christ as man's moral and ethical example – as our means of "final justification" at God's judgment bar.[59] As one conservative theologian has put it, neo-liberalism makes Jesus Christ little more than "the first Christian."[60]

57. Machen, *Christianity and Liberalism*, 117-120.

58. As, for example, John O. Kinnaird, quoted Robbins, *A Companion to The Current Justification Controversy*, 55-56; and Norman Shepherd, *The Call of Grace*, 13-20.

59. Norman Shepherd, *Thirty-four Theses on Justification in Relation to Faith, Repentance, and Good Works*.

60. R. Scott Clark (Associate Professor of Historical and Systematic

Neo-liberalism's gospel is "another gospel, which is not another" and comes under the strongest possible condemnation of the Lord of the Church (*Galatians* 1:6-10). Yet the Orthodox Presbyterian Church has for the past three decades permitted precisely such malignant teachings to grow and spread, without censure or correction, and has provided the cloak under which this evil has grown.

Neo-Liberalism's False Confessional Unity

The old liberalism and today's neo-liberalism seek to unify truth and falsehood under the same confessional tent.

The liberalism of the early twentieth century said that doctrinal inclusivism promoting "unity of spirit" was far more important than careful agreement on doctrinal foundations.[61] Today's neo-liberalism asserts that those who preach another gospel can peacefully coexist in the same church with those who hold the truth. It says that together they must "await development of a consensus"[62] on issues of fundamental doctrine that are in fact forever settled in the Word of God.

As we said at the beginning of this book, neo-liberals pretend to be what they are not, and profess to believe what they do not. Neo-liberals profess to believe in the God of the Bible, but they teach an unknowable God of their own

---

Theology, Westminster Seminary in California) in *The Foolishness of the Gospel: Covenant and Justification Under Attack* (Escondido, California: Westminster Seminary California, 2004), audio cassette no. 6, side B.

61. Edwin H. Rian, *The Presbyterian Conflict* (Philadelphia: The Committee for the Historian of the Orthodox Presbyterian Church, [1940] 1992), 35.

62. Frame, Foreword to *Backbone of the Bible*, xi.

imagining. Neo-liberals profess to know the truth, but they teach that for man there is only an analogy or analogies of the truth. Neo-liberals profess salvation by faith in Christ alone, but they teach salvation by Christ plus man's faithfulness. Neo-liberals profess to believe in the authority of Scripture, but they teach the primacy of human scholarship. Neo-liberals profess to hold to the truth, but they teach that the truth can be contradictory. Neo-liberals profess to believe the words of Scripture and profess loyalty to the doctrines affirmed in their confessions, but by twisting the words of both they create doctrines that are supported by neither. Neo-liberals profess to preach the all-sufficiency of Christ, but they teach the insufficiency of His obedience for the salvation of souls. Neo-liberals profess to believe in full assurance of salvation, but they teach that the believer can never be assured.

Because of their duplicity, neo-liberals can speak to unsuspecting conservatives in the church in a way that makes them think the neo-liberals are actually "one of us" – thus muting opposition, and leading the unwary to accommodate or even collaborate in their apostasy. Scripture condemns such deceitfulness:

> But there were also false prophets among the people, even as there will be false teachers among you, who will secretly bring in destructive heresies, even denying the Lord who bought them, and bring on themselves swift destruction. And many will follow their destructive ways, because of whom the way of truth will be blasphemed....
>
> While they promise them liberty, they themselves are slaves of corruption; for by whom a person is overcome, by him also he is brought into bondage. For

if, after they have escaped the pollutions of the world through the knowledge of the Lord and Savior Jesus Christ, they are again entangled in them and overcome, the latter end is worse for them than the beginning [2 *Peter* 2:1-2, 18-20].

To paraphrase Machen, conservatives today do not presume to say whether any individual who has embraced neo-liberalism, or has aided and abetted its spread, will be saved or not. God alone decides such questions, and on the last day Christ will make that righteous judgment plain to all when He places the justified saints on His right hand. Some who have gone after these errors may yet repent, and that is our hope and prayer. *But on the authority of Scripture, one thing is perfectly plain even now: Whether or not some neo-liberals are Christians, neo-liberalism is not Christianity. And those who continue to reject Christianity will be lost.*

The marks of neo-liberalism are now the marks of the Orthodox Presbyterian Church. The OPC has quietly permitted foundational doctrines of authentic Biblical Christianity to be gradually supplanted by subtle but increasingly deadly counterfeits. It began in the seminaries, particularly Westminster in Philadelphia. And as seminary graduates influenced by these counterfeits entered pulpits in the Orthodox Presbyterian Church, the Presbyterian Church in America, and elsewhere, and came to hold positions of influence on boards and committees, the cancer spread.

For over thirty years, the OPC's sessions, presbyteries, and general assemblies have failed to rid the denomination of neo-liberalism through Biblical discipline. Because of their failure, the cancer has spread beyond the OPC into other denominations. The OPC bears heavy responsibility for this plague in the body of Christ. Honest examination demonstrates that the OPC as a denomination no longer bears the marks of a true church of Jesus Christ. But sadly, the predominant attitudes among the ministers, elders, and congregations of the OPC are ignorance, complacency, and denial. And equally sadly, there is no sign of denominational repentance. The OPC is ignoring the errors of history.

Chapter 3

Those Who Ignore the Errors of History...

Remember the days of old,
Consider the years of many generations.
Ask your father, and he will show you;
Your elders, and they will tell you.
Deuteronomy 32:7

It is well said that those who refuse to learn from the mistakes of history are condemned to repeat them. Perhaps nowhere has this been true more often than in the history of the church. The most serious and damaging mistakes of church history have been heresies regarding the Gospel. As such, they are far worse than mere mistakes. They are among the greatest sins of church history.

Perversions of the Gospel have consistently shared two characteristics: They denigrate the person and work of Jesus Christ in salvation, and they elevate the person and work of sinful man. And beneath historical heresies concerning the Gospel, we find a common root cause: The promulgators forsake sound principles for interpreting Scripture. Heresy assigns the word of man greater authority than the Word of God.

In this chapter and the next, we shall examine two areas in which the OPC is repeating the mistakes of church history. First, many past heresies regarding the Gospel and

Scripture have found new life in neo-liberal theology within the OPC. Second, the OPC has embraced the false principles of the old liberalism. In this regard we shall look closely at the infamous *Auburn Affirmation* of 1924, and see how the OPC has, to the peril of the church, embraced every underlying principle of that liberal manifesto of three generations ago.

Historical Errors Repeated: The Gospel

Perversions of Gospel doctrine appeared in the early church, even before the New Testament was completed. The Galatian heresy taught that the Gospel was the continuation of the law, not distinct from it. The preachers of "another gospel" in the church's first decades believed that Judaism with its system of law-observance continued to possess merit in itself. Christianity was merely a continuation of Judaism, and Jesus was in effect the first Christian. This heresy was condemned by the first council at Jerusalem in *Acts* 15, and by Paul in his epistles.

From the fifth century onward, Pelagianism has denied the imputation of sin to all of mankind through the federal headship of Adam (1 *Corinthians* 15:22), and has asserted that men advance in holiness by their own merits, with the aid of the law. Pelagianism teaches that the law, as well as the Gospel, gives entrance to Heaven. Semi-Pelagianism asserts that salvation is a cooperative effort involving the work of Christ and the good works of men. This is the doctrine of Roman Catholicism.

Socinianism, a heresy at the time of the Reformation, said that Jesus was principally a prophet who taught a new form of the law and provided the example of a holy life. Socinianism denied man's total inability to save himself, and denied the doctrine of justification by faith alone.

Sacramentalism, which developed mainly within Roman Catholicism, is the false teaching that the saving grace of Christ is transmitted to men through baptism and the Lord's Supper. Sacramentalism also appears in such nineteenth-century Protestant heresies as the Oxford Movement in England and the Mercersburg Theology of John Williamson Nevin and Philip Schaff in the United States.

Sacerdotalism, a companion heresy, teaches that members of a human priesthood can act as salvific mediators between God and man.

Sacralism is the heresy that men may become Christians merely by entering into nominal Christianity as a common religion, chosen and shaped by the leaders of their society, to which all members of that society are expected to subscribe. In historical terms, sacralism is associated with the mass "conversions" that took place when medieval monarchs adopted nominal Christianity in their realms. All their subjects were expected to adopt the new state religion. Sacralism influenced the establishment of official state churches in many nations of Europe. The first clause of the First Amendment to the United States Constitution ("Congress shall make no law respecting an establishment of religion") was designed to prevent state-sponsored sacralism in this country.

All of these heresies reappear in the neo-liberal errors currently being taught in the OPC and beyond. As in the Galatian heresy, Pelagianism, and Socinianism, neo-liberalism confuses law and Gospel. Like Socinianism, neo-liberalism effectively views Jesus Christ as little more than the first Christian, man's ethical and moral example in achieving "final justification." Like semi-Pelagianism, neo-liberalism views man as cooperating with God in salvation. Like sacramentalism, neo-liberalism says that baptism "is the moment when we see the transition from death to life and a person is saved."[1] This logically entails sacerdotalism, because neo-liberals are in fact saying that the one who administers baptism is a salvific mediator, no different in principle from a Roman priest.

Neo-liberalism introduces a not-so-subtle form of sacralism through its distortion of "living in covenant," which we touched upon in the discussion of the Shepherd-Gaffin view of man and salvation in chapter two. Neo-liberal sacralism stems from its perversion of the Biblical doctrines of the Covenant of Works and the Covenant of Grace, and of the Old and New Testament administrations of the latter.

In the neo-liberal view, Christianity becomes Christendom, a social order characterized by membership in a "covenant community." Church members enter this "covenant community" (which bears only slight resemblance to the authentic Biblical covenants) by means of baptism. They remain "in covenant" by partaking of the Lord's Supper and by "covenant faithfulness" – the neo-liberal code words for justification by law-keeping. The shape of the "covenant" is based on the opinions of the leaders of the church rather than on Scripture alone. The leaders of the church admit men to the covenant and they exclude men from the covenant, usurping the office of the Holy Spirit.

In medieval sacralist Europe, nominally Christian kings held the threat of physical death over subjects who did not conform to the state religion. Modern sacralist neo-liberalism places members of its "covenant community" under the threat of spiritual death through excommuni-

1. Norman Shepherd, *The Call of Grace*, 94.

cation. It teaches that there is no salvation outside the visible church. It places the people of God under covenant curses within the communal context. The vehicle for this threat is the un-Biblical confusion of law and Gospel.

This form of sacralism is being openly promoted in the OPC. In August 2003, the Southern California Center for Christian Studies, a ministry of Bayview Orthodox Presbyterian Church in Chula Vista, California, held a conference called "Contemporary Perspectives in Covenant Theology" to promote the neo-liberal apostasy. Speakers included Norman Shepherd and Roger Wagner, Bayview's pastor, who is also the president of SCCCS. Conference presentations were later published in book form. In one of them, Randy Booth placed members of the "covenant" under its curses:

> We have thought too long only in terms of covenant blessings. As Bahnsen[2] put it: "The covenant of grace curses people who have the privilege of being among God's people on earth, distinguished from the world, and yet don't live up to what He teaches." [3]

> To be covenantally united with God, although intended by God to bring favor and blessing to His chosen people, carries as well the threat of judgment and curse. God's covenant involves blessing and cursing, depending upon whether one is a covenant-keeper or a covenant-breaker.[4]

2. Dr. Greg L. Bahnsen (1948-1995), Westminster Seminary graduate, OPC minister, disciple of Norman Shepherd, founder of SCCCS, leading promoter of the philosophy of Cornelius Van Til.

3. Randy Booth, "The Sensible Covenant" in *Backbone of the Bible: Covenant in Contemporary Perspective,* 31.

4. Booth, 31. This is also a theme of Cornelius Van Til.

To be in covenant with God, therefore, does not automatically imply eternal salvation – certainly not for covenant-breakers.[5]

The Church must speak when one of its own (or a group of its own) defiles the covenant. It is an abomination to assume the name of Christ and then to profane that name. Recognizing that someone is in the covenant is not the same as saying he is faithful to the covenant. We should not advocate an undiscerning group-hug. We want unity, but we want it on Christ's terms. We long for Christendom to be united, but that unity will come only when covenant disloyalty is rebuked and repented of.

Reformation is an ongoing work. It is accomplished only by declaring the good news of God's covenant law....[6]

Neo-liberalism's sacralist view of the "covenant" disregards the Apostle Paul's instruction – in response to the Galatian heresy – regarding the stark contrast between the curse of the law and the blessings of the Gospel in Christ:

For as many as are of the works of the law are under the curse; for it is written, "Cursed is everyone who does not continue in all things which are written in the book of the law, to do them." But that no one is justified by the law in the sight of God is evident, for "the just shall live by faith." Yet the law is not of faith, but "the man who does them shall live by them."

5. Booth, 32.

6. Booth, 33. Of course, law – commands – are not good news, for they are not news at all.

74

Christ has redeemed us from the curse of the law, having become a curse for us... [*Galatians* 3:10-13].

Other neo-liberals are more blatant than Booth or Bahnsen in their sacralism. Federal Visionist Steven M. Schlissel, pastor of the independent Messiah's Congregation in Brooklyn, New York, is a gifted speaker who has developed a strong following in the OPC and PCA. Schlissel states the neo-liberals' sacralist view of "covenant" even more plainly:

The "bilateral nature" of the covenant means that man is compacted into a covenant of mutual obligations, and is therefore accorded a decisive role in securing its promises. Man is required to fulfill what is due and to request thereupon his due.... This turns Christianity into a congregation of obeyers rather than a congregation of believers.[7]

In a lecture called "Covenant Hearing" at the Auburn Avenue Pastors Conference in January 2002, Schlissel said:

I want to suggest that a failure of covenant consciousness in our churches has led in large measure to this condition of widespread anti-Christianity today. A historian of note has written that the "great missionary expansion of the nineteenth century was everywhere based upon the principle of individual conversion, and this was marked by an introspective psychological approach and an intensely personal view of conversion and salvation. There is a fundamental contrast between this approach

7. Steven M. Schlissel, "A New Way of Seeing?" in *The Auburn Avenue Theology, Pros & Cons: Debating the Federal Vision*, 23. Here he is approvingly paraphrasing material from an essay by the Lutheran theologian Armand J. Boehme.

and the collective or communal (or what we would call covenantal) form of expression, which had dominated the Christian world for upward of one thousand years."

Western Christendom was not built up by the method of individual conversions; rather, it was a way of life that the people accepted as a whole, often by the decision of their rulers. When accepted, Christianity affected the whole life of society by the change of their institutions and laws. It is easy to condemn this type of corporate Christianity as superficial, external, or even sub-Christian, but at least it means that Christianity is accepted as a social fact affecting every side of life and not merely as an opinion or a specialized group activity or even a hobby. If we want to know how a nation that was largely uniformly Christian in its self-understanding has become anti-Christian, we need look no further than this individualized conception of God's dealings, which was heavily promoted in the nineteenth century.[8]

Neo-liberalism's covenantal sacralism places the church once again in the Middle Ages, and once again under the yoke of sacerdotalism, sacramentalism, and clericalism, the establishment of the clergy as a ruling class. The commandment of Jesus Christ is in stark contrast:

> You know that the rulers of the Gentiles lord it over them, and those who are great exercise authority over them. Yet it shall not be so among you; but whoever desires to become great among you, let him be your servant. And whoever desires to be first among you, let

8. Steven M. Schlissel, "Covenant Hearing," a lecture given at the Auburn Avenue Pastors Conference, 2002. From a transcript published by the author at www.messiahnyc.org/mediaview.asp?id-12.

him be your slave – just as the Son of Man did not come to be served, but to serve, and to give His life a ransom for many [*Matthew* 20:25-28].

Historical Errors Repeated: Scripture

Heresies regarding the Gospel spring from rejection of sound principles for interpreting Scripture.[9] This problem likewise manifested itself from the earliest days of the church, and it appears in the neo-liberalism of the OPC today.

Gnosticism is based on the propositions that God is unknowable, and that belief founded on a reasoned interpretation of Scripture is somehow unspiritual or inferior to a supposed extra-Biblical "higher knowledge." Although Gnosticism did not emerge as a movement in the church until the second century, the Holy Spirit through the Apostle Paul anticipates it in warning against "the profane and idle babblings of what is falsely called knowledge" – in the original, *gnoseos* (1 *Timothy* 6:20).

Like Gnosticism, dialectical theology asserts the deficiency of propositional truth. Neo-liberalism's dialectical theology says that Scripture is full of paradoxical statements about God, man, creation, Christ, and salvation, and that embracing these paradoxes yields "truth." Dialectical theology claims to synthesize or combine opposing doctrinal positions without resolving the inherent conflicts between them. This grants men a license to give new and un-Biblical meanings, without regard to context, to doctrinal terms that are clearly defined within the Scriptures.

9. See chapter eight for a discussion of these principles.

The philosophies of Bavinck and Van Til, discussed in chapter two, reflect the influence of a dialectical approach to theology.

Postmodernism has carried the interpretive heresies of Gnosticism and dialectical theology to new depths. In post-modern thinking there is no single reality, there are only "realities" in the plural. There are as many legitimate inter-pretations of Scripture as there are individual interpreters, or communities of interpreters. The only absolute, certain, or fixed principle is that *there are no absolute, certain, or fixed principles* – only varying but equally legitimate perspectives. In such a self-contradictory and irrational atmosphere, whatever "principles" of Biblical interpretation one may choose to hold are in fact merely the *preferences* of the com-munity of interpreters in which one chooses to participate. There are no fixed rules having their sure foundation in the transcendent and self-interpreting *Logos*.

Many conservatives in the church wish to think that the influences of postmodernism have not penetrated the theo-logy of denominations like the OPC. They should think again. The OPC's 2004 *Report of the Committee to Study the Views of Creation* reflects a philosophy steeped in post-modernism. It approvingly quotes a 1968 Presbytery of Southern California report: "We recognize different inter-pretations of the word 'day' [in *Genesis* 1] and do not feel that one interpretation is to be insisted upon to the exclusion of others." The 2004 OPC *Report* then goes on to say,

> Here is where the Orthodox Presbyterian Church appears to be presently divided. Must one interpretation of the character of the days of creation be accepted to the exclusion of the others? In recent practice some presby-

teries in the church have so insisted, to the chagrin of other presbyteries. [10]

Taking the side of those "chagrined" presbyteries, the 2004 *Report* commends what it clearly sees as the majority in the OPC, which

> has cultivated a community of interpretation that has sustained confessional integrity among its ministerial membership without imposing over-exacting standards.... The most important factor in establishing and maintaining the community of interpretation has been the function of Westminster Theological Seminary in Philadelphia as the OPC's *de facto* denominational seminary...*inducting Orthodox Presbyterian ministerial candidates into a culture of interpretation.*[11]

A popular American restaurant chain advertises using the slogan, "No Rules, Just Right." That may be an appealing catch phrase for a business where customer taste is the highest standard. But where God's Word is concerned, the induction of ministerial candidates into a dialectical, postmodern, no-rules-just-right "culture of interpretation" is the kind of vain philosophy that Scripture warns against:

> Beware lest anyone cheat you through philosophy and empty deceit, according to the tradition of men, according to the basic principles of the world, and not according to Christ [*Colossians* 2:8].

---

10. "Report of the Committee to Study the Views of Creation" (*Commissioners' Workbook for the 71st General Assembly of the Orthodox Presbyterian Church*, 2004), 1604.

11. *Report*, 1607. Emphasis in the original.

This kind of thinking has no place among those who claim to stand for the full authority and inerrancy of the Scriptures. Yet the OPC's 2004 General Assembly legitimized such thinking when it commended this *Report* to its churches. This on-the-record endorsement of interpretive heresy became possible because Westminster Seminary in Philadelphia has, in the *Report's* own words, "inducted" OPC ministerial candidates into such a "culture of interpretation" for several decades.

Because they have been steeped in this culture of interpretation, it is no surprise that many "Timothys" who have left Westminster Theological Seminary to enter the pulpits of the OPC during the past thirty years have been largely incapable of heeding the Apostle Paul's warning to their namesake of old:

> O Timothy! Guard what was committed to your trust, avoiding the profane and idle babblings and contradictions of what is falsely called knowledge – by professing it some have strayed concerning the faith [1 Timothy 6:19-20].

Chapter 4

Embracing the Principles of the Auburn Affirmation

Do not be unequally yoked together with unbelievers.
For what fellowship has righteousness with lawlessness?
And what communion has light with darkness?
And what accord has Christ with Belial?
Or what part has a believer with an unbeliever?
And what agreement has the temple of God with idols?
2 Corinthians 6:14-16

In early 1924, liberals in the Presbyterian Church in the U. S. A. published a manifesto of their false principles that came to be known as the *Auburn Affirmation*.[1] The subsequent acceptance of this landmark document in the PCUSA, and the fact that none of its signers was ever disciplined by the church, revealed the extent to which the cancer of the old liberalism had corrupted the denomination over the preceding three generations.

As yet, the neo-liberalism that has sapped the spiritual vitality of the OPC during the past thirty years has no direct equivalent to the *Auburn Affirmation* – a single document reducing such false principles to a few pages in contemporary terms. But there is abundant evidence that the OPC

---

1. The *Auburn Affirmation* is reproduced in full in Appendix A.

has embraced the underlying principles of the *Auburn Affirmation*, and their corrupting influence is now widespread. The OPC has repeated this mistake of history.

The publication of the *Auburn Affirmation* was one of the key events leading to the secession of conservatives from the PCUSA to form the OPC in 1936. A detailed account of those events is beyond the scope of this book, but it is important background for readers of this book. The books and articles listed below[2] more fully describe the PCUSA's descent into liberalism, the tepid response of the majority of

2. Gordon H. Clark, *The Auburn Heresy* (Committee on Christian Education, Orthodox Presbyterian Church, www.opc.org/cce/clark.html).

John P. Galbraith, *Choose Ye This Day! An Analysis of Reasons Why Christians Should Separate from the Presbyterian Church in the U. S. A.* (Committee on Christian Education, Orthodox Presbyterian Church, www.opc.org/cce/choose_ye.html).

Galbraith, *Why the Orthodox Presbyterian Church?* (Committee on Christian Education, Orthodox Presbyterian Church, www.opc.org/cce/WhyOPC.html).

D. G. Hart, ed., *J. Gresham Machen: Selected Shorter Writings* (Phillipsburg, New Jersey: P&R Publishing, 2004).

Hart, *Defending the Faith: J. Gresham Machen and the Crisis of Conservative Protestantism in America* (Grand Rapids, Michigan: Baker Books, 1994).

Hart & John Muether, *Fighting the Good Fight: A Brief History of the Orthodox Presbyterian Church* (Philadelphia: The Committee for the Historian of the Orthodox Presbyterian Church, 1995).

J. Gresham Machen, *Christianity and Liberalism* (Grand Rapids, Michigan: Wm. B. Eerdmans Publishing Co., [1923] 1999).

Machen, *What Is Faith?* (Carlisle, Pennsylvania: The Banner of Truth Trust, [1925] 1991).

Edwin H. Rian, *The Presbyterian Conflict* (Philadelphia: The Committee for the Historian of the Orthodox Presbyterian Church, [1940] 1992).

Ned B. Stonehouse, *J. Gresham Machen: A Biographical Memoir* (Carlisle, Pennsylvania: The Banner of Truth Trust, [1954] 1998).

its pastors and elders, and the struggles of those who remained true to Scripture.

To understand what has happened to the OPC, it is important to understand the eight principles that were encapsulated in the *Auburn Affirmation* and their corrupting parallels in the OPC today.

The Auburn Affirmation: Background

The spiritual crisis that brought about the separation of conservatives from the PCUSA in the mid-1930s was three generations in the making. It became increasingly public between 1900 and 1935 as a spirit of un-Biblical pluralism and "tolerance" – actually a rising tide of *intolerance* of authentic Biblical Christianity – finally destroyed the PCUSA's already-weakened foundations.

The *Auburn Affirmation* was not the first visible symptom of the long-developing cancer. A few conservatives had recognized the signs of spiritual rot much earlier. In 1893 Dr. Charles A. Briggs of Union Theological Seminary was convicted of heresy and removed from the ministry for teaching that the Bible was not inerrant. Several other liberals were also convicted and removed from their pulpits during the 1890s, but many more remained.[3]

By the time the *Auburn Affirmation* appeared in 1924, as Machen and others recognized in retrospect, the malignancy of liberalism had spread so far that it was too late to rid the PCUSA of it.[4] By the middle 1930s, there was no

---

3. Carl McIntire, *The Death of a Church* (Collingswood, New Jersey: Christian Beacon Press, 1967), 117-124.

4. Rian, *The Presbyterian Conflict*, 4-25; Stonehouse, *J. Gresham Machen*, 351-364.

room for doubt. Dr. George A. Buttrick of Madison Avenue Presbyterian Church wrote his book *The Christian Fact and Modern Doubt,* in which he denied the inerrancy of Scripture, the historicity of the first eleven chapters of *Genesis,* the doctrine of the federal headship of Adam, and the historicity of Christ's resurrection. Heresy charges were filed against him, but the PCUSA refused to hear the case. The charges were simply buried.[5] Buttrick remained in his pulpit for nearly thirty years, served as a visiting professor of Christian morals at Harvard, and also served into the 1960s as general editor of the *Interpreter's Bible* and the *Interpreter's Dictionary of the Bible.*

When the *Auburn Affirmation* was first published in January 1924, it included the names of 150 signers, all of them minister in the PCUSA. By May of 1924 the number of signers had grown to nearly 1,300 ministers and ruling elders. This number, though substantial, constituted no more than 15 percent of the PCUSA's ordained ministers and ruling elders at the time.[6] But the *Auburn Affirmation* was to exert an influence on the denomination well beyond those numbers.

The *Affirmation* proclaimed itself to be "designed to safeguard the unity and liberty of the Presbyterian Church in the United States of America." In reality, it was a declaration of the underlying principles of the old liberalism. Far from being an affirmation of truth, it was a denial of the foundations of the faith. As one minister put it, "The *Affirmation* revealed the campaign strategy of the modernists.

5. McIntire, *The Death of a Church,* 132-142.

6. Charles E. Quirk, "A Statistical Analysis of the Signers of the Auburn Affirmation," *The Journal of Presbyterian History* (Volume 43:3, September 1965), 149-196.

The attack on historic Christianity was not to be an open, forthright one. It was to be a denial of the faith by feigned affirmations."[7] It received substantial public and private support from so-called moderates within the PCUSA, and even from some who styled themselves conservatives.[8]

Reading the *Affirmation* at a distance of 80 years, vigilant Bible-believing Christians recognize it as a frontal attack on the inerrancy of Scripture, the virgin birth of Christ, justification by faith alone, the bodily resurrection of Christ, and the reality of His miracles. They also recognize its underlying principles. But the majority of men in the PCUSA of the 1920s and 1930s were not so discerning. Many were taken in by the subtlety of the *Affirmation*. As Gordon H. Clark said in 1935, "the *Auburn Affirmation* is a cleverly written document with some pious phraseology slightly obscuring its real intent."[9]

Its writers and signers, men who openly denied the true Gospel, struck the pose of faithful men who were allegedly victims of ecclesiastical injustice. But the alleged "injustice" consisted of the efforts of faithful men to rid the church of heresy. The Auburn liberals said they felt bound, in view of "persistent attempts to divide the church and abridge its freedom," to express their "convictions." They insisted that

7. Robert K. Churchill, *Lest We Forget: A Personal Reflection on the Formation of the Orthodox Presbyterian Church* (Philadelphia: Committee for the Historian of the Orthodox Presbyterian Church, 1997), 65.

8. Charles E. Quirk, "Origins of the Auburn Affirmation," *The Journal of Presbyterian History* (Volume 53:2, Summer 1975), 120-142.

9. Gordon H. Clark, *The Auburn Heresy*, an address given at a meeting of Presbyterian laymen in Philadelphia, February 28, 1935, and later published in the *Southern Presbyterian Review* in July 1946. Reproduced at www.opc.org/cce/clark.html.

We do not desire liberty to go beyond the teachings of evangelical Christianity. But we maintain that it is our constitutional right[10] and our Christian duty within these limits to exercise liberty of thought and teaching, that we may more effectively preach the gospel of Jesus Christ, the Saviour of the World.

...[W]e deplore the evidences of division in our beloved church, in the face of a world so desperately in need of a united testimony to the gospel of Christ. We earnestly desire fellowship with all who like us are disciples of Jesus Christ. We hope that those to whom this Affirmation comes will believe that it is not the declaration of a theological party, but rather a sincere appeal, based on the Scriptures and our standards, for the preservation of the unity and freedom of our church, for which most earnestly we plead and pray.

Under this cloak, they sought redress of those alleged injustices. In the *Affirmation* they clothed deadly error in affirmative language, stressing the word "liberty," used nine times in the document. They called on the PCUSA to "safeguard the unity and liberty" of the church and to "safeguard the liberty of thought and teaching of its ministers."

Taken in by that subtlety, the majority in the PCUSA adopted a posture of tolerance and accommodation, if not outright support, toward the *Auburn Affirmation*'s signers and their wicked propositions. They turned a deaf ear toward the Holy Spirit's warnings and admonitions regarding the subtlety of false teachers:

10. Here they referred to the constitution (*i.e.*, the *Form of Government, Book of Discipline*, and confessional standards) of the PCUSA.

Now the Spirit expressly says that in latter times some will depart from the faith, giving heed to deceiving spirits and doctrines of demons, speaking lies in hypocrisy, having their own conscience seared with a hot iron [1 *Timothy* 4:1-2].

But there were also false prophets among the people, even as there will be false teachers among you, who will secretly bring in destructive heresies, even denying the Lord who bought them, and bring on themselves swift destruction. And many will follow their destructive ways, because of whom the way of truth will be blasphemed. By covetousness they will exploit you with deceptive words; for a long time their judgment has not been idle, and their destruction does not slumber [2 *Peter* 2:1-3].

I found it necessary to write to you exhorting you to contend earnestly for the faith which was once for all delivered to the saints. For certain men have crept in unnoticed [*Jude* 3-4].

But evil men and impostors will grow worse and worse, deceiving and being deceived [2 *Timothy* 3:13].

For such are false apostles, deceitful workers, transforming themselves into apostles of Christ. And no wonder! For Satan himself transforms himself into an angel of light [2 *Corinthians* 11:13-14].

Now this I say lest anyone should deceive you with persuasive words [*Colossians* 2:4].

The *Auburn Affirmation* made the case for the presservation of a doctrinal pluralism within the PCUSA that was already well established, as we shall see shortly. The signers sought to protect and expand the big theological tent they had been spreading through incremental advances for many years. Under this big tent, in the name of "the unity and freedom of our church," it would be acceptable to permit multiple conflicting interpretations of the foundational doctrines of Scripture. There would be no single standard of truth, but ministers and communities of ministers could arrive at their own "truth" – all the while professing loyal adherence to Scripture and to the confessional standards of the church.

On the surface, the writers of the *Auburn Affirmation* addressed certain issues and controversies that had arisen in the PCUSA in the first two decades of the twentieth century. These issues were indicated by sub-headings in the text of the Affirmation. But the sub-headings masked the writers' true intent. Woven into the text of the document was a structure of false and deadly principles that went largely unchallenged at the time, except by a small number of conservatives.

It is those underlying principles of the old liberalism that are important to our present historical study. The reason is that they are also the underlying principles of the neo-liberalism that has corrupted the OPC.

In the remainder of this chapter we shall uncover those false principles, quoting appropriate passages from the *Auburn Affirmation*, with explanatory notes and comments.

Conceal Liberalism's True Colors

The first false principle emanating from the Auburn Affirmation was that liberals are sound men, true disciples of Christ, true defenders of the faith, and true adherents of the Reformation. The Auburn liberals said:

> At the outset we affirm and declare our acceptance of the *Westminster Confession of Faith,* as we did at our ordinations, "as containing the system of doctrine taught in the Holy Scriptures." We sincerely hold and earnestly preach the doctrines of evangelical Christianity, in agreement with the historic testimony of the Presbyterian Church in the United States of America, of which we are loyal ministers. For the maintenance of the faith of our church, the preservation of its unity, and the protection of the liberties of its ministers and people, we offer this *Affirmation.*

Today in the OPC, neo-liberals and their supporters use the same ploy to claim liberty to preach another gospel. Neo-liberals pervert point after point of Scriptural terminology. In the name of unity, they claim the right of existence and toleration for conflicting versions of "truth" within the church. All the while they claim to be loyal to the Scriptures and loyal to the doctrinal standards of their church, true defenders of the faith, true disciples of Christ, and true sons of the Reformation. But while promising liberty, they themselves are the slaves of corruption (2 *Peter* 2:1).

Put a Positive "Spin" on Doctrinal Compromise

The second false principle propagated by the Auburn liberals was that doctrinal compromise is a positive development for the sake of unity and growth.

The Auburn liberals were referring to the doctrinal compromises of the 1800s through the early 1900s in the PCUSA.[11] What were those compromises? In 1801, the

---

11. A somewhat more detailed discussion of these compromises

89

PCUSA united with New England Congregationalists who embraced Hopkinsianism, a system of theology based not on Scripture but on a fusion of the Bible and abolitionist political philosophy. Hopkinsianism was the historical descendant of many older heresies. Among other things Hopkinsianism denied human depravity, the imputation of sin through the federal headship of Adam, and the imputation of the righteousness of Christ as the federal head of believers. Hopkinsianism taught justification by faith plus works.

In 1837 the PCUSA General Assembly abrogated the 1801 union with the liberal Congregationalists. But the liberals had already done great damage. Some remained in PCUSA pulpits after the 1837 split. Men from the liberal wing had infiltrated existing colleges and seminaries and founded new ones – including Auburn Theological Seminary in New York, from which would come, three generations later, the infamous *Affirmation*.

In 1869, the liberals who had been put out of the PCUSA in 1837 were allowed to return to the denomination in full force, and by then, in larger numbers.

In 1889, the repatriated liberals and their supporters attempted to revise the *Westminster Confession of Faith* to gain official standing for some of their un-Biblical views. The General Assembly appointed a committee to prepare the revisions, and in 1892 the proposed compromises were circulated to the presbyteries but subsequently rejected. But this was a hollow victory for conservatives. They succeeded only because many liberals joined them in opposing the

---

appears in John P. Galbraith's *Why the Orthodox Presbyterian Church?* (Committee on Christian Education, Orthodox Presbyterian Church, www.opc.org/cce/WhyOPC.html).

doctrinal compromises, but for a far different reason – for the liberals, the changes had not gone far enough.

In the late 1890s, discussions began with the goal of reunion between the PCUSA and the Cumberland Presbyterian Church. The CPC had been founded by men who had broken away from the PCUSA in 1810 to form a more liberal group. It became obvious that reunion would necessitate doctrinal compromise. Thus, in 1903 the liberals succeeded in having the PCUSA revise the *Confession of Faith*. Among other things, those revisions opened the door to a denial of the federal headship of Christ and the imputation of His righteousness to sinners. They also opened the way to increased acceptance of a doctrine of salvation that accorded a role to man's works alongside Christ's atonement.

By 1918-1920, the spirit of compromise had permeated the PCUSA to such an extent that a "Plan of Organic Union" with other churches, spanning the full spectrum from conservative to extremely liberal, was approved by over 100 presbyteries representing approximately one-third of the denomination. The creedal basis of the proposed union was a pseudo-Christian declaration to which even a Roman Catholic could have subscribed. In this, it prefigured the *Evangelicals and Catholics Together* and *The Gift of Salvation* declarations of the late twentieth century.

As with all such compromise documents, what it said was less significant than what was *not* said, especially concerning the Gospel and the Scriptures. The proposed creedal basis of union spoke of "God's eternal purpose of salvation" but said nothing of justification by faith in Christ alone apart from works. It said that the Scriptures merely contained God's revealed will, but said nothing of their inerrancy, infallibility, or full sufficiency as the believer's rule of faith and practice.[12]

In 1920 this plan of union was voted down in the PCUSA. But once again it was a hollow victory for true conservatives. Many who called themselves doctrinal conservatives opposed the plan not because it embodied serious doctrinal compromise, but mainly because it meant union with non-Presbyterian groups!

The Auburn liberals portrayed these decades of growing compromise on the Gospel, the Scriptures, and other foundational elements of doctrine as healthy developments. In the *Affirmation* they wrote:

> Of the two parts into which our church was separated from 1837 to 1870, one held that only one interpretation of certain parts of the *Confession of Faith* was legitimate, while the other maintained its right to dissent from this interpretation. In the Reunion of 1870 they came together on equal terms, "each recognizing the other as a sound and orthodox body." The meaning of this, as understood then and ever since, is that office-bearers in the church who maintain their liberty in the interpretation of the *Confession* are exercising their rights guaranteed by the terms of the Reunion.
>
> A more recent reunion also is significant, that of the Cumberland Presbyterian Church and the Presbyterian Church in the United States of America, in 1906. This reunion was opposed by certain members of the Presbyterian Church in the United States of America, on the ground that the two churches were not at one in doctrine; yet it was consummated. Thus did our

12. *Minutes of the General Assembly of the PCUSA*, 1920, Part 1, 118.

church once more exemplify its historic policy of accepting theological differences within its bounds and subordinating them to recognized loyalty to Jesus Christ and united work for the kingdom of God.

Likewise, the OPC has maintained doctrinal pluralism on the Gospel and other foundational matters for over thirty years. Men who hold the truth on the foundations of the faith have chosen to coexist with neo-liberals in their presbyteries; they have served together with them on the OPC's boards, committees, and commissions; they have met together with them year after year as commissioners to its General Assemblies – all as if nothing were wrong.

They ignore the mistakes of their own church history. Like their counterparts in the PCUSA three generations ago, most conservatives in the OPC during the past thirty years have misguidedly subordinated differences that clearly cross the divide between truth and error, in the name of "loyalty to Jesus Christ and united work for the kingdom of God." In making common cause with neo-liberals they have, as Machen put it, been "indifferent to the question whether the gospel is true or false." And when they bow together in prayer with their neo-liberal counterparts, as Machen said, "that is not Christian prayer; it is bowing down in the house of Rimmon."[13]

Denigrate the Doctrine of Inerrancy

The third false principle propagated via the Auburn Affirmation was that Scripture is not inerrant, nor is it subject to fixed, self-derived rules of interpretation. Therefore, men can

13. Machen "The Defense of the Faith" in *J. Gresham Machen: Selected Shorter Writings*, 147.

teach whatever they want from Scripture so long as they claim
that they do so under the guidance of the Holy Spirit.

The signers of the *Auburn Affirmation* attacked the doctrine of inerrancy head-on:

> There is no assertion in the Scriptures that their
> writers were kept "from error." The Confession of Faith
> does not make this assertion; and it is significant that
> this assertion is not to be found in the Apostles' Creed
> or the Nicene Creed or in any of the great Reformation
> confessions. The doctrine of inerrancy, intended to en-
> hance the authority of the Scriptures, in fact impairs
> their supreme authority for faith and life, and weakens
> the testimony of the church to the power of God unto
> salvation through Jesus Christ. We hold that the Gen-
> eral Assembly of 1923, in asserting that "the Holy Spirit
> did so inspire, guide and move the writers of Holy
> Scripture as to keep them from error," spoke without
> warrant of the Scriptures or of the *Confession of Faith*.
> We hold rather to the words of the *Confession of Faith*,
> that the Scriptures "are given by inspiration of God, to
> be the rule of faith and life" (*Conf.* I, ii).

Most people in the OPC think that their denomination
and Westminster Theological Seminary are still bulwarks of
Biblical inerrancy. They should think again. As we have seen
and shall see again in chapter eight, the 2004 OPC Creation
Study Committee *Report* is an attack on inerrancy. But it is
not the first by far. For many years the *Westminster Theological Journal* has published essays by the skeptic Paul H.
Seely, a Westminster graduate, attacking the doctrine of
inerrancy.[14] In the Fall 2004 issue of *WTJ* Seely states that

14. In 1991, 1992, 1997, 2001, and 2004.

"the description of the extent of the flood in *Gen* 6-9 is not at all supported by archaeology. It is, in fact, falsified by archaeology."[15] And in case we might miss his point that the Bible is not inerrant, he says a few pages later that "archaeology, glaciology, and geology falsify the catastrophic dimensions of the flood as given in *Gen* 6-9."[16] For Seely, the *Genesis* flood account is useful only for its spiritual lessons, not its historicity.

In another *Westminster Theological Journal* essay, Seely denies the historicity of the *Genesis* record of the division of human language at the time of the building of the Tower of Babel. Seely cites as his main support not the Scriptures, but the arguments of secular scholars, many of whom are evolutionists, some of them atheists or agnostics, with no interest (to say the least) in submitting to the authority of the Word of God.[17] Denial of the historicity of the *Genesis* flood account is a major component of their arguments. Seely and those he adopts as allies place the so-called wisdom of unregenerate men in judgment over the Scriptures. Seely sees the Babel account as only a "revelation of God as sovereign over the affairs of men" accommodating Israel's supposed understanding of the Earth "as a flat disc floating on a very deep ocean."[18] How short is the distance between

15. Paul H. Seely, "Noah's Flood: Its Date, Extent, and Divine Accommodation" in *Westminster Theological Journal*, Vol. 66, Fall 2004, 301.

16. For a refutation of this assertion, see John C. Whitcomb and Henry M. Morris, *The Genesis Flood: The Biblical Record and Its Scientific Implications* (Phillipsburg, New Jersey: Presbyterian and Reformed Publishing Co., 1961) and John D. Morris, *The Young Earth* (Colorado Springs, Colorado: Master Books, 1994).

17. Seely, "The Date of the Tower of Babel and Some Theological Implications" in *Westminster Theological Journal*, Vol. 63, No. 1, Spring 2001, 15-38.

18. Seely, 29.

calling the Scriptures an analogy of an unknowable truth, after the Van Tilian model, and calling them a collection of spiritually useful myths!

In this regard, Seely echoes the words of Dr. George A. Buttrick, a leading liberal of the PCUSA in the 1930s:

> The Old Testament...at its best [is] the reverent attempt of a primitive mind to explain in story-form the encompassing and indwelling Mystery. Whence came different languages? Impious men built a tower, intending to reach heaven and dispute the throne with God; so He broke their tower, and for penalty laid on them confusion of tongues. Only a dull mind could try to find history or science in that story, but only a dead mind could miss its moral and spiritual truth.[19]

Dr. Harold Lindsell cited Seely's outright denial of Biblical inerrancy in his 1976 book, *The Battle for the Bible*. He quotes another essay by Seely in which the Westminster Seminary alumnus says:

> The relationship of science to Scripture is this: The Bible gives redemptive truth through the scientific thoughts of the time without ever intending that those scientific thoughts should be believed as inerrant.... The aim of the Bible is to give redemptive truth. It never intended to teach science; nor does it ever claim to be "inerrant whenever it touches on science." It does not correct the errant science of the time in which it was written, but rather incorporates that pre-scientific science in its redemptive message.... To insist that the Bible be

19. George A. Buttrick, *The Christian Fact and Modern Doubt* (New York: Charles Scribner's Sons, 1935), 176.

inerrant every time it touches on science is to insist on an *a priori* doctrine that has been read into the Bible.[20]

Dr. Peter E. Enns,[21] a Westminster Seminary professor and present editor of its *Theological Journal*, presents an argument very similar to Seely's in a 2003 article:

> The purpose of speaking of an inerrant Scripture is not to generate an abstract comment about the church's sacred book, but it is to reflect on our doctrine of God, that is, that God does not err. But such a confession does not determine the *manner* in which the notion of an inerrant Scripture is articulated. It may very well be that the very way in which God "does not err" is by participating in the cultural conventions of the time.... The Bible is not inerrant because it conforms to some notion of how we think something worthy of the name "Scripture" should behave....
>
> The issue, therefore, is not *whether* Scripture is "inerrant" nor certainly whether the God who speaks therein is "inerrant," but the *nature* of the Scripture that the inerrant God has given us. And this is something the church proclaims to itself and the world by faith. Scripture is not "inerrant" *because* it can be shown that

20. Paul H. Seely, essay in the *Journal of the American Scientific Affiliation*, as quoted in Harold Lindsell, *The Battle for the Bible* (Grand Rapids, Michigan: Zondervan, 1976), 130-131.

21. B. A., Messiah College, 1982; M. Div., Westminster Theological Seminary, 1989; M. A., Harvard University, 1993; Ph. D., Harvard University, 1994; Teaching Fellow, Harvard University, 1990-1994; Editor, *Westminster Theological Journal*, 2000 – present; Professor of Old Testament, Westminster Theological Seminary, 1994 – present.

there really is no "synoptic problem"[22] or that the Apostles are doing faithful grammatical-historical exegesis.[23]

Such an *a priori* doctrine is not, as Seely and Enns have it, something "that has been read into the Bible" or something that "conforms to some notion of how we think something worthy of the name 'Scripture' should behave." It simply affirms the nature of God who speaks, who cannot err or lie in His Word.

If God has at any point incorporated erroneous human beliefs into the teaching of Scripture, at that point we cannot trust the Bible. If we cannot trust the Bible at even one single point, God is a liar, for He tells us that the whole of His Word is trustworthy. If God is a liar, we cannot be certain of His word at *any* point, and therefore we cannot trust His Word at all. Yet the purportedly "conservative" *Westminster Theological Journal* has permitted this outright denier of the inerrancy of Scripture to repeatedly publish his attacks on the Bible in its pages, and its own editor echoes his position.

Enns expands his attack on inerrancy in his book, *Inspiration and Incarnation: Evangelicals and the Problem of the Old Testament*. The title reflects Enns' exposure to liberal theology during his graduate studies at Harvard:

> While I was in graduate school, one of my professors (a traditional Jewish scholar) said something that

22. Elsewhere in this essay Enns alleges that there are factual inconsistencies among the accounts of the writers of the four Gospels and elsewhere in the Bible, and that these need not be harmonized.

23. Peter Enns, "Apostolic Hermeneutics and an Evangelical Doctrine of Scripture: Moving Beyond a Modernist Impasse," in *Westminster Theological Journal*, Volume 65, No. 2, Fall 2003, 263-288; also online at www.wts.edu/publications/articles/enns-impasse-p.html. Emphases in the original.

has stuck with me. This may sound terribly self-absorbed, but it was one of those "aha" moments that generate a process of rethinking a few things. [My professor said that] "For Jews, the Bible is a problem to be solved. For Christians, it is a message to be proclaimed."[24]

Enns clearly comes down on the side of the Bible as a "problem to be solved." On what basis does he claim, as his book title states, that there is a "problem of the Old Testament?" Enns reminds us that there have been numerous archeological discoveries in the past 150 years. But the archaeological data are not his principal concern. More important to Enns are the conclusions of unbelieving scholars about those discoveries.

And what, in Enns' view, is the "problem of the Old Testament"? He never really defines it except in terms of three purported "discoveries": 1. that the Old Testament contains myths, particularly in its earliest chapters;[25] 2. that there is theological diversity, even contradiction, in the Old Testament;[26] and 3. that the New Testament writers handled Old Testament passages in ways that are hermeneutically inconsistent.[27] Space does not permit us to deal with all three false assertions at length. In this chapter we shall briefly discuss his theory of Old Testament mythology. In chapter eight we shall examine his view of the New Testa-

24. Peter E. Enns, *Inspiration and Incarnation: Evangelicals and the Problem of the Old Testament* (Grand Rapids, Michigan: Baker Academic, 2005), 71.

25. Enns, 40*ff.*

26. Enns, 109.

27. Enns, 133*ff.*

ment writers' use of the Old. But we can summarize Enns' proposed solution to the purported "problem of the Old Testament" thus: Evangelicals must adjust their thinking about Scripture to incorporate unbelieving scholars' anti-supernatural "spin" on the discoveries of the past 150 years.

It is true that there have been vast and important archaeological discoveries during the past 150 years that have a direct or indirect relationship to the pages of Scripture. Two that Enns mentions are the discovery of the law code of Hammurabi, which is thought to predate the Mosaic law[28] and is similar to it in some details, and the discovery of various Near Eastern accounts of creation and the flood which, though pagan and in many cases childishly fanciful, bear some resemblances to the *Genesis* accounts. The question is, what does the believer do with these discoveries? Enns chooses to focus, not on interpreting these discoveries in light of Scripture, but on interpreting Scripture in light of what liberals claim these discoveries tell us about Scripture. Many liberal scholars – who as unbelievers are predisposed to do so – conclude that the Mosaic law is based on or plagiarized from Hammurabi's code, and that Biblical creation and flood accounts are based on pagan myths. For them, the Bible is a human and not a divine book.

Enns makes no serious effort to refute these conclusions of liberal scholarship, which are not new and have been well refuted by others.[29] Rather, his starting point is

28. Recently-discovered data which have altered archaeologists' thinking on the chronologies of neighboring empires have also raised questions on the dating of the code of Hammurabi.

29. See, for example, John C. Whitcomb, *The Early Earth* (Grand Rapids: Baker Book House, 1986); Whitcomb and Henry M. Morris, *The Genesis Flood* (Phillipsburg, New Jersey: Presbyterian & Reformed,

that evangelicals must engage in a "conversation" through which they can reconcile their doctrinal positions with the liberals' wrong conclusions. And how shall we do that? Enns begins by telling us what we must *not* do:

> Much of the theological landscape of the twentieth and into the twenty-first centuries was dominated by a "battle for the Bible." The terms are familiar: liberal vs. conservative, modernist vs. fundamentalist, mainline vs. evangelical, progressive vs. traditionalist. Such labels may serve some purpose, but they more often serve to entrench rather than enlighten.[30]

Instead, says Enns, we must accommodate those "who desire to maintain a vibrant and reverent doctrine of Scripture [something he does not define], but who find it difficult to do so because they find familiar and conventional approaches to newer problems to be unhelpful."[31]

Enns asserts that "what is needed is to move beyond both sides [liberal and conservative] by thinking of better ways to account for some of the data." He further explains:

> To put it another way, my aim is to allow the collective evidence to affect not just how we understand a biblical passage or story here and there within the parameters of earlier doctrinal formulations. Rather, I

1961); Morris, *Many Infallible Proofs* (El Cajon, California: Master Books, 1974); Don Batten, ed., *The Revised and Expanded Answers Book* (Master Books, 1990).

30. Enns, 14.

31. Enns, 13.

want to move beyond that by allowing the evidence to affect how we think about what Scripture as a whole *is*.[32]

In other words, we must synthesize conservative and liberal positions and arrive at a new doctrine of Scripture. When Enns is finished, the new doctrine of Scripture he espouses looks much like that of the Auburn Affirmationists. The doctrine of Scripture as the self-attesting Word of God is completely absent from Enns' book. He includes an extensive glossary of key terms and concepts used in the book, but three are conspicuous by their absence: inspiration, inerrancy, and infallibility.

Like the Auburn Affirmationists, Enns begins with some disturbing statements about the Bible:

> On the one hand, I am very eager to affirm that many evangelical instincts are correct and should be maintained, for example, the conviction that the Bible is ultimately from God and that it is God's gift to the church. Any theories concerning Scripture that do not arise from these fundamental instincts are unacceptable.[33]

The un-careful reader might equate Enns' "conviction that the Bible is ultimately from God" with inspiration, but, as we shall see, that is not the case. Further, he reduces the idea that "the Bible is ultimately from God" to the level of an *instinct*, rather than the unequivocal statement of God in Scripture itself (2 *Timothy* 3:16). Enns continues:

> On the other hand, how the evangelical church *fleshes out* its doctrine of Scripture will always have somewhat of a provisional quality to it. This is not to say

32. Enns, 15. Emphasis in the original.
33. Enns, 13-14.

that each generation must disregard the past and start afresh, formulating ever-new doctrine, bowing to all the latest fads. But it is to say that at such time when new evidence comes to light, or old evidence is seen in a new light, we must be willing to engage that evidence and adjust our doctrine accordingly.[34]

In other words, our doctrine of Scripture cannot be fixed, and based on Scripture alone. It must always be tentative as we await new extra-Biblical discoveries and unbelieving scholars' pronouncements about them. We must base our doctrine of Scripture, not on what Scripture says as its own infallible interpreter, but upon "new evidence" – actually unbelieving scholars' "spin" on that evidence.

Therefore, for Enns, it is not a problem to say that the early chapters of *Genesis* contain myths. How so? Under a subheading, "Is *Genesis* Myth or History?" Enns explains:

> This has certainly been a pressure issue among evangelicals, for, if *Genesis* is myth, it seems to bring the Bible down to the level of other ancient literature.
>
> Taking the extrabiblical evidence into account, I question how much value there is in posing the choice of *Genesis* as either myth or history. This distinction seems to be a modern invention. It presupposes – without stating explicitly – that what is historical, in a modern sense of the word, is more real, of more value, more like something God would do, than myth. So, the argument goes, if *Genesis* is myth, then it is not "of God." Conversely, if *Genesis* is history, only then is it something worthy of the name "Bible"....

34. Enns, 14. Emphasis in the original.

But one might ask *why* it is that God *can't* use the category *we* call "myth" to speak to *ancient* Israelites....

We must begin our thinking by acknowledging that the ancient Near Eastern myths are almost certainly older than the *versions* recorded for us in the Bible.[35]

In other words, the content of the early chapters of *Genesis* – Enns makes it clear he has in mind the creation and flood accounts – consists of *versions* of ancient Near Eastern myths. And, Enns goes on to say as he did in the article we cited earlier, God did this so that He could accommodate Himself and His message to the times, even though that involved the incorporation of scientific error.

Therefore, the question is not the degree to which *Genesis* conforms to what we would think is a proper description of origins. It is a fundamental misunderstanding of *Genesis* to expect it to answer questions generated by a modern worldview, such as whether the days of creation were literal or figurative, or whether the days of creation can be lined up with modern science, or whether the flood was local or universal. The question that *Genesis* is prepared to answer is whether Yahweh, the God of Israel, is worthy of worship....

Enns does not dare to explain how a God who uses falsehood to communicate His message could be "worthy of worship." He continues:

The point I would like to emphasize, however, is that such a firm grounding in ancient myth does not make *Genesis* less inspired; it is not a concession we must put

35. Enns, 49-50. Emphases in the original except in last sentence.

up with or an embarrassment to a sound doctrine of Scripture. Quite to the contrary, such rootedness in the culture of the time is precisely what it means for God to speak to his people.

...The phrase *word of God* does not imply disconnectedness to its environment.... And if God was willing and ready to adopt an ancient way of thinking, we truly hold a very low view of Scripture indeed if we make that into a point of embarrassment.[36]

Later in the book, Enns says:

The messiness of the Old Testament, which is a source of embarrassment to some, is actually a positive. On one level it may not help with a certain brand of apologetics, where we use the so-called perfection of the Bible to prove to nonbelievers that Christianity is true.[37]

It is Enns' low view of God and His Word, not conservatives' high view of Scripture, which is an embarrassment. Let us repeat: If God has at *any* point subordinated the words or teaching of Scripture to erroneous human beliefs, at that point we cannot trust the Bible. If we cannot trust the Bible at even one single point, God is a liar. If God is a liar, we cannot be certain of His word at *any* point.

One wonders if the two-thirds of OPC ministers who are Westminster Theological Seminary graduates ever read their *alma mater's* journal, or the books being produced by its faculty. If they do, the lack of outrage would indicate that Westminster has been so effective "in inducting Orthodox Presbyterian ministerial candidates into a culture of inter-

36. Enns, 55-56.
37. Enns, 109.

pretation"[38] that it has become difficult if not impossible for many of these men to see the problem.

In addition to their frontal attack on Biblical inerrancy three generations ago, the Auburn liberals also launched a more subtle attack on the authority of Scripture in their *Affirmation*:

> Accordingly our church has held that the supreme guide in the interpretation of the Scriptures is not, as it is with Roman Catholics, ecclesiastical authority, but the Spirit of God, speaking to the Christian believer. Thus our church lays it upon its ministers and others to read and teach the Scriptures as the Spirit of God through His manifold ministries instructs them, and to receive all truth which from time to time He causes to break forth from the Scriptures.

On the surface, this statement seems to support the Reformation principle of the right of private judgment, but it actually perverts it. The right of private judgment – and the companion responsibility of Christ's ministers to teach faithfully from the Scriptures – is never meant to be divorced from the principle that Scripture is its own infallible interpreter. But that principle found no place in the Auburn liberals' thinking. Nor do men have the right, as the Auburn liberals insisted, to attribute to the Holy Spirit the "breaking forth" of "truth" that is clearly contrary to the self-attesting Word. That is blasphemy.

Sadly, the same spirit increasingly holds sway in the OPC. As we have seen, and shall see in more detail in chapter eight, the frontal attack on inerrancy is not a thing of the past. But over the last thirty years, the main line of

---

38. *Report of the Committee to Study the Views of Creation*, 1607.

neo-liberal attack on Scripture has been the more subtle dialectical/postmodern approach. Many men associated with Westminster Seminary in Philadelphia and serving in OPC and PCA pulpits have effectively abandoned the principles of grammatical-historical interpretation, where words have but one meaning in context, based on the principle that Scripture itself is its only infallible interpreter.

Instead, like the old PCUSA liberals, today's neo-liberals have invented a "right" for men at WTS and in the pulpits to hold variant and conflicting versions of "truth" concerning the days of creation, the meaning of baptism, the meaning of justification by faith, the meaning of the covenants, the basis of the believer's right standing at the Last Judgment, and many other doctrines. And many in the OPC have bought into that newly-invented "right" by doing nothing in the face of growing error.

Deny That Any Doctrine Is Essential

The fourth false principle propagated in the Auburn Affirmation was that there is no such thing as essential doctrine. Any such statement by a council or assembly is, they insisted, merely an opinion. Thus the Auburn Affirmation:

> While it is constitutional for any General Assembly "to bear testimony against error in doctrine," (*Form of Govt.* XII, v), yet such testimony is without binding authority, since the constitution of our church provides that its doctrine shall be declared only by concurrent action of the General Assembly and the presbyteries. Thus the church guards the statement of its doctrine against hasty or ill-considered action by either General Assemblies or presbyteries. From this provision of our constitution, it is evident that neither in one General

> Assembly nor in many, without concurrent action of
> the presbyteries, is there authority to declare what the
> Presbyterian Church in the United States of America
> believes and teaches; and that the assumption that any
> General Assembly has authoritatively declared what
> the church believes and teaches is groundless. A
> declaration by a General Assembly that any doctrine is
> "an essential doctrine" attempts to amend the consti-
> tution of the church in an unconstitutional manner.

The Auburn liberals' argument was specious, and was
also a faulty view of Presbyterian government. The issue
was not the constitutional authority of statements by
assemblies, but the binding authority of the Word of God,
and the authority of the church under the headship of
Christ to require conformity to the system of doctrine
revealed in Scripture among its ordained men.

If the Bible is not inerrant, if it is not subject to fixed, self-
derived rules of interpretation, and if there is no such thing
as an essential doctrine, one wonders how there can be any
place at all for a "testimony against error in doctrine." But
such contradictions were possible because the old liberals
implicitly rejected systematic theology. Systematic theology
is founded on the principle that the Scriptures reveal a God-
ordained, ordered, coherent, and unchanging system of
doctrine, and that by nature this system has essential or
foundational elements.

The paleo-liberals' opposition to systematic theology is
reflected today in the so-called Biblical Theology movement.
This movement's adherents include many neo-liberals in the
OPC, PCA, and at Westminster Seminary in Philadelphia,
and even some conservatives. Proponents of the present-
day Biblical Theology movement assert that it is somehow

more concerned with the text of Scripture than is systematic theology. The Biblical Theology movement also insists on studying "theologies" in the plural and in semi-isolation – the "theology of Paul" – the "theology of Peter" – the "theology of John" – the "theology of James" – or even the "theology of Jesus."

The Biblical Theology movement relegates the doctrine of God the Holy Spirit's primary authorship of *all* of Scripture, through His supernatural inspiration of its very words, to secondary status. Human authorship becomes the primary focus. In such an atmosphere, theologians can stand in judgment of the Scriptures rather than submitting to the judgment of the Word. Dialectical theology can flourish, and with it the implicit – and sometimes explicit – denial of the overall unity and coherence of Scripture. From there it is a small step to the false conclusion that there is no single, God-articulated, uniquely valid system of doctrine – but rather multiple, humanly-articulated systems that can each rightfully claim to be valid. Dr. Thomas K. Ascol observes:

> If there is no overall unity in the Bible, no coherence in all its parts, then the systematic theologian is on a fool's errand.
>
> This is precisely the conclusion of much of the modern theological world....
>
> At the same time that systematic theology was falling into disfavor, the study of Pauline, Petrine, Johannine, etc., theologies was growing in popularity. Thus this kind of "biblical" theology has been heralded as the proper domain of the legitimate theologian and the study of systematics has been relegated to the realm of philosophy (where "systems" are acceptable).

Such conclusions can stand only when their presuppositions are left unchallenged. For if the Bible is without genuine discrepancy, inconsistency, or error, then the analytical search of its text for a system of truth is not only legitimate, it is mandatory. If God has consistently, albeit progressively, revealed His truth to us in the Scriptures, then it is incumbent that we analyze the whole Bible when seeking to know His mind on any particular point.

It is specious to argue that "biblical" theology is by definition more concerned with the Bible than is "systematic" theology. Both [in their legitimate forms] are concerned with the text of Scripture. It is the comprehensive, coherent teaching of that text which concerns the latter. Careful exegesis is no more valued by one than the other, and neither can be slighted in any thorough study of God's Word.

Systematic theology is a necessary discipline in the pursuit of both knowing and proclaiming the whole counsel of God. It will curb careless exegesis which results in fanciful, contradictory expositions of various texts. Where it is depreciated doctrinal instability prevails, and God's people are robbed of Christian vitality.[39]

And this is precisely the case today in the Orthodox Presbyterian Church, at Westminster Seminary in Philadelphia, and beyond.

39. Thomas K. Ascol, "Systematic Theology and Preaching" in *The Founders Journal*, Issue 4, Spring 1991, reproduced at www.founders.org/FJ04/editorial_fr.htm.

Never Let Anyone Call Heresy by Its Right Name

A fifth false principle of the Auburn liberals was that assemblies of the church (and, by implication, individual ministers, elders, and sessions) cannot call error that which Scripture plainly calls error, without formal judicial process.

This false principle derives from the preceding one. Again, quoting the *Auburn Affirmation*:

> The General Assembly of 1923, in asserting that "doctrines contrary to the standards of the Presbyterian Church" have been preached in the pulpit of the First Presbyterian Church of New York City, virtually pronounced a judgment against this church. The General Assembly did this with knowledge that the matter on which it so expressed itself was already under formal consideration in the Presbytery of New York, as is shown by the language of its action. The General Assembly acted in the case without giving hearing to the parties concerned. Thus the General Assembly did not conform to the procedure in such cases contemplated by our Book of Discipline, and, what is more serious, it in effect condemned a Christian minister without using the method of conference, patience and love enjoined on us by Jesus Christ. We object to the action of the General Assembly in this case, as being out of keeping with the law and spirit of our church.

The Auburn liberals were referring to the case of Dr. Harry Emerson Fosdick, who preached at First Presbyterian Church in New York City in the 1920s. Fosdick denied, among other truths, the virgin birth of Christ, the inerrancy of Scripture, the propitiatory nature of the atonement, and the doctrine of justification by faith alone. Although men in other parts of the church spoke out against him, the Presbytery of New York had in fact refused to take positive action against him or the session of his church. In his widely-circulated sermon "Shall the Fundamentalists Win?" Fosdick called for pluralism within the PCUSA – tolerance of liberal views like his alongside orthodox positions, and the long-term development of consensus doctrinal positions.[40]

In much the same way, neo-liberals associated with the OPC and Westminster Seminary say that we must "await development of consensus" (as we quoted John Frame earlier) on doctrines that are clearly and forever settled in the Word of God. (We shall see this in greater detail as we examine the heresy of perspectivalism in chapter eight.)

Today in the OPC, and elsewhere in the Reformed and larger evangelical world, there is great resistance to the use of the term "heresy." Neo-liberals cry foul whenever that label is applied to their false teachings. But worse yet, critics of neo-liberalism seem afraid to use it. Directly echoing the *Auburn Affirmation*, Dr. James S. Gidley, writing in the June 2004 issue of the OPC's *New Horizons* magazine, publicly declared the neo-liberals' heretofore unwritten rule that heresy cannot be called by its right name:

> ...[N]o individual elder or minister, or group of ministers and elders not constituted as a court of the church, can lawfully declare someone to be a heretic or to be guilty of censurable error.[41]

---

40. Harry Emerson Fosdick, "Shall the Fundamentalists Win?" in *The Riverside Preachers*, Paul Sherry, ed., (New York: Pilgrim Press, 1978), 27-38.

41. James S. Gidley, "Quick to Hear, Slow to Speak, Slow to Anger" in *New Horizons*, Volume 25, No. 6, June 2004, 9.

In a letter to the editor of *New Horizons*, Dr. John W. Robbins responded,

> This rule is without Scriptural support, and Mr. Gidley, tellingly, cites no Scripture to support it. Therefore, there is no reason to accept the Gidley Rule.
>
> Second, there are many passages of Scripture which deny this rule. Both Christ and the apostles not only expect individual officers in the church to recognize false teaching and teachers and to warn the flock of God against them, but also expect ordinary Christians to make such judgments about teachers. Far from Christ and the apostles espousing a "hermeneutic of trust," to use a phrase that the OPC's Committee on Creation has recently used, the command of Christ and the apostles to all Christians is a hermeneutic of skepticism: "Believe not every spirit," "test the spirits," do not believe even an angel from heaven or an apostle or "those who seem to be something" (*Gal.* 2:6), if they depart from Scripture and the Gospel.
>
> Third, the Gidley Rule would make all discipline for doctrinal error impossible, for in order for ecclesiastical discipline to begin, some individual who, by definition, is not constituted as a court of the church must declare a teacher to be guilty of censurable error or heresy, and such a declaration must be made publicly. Mr. Gidley's Rule is a catch-22.
>
> Fourth, Gidley's Rule condemns the actions of J. Gresham Machen and many others in the Presbyterian Church in the 1920s and 1930s who declared teachers in that church to be guilty of censurable error

and heresy. Gidley's Rule implies that the OPC is founded on illegal and sinful actions.[42]

Promote Doctrinal Pluralism

A sixth and related false principle articulated by the Auburn liberals was that the church, in the name of "liberty and unity," far from requiring conformity in doctrine from its ministers and elders, must permit the development and propagation of multiple conflicting theories about "great facts and doctrines." Thus the *Auburn Affirmation*:

> The General Assembly of 1923 expressed the opinion concerning five doctrinal statements that each one "is an essential doctrine of the Word of God and our standards." On the constitutional ground which we have before described, we are opposed to any attempt to elevate these five doctrinal statements, or any of them, to the position of tests for ordination or for good standing in our church.
>
> Furthermore, this opinion of the General Assembly attempts to commit our church to certain theories concerning the inspiration of the Bible, and the Incarnation, the Atonement, the Resurrection, and the Continuing Life and Supernatural Power of our Lord Jesus Christ. We hold most earnestly to these great facts and doctrines; we all believe from our hearts that the writers of the Bible were inspired of God; that Jesus Christ was God manifest in the flesh; that God was in Christ, reconciling the world unto Himself, and through Him we have our redemption; that having died for our sins

42. John W. Robbins, "Declaring Error" in *New Horizons*, Volume 25, No. 9, October 2004, 21-22.

He rose from the dead and is our everliving Saviour; that in His earthly ministry He wrought many mighty works, and by His vicarious death and unfailing presence He is able to save to the uttermost. Some of us regard the particular theories contained in the deliverance of the General Assembly of 1923 as satisfactory explanations of these facts and doctrines. But we are united in believing that these are not the only theories allowed by the Scriptures and our standards as explanations of these facts and doctrines of our religion, and that all who hold to these facts and doctrines, whatever theories they may employ to explain them, are worthy of all confidence and fellowship.

The statement that the liberals "hold most earnestly to these great facts and doctrines" was a bald-faced lie. Fosdick, for example, said that "To believe in virgin birth as an explanation of great personality is one of the familiar ways in which the ancient world was accustomed to account for unusual superiority" and that Jesus was only virgin-born in the same sense that "Pythagoras was called virgin born, and Plato, and Augustus Caesar, and many more."[43] In the liberal no-rules world of the 1920s, as in the neo-liberal no-rules world of the present-day OPC, unity on "great facts and doctrines" was to be based on a lowest common denominator where those doctrines cease to have any fixed and univocal meaning.

43. Fosdick, "Shall the Fundamentalists Win?"

Broaden the Definition of Christianity

A seventh and corollary false principle of the Auburn liberals was that the church must have a broad definition of "evangelical Christianity" and therefore of the Gospel, employing words that men can all agree to use, even though they mean different things by them, whether Scripture supports what they mean or not. The *Auburn Affirmation* declared:

> We do not desire liberty to go beyond the teachings of evangelical Christianity. But we maintain that it is our constitutional right and our Christian duty within these limits to exercise liberty of thought and teaching, that we may more effectively preach the gospel of Jesus Christ, the Saviour of the World.

The echo of this thinking in the OPC today means that the denomination can supposedly tolerate the presence of those who teach salvation by baptism, and justification by faith-plus-works, alongside those who teach salvation by grace through faith in Christ alone. And, the denomination can supposedly tolerate those who teach that an "inspired" and "inerrant" Word of God contains myths, alongside those who understand that to profess such a doctrine is to say that God is a liar.

Champion Unity at the Expense of Truth

The OPC as a body has also accepted the Auburn liberals' final false principle: *Unity is more important than truth – because there is no fixed truth, but rather many "theories" about the truth. Therefore, in the name of "liberty and unity" precise definition of the Gospel is unhealthy. Efforts to defend a single definition of Biblical truth that is based on sound principles of interpretation are schismatic.* The Auburn liberals wrote:

116

Finally, we deplore the evidences of division in our beloved church, in the face of a world so desperately in need of a united testimony to the gospel of Christ. We earnestly desire fellowship with all who like us are disciples of Jesus Christ. We hope that those to whom this Affirmation comes will believe that it is not the declaration of a theological party, but rather a sincere appeal, based on the Scriptures and our standards, for the preservation of the unity and freedom of our church, for which most earnestly we plead and pray.

Conservatives' Ineffectual Response

What was the reaction to the *Auburn Affirmation* in the 1920s? Machen (who had published his book *Christianity and Liberalism* just a few months before the *Affirmation* appeared) focused on the key issue of truth versus error, light versus darkness, authentic Biblical Christianity versus the counterfeit of liberalism. In this he was joined by a relative handful of other conservatives.

But sadly, most conservatives put false unity and false Presbyterianism above the truth. Though they were opposed to the liberals' assertions in the *Affirmation*, they allowed themselves to be distracted by the non-issue of the PCUSA General Assembly's supposed lack of constitutional authority to call heresy by its right name. Amazingly, Edwin H. Rian, writing an official history published by the OPC in 1940, also focused on this point, saying, "The weight of the law [that is, church law] seems to be on the side of the *Auburn Affirmation*"![44]

Conservatives had considered publishing a counter-

44. Rian, *The Presbyterian Conflict*, 26.

affirmation, and Machen had drafted one.[45] Machen also sought to rally conservatives through several magazine articles and many personal contacts. But conservatives came to the faulty conclusion that they would "be on stronger ground in not making any formal, signed reply."[46]

Incredibly, conservatives, in the name of good churchmanship, then joined so-called moderates in shielding the liberals from church discipline. By unanimous vote, the PCUSA General Assembly refused to act on an overture that could have resulted in sanctions against the Auburn liberals.[47] No signer of the *Auburn Affirmation* was ever charged with heresy in his own presbytery. Rian writes:

> ...[T]he question has often been asked, "Why was not some action taken against the *Auburn Affirmation* and its signers?".... The fact remains that as far as the record is concerned, there was no protest and no dissenting vote. It is also surprising that very little or no comment is made concerning this overture in the report of the proceedings of the general assembly in such a magazine as *The Presbyterian*, which was then the most aggressive organ for the faith....
>
> There seems to be no sound explanation of this action and attitude of the conservatives except that they made a grave mistake. No advice was given to the church concerning the *Auburn Affirmation* and, as a result, the matter has troubled the church ever since.[48]

---

45. Ned B. Stonehouse, *J. Gresham Machen, A Biographical Memoir* (Grand Rapids, Michigan: William B. Eerdmans, 1954), 366-368.

46. Stonehouse, 366-367.

47. Rian, *The Presbyterian Conflict*, 33-34.

48. Rian, 34.

That is still true. The legacy of conservatives' tepid response to the *Auburn Affirmation* troubles the OPC today. Its own response to the neo-liberal apostasy is likewise feeble and irresolute. The most "decisive" response to teachings that are clearly heresies regarding the Gospel – the doctrines of the Shepherdites, the Federal Vision, and the so-called New Perspective on Paul – has been to lend undeserved validity to those teachings by erecting a committee which includes neo-liberals and their fellow travelers, and giving it two years to study those false doctrines. This fact, possibly more than any other, exposes the depth of the OPC's spiritual crisis. As Martyn Lloyd-Jones said:

> To regard a church, or a council of churches, as a forum in which fundamental matters can be debated and discussed...is sheer confusion and muddled thinking. There is to be no discussion about "the foundation".... If men do not accept that, they are not brethren and we can have no dialog with them. We are to preach to such and to evangelize them.
>
> ...Those who question and query, let alone deny, the great cardinal truths that have been accepted throughout the centuries do not belong to the church, and to regard them as brethren is to betray the truth.... [T]he apostle Paul tells us clearly what our attitude to them should be: "A man that is an heretick after the first and second admonition reject" (*Tit.* 3:10). They are to be regarded as unbelievers who need to be called to repentance and acceptance of the truth as it is in Christ Jesus. To give the impression that they are Christians with whom other Christians disagree about certain matters is to confuse the genuine seeker and enquirer who is outside [and, to confuse true believers within

119

the church – pme]. But such is the position prevailing today. It is based upon a failure to understand the nature of the New Testament church which is "the pillar and ground of the truth" (1 Tim. 3:15). In the same way it is a sheer waste of time to discuss or debate the implications of Christianity with people who are not agreed as to what Christianity is. Failure to realize this constitutes the very essence of the modern confusion.[49]

By exchanging the principles of the Reformation for the principles of the *Auburn Affirmation*, the Orthodox Presbyterian Church is repeating the mistakes of history – the history that led to its own founding in 1936.

Clearly, the OPC's present-day neo-liberalism shares both the core characteristics and the underlying principles of the PCUSA's old liberalism three generations ago. And as we have also seen, the environment in which neo-liberalism has grown up in the OPC is much like the environment in which the old liberalism grew and flourished. That environment is principally characterized by a lack of discernment and vigilance – a failure to see the attacks on the truth for what they are – and a lack of resolve to take decisive action to preserve the truth whatever the cost.

The clear evidence of the OPC's lack of will to stand for the truth begins with its failure to rid itself of the false teachings of Norman Shepherd.

---

49. Lloyd-Jones, "The Basis of Christian Unity" in *Knowing the Times*, 161.

Chapter 5

The Shepherd Controversy: Entry of Another Gospel

> *There are some who trouble you*
> *and want to pervert the gospel of Christ.*
> *But even if we, or an angel from heaven,*
> *preach any other gospel to you than what*
> *we have preached to you, let him be accursed.*
> *Galatians 1:7-8*

For over thirty years, the Orthodox Presbyterian Church has permitted two ways of salvation to be preached from its pulpits and taught in the seminary that has trained nearly two-thirds of its ministers. That pluralism, which has now thoroughly corrupted the denomination, first manifested itself in the Shepherd controversy beginning in 1975.

The Authentic Gospel

As we saw in chapter two, Norman Shepherd and his followers deny the authentic Gospel of justification by faith alone. Since there is much confusion today about this doctrine – and because Shepherd and his followers use the phrase but redefine the words – let us be clear as to what we mean by "justification by faith alone." And to be clear, we must have Scripture, not the words of men, as our authority. According to Scripture, justification is a once-for-all judicial

121

act of God at the conversion of the sinner.[1] In this act God graciously declares the guilty sinner to be righteous – not guilty before His judgment bar, where the standard is perfect holiness – on the basis of the merits of Jesus Christ alone, imputed, not infused, to the sinner. Scripture declares that faith, and faith alone, is the instrument of the believer's justification. This faith is absolutely naked faith – it is unadorned, unembellished, empty-handed belief in the person and work of Christ to save sinners. That faith is itself the gift of God, and has nothing to do with works, so that no one can boast that he added one iota to the righteousness of Christ. This faith is given to the sinner, who was spiritually dead but has now been made alive, by a gracious unilateral act of the Holy Spirit.

In justification by faith, a great legal exchange takes place. The sins of the sinner are imputed to Jesus Christ, who has made full and final atonement for them. At the same time, the perfect all-sufficient righteousness of Christ is imputed to the undeserving, hopeless sinner. The believing sinner now wears the robe of Christ's righteousness, and need not – indeed cannot – add any garment of his own. To attempt to do so would be to deny the sufficiency of Christ.

Let us also be clear that Scripture knows nothing of "easy believism." This is the false teaching that one can profess a "faith" in Christ that is a mere formula of words and not the result of the regenerating work of God. Scripture knows nothing of "easy believism," not because genuine faith involves works, but because genuine faith is

1. The discussion that follows is based on passages such as *Isaiah* 61:10; *John* 3:18 and 3:36; *Romans* 3:22-28, 4:1-8, 5:1-20, and 8:28-39; *1 Corinthians* 1:30-31; *2 Corinthians* 5:16-21; *Galatians* 3:1-13; *Ephesians* 1:13-2:10; *Philippians* 3:9; *Titus* 3:5-11; *Hebrews* 10:11-39; *Revelation* 19:5-8.

God-given faith. It is impossible for the natural man to believe the Gospel. Belief is no mere formula of words originating in the sinful heart of man by his own will. The one who truly believes is God's workmanship from beginning to end. He has been created in Christ Jesus before the foundation of the world to do good works – the works which God prepared beforehand for him to do *after* he has been justified by faith alone. If the sinner has truly believed – has exercised God-given faith in Christ and not a counterfeit – then a changed life will follow as surely as day follows night. But the changed life – his sanctification by the work of the Holy Spirit – does not justify the believer in the sight of God. It is the result, not the cause, of his salvation.

And when the Day of Judgment comes,[2] the very first thing the Lord Jesus Christ will do is to place His sheep on His right hand. The sheep are already the sheep, and always have been. Their status is already known. They are already justified. They await no further evaluation in order to inherit the kingdom of God. They are invited without question to inherit the kingdom prepared for them from the foundation of the world.

On that day the wicked will plead their good works as justification before the Lord, but to no avail. On the Last Day, those who plead their good works under the law will be among those whom the Lord condemns as lawless: "I never knew you; depart from Me, you who practice lawlessness" (*Matthew* 7:23).

At the Judgment the justified will continue to reiterate their failings. They will continue to say with Paul (*Philip-*

2. *Matthew* 7:21-23 and 25:31-36.

pians 3:9), that they do not have a righteousness of their own. They came to Christ empty-handed at their conversion; they will come to Him empty-handed at the Judgment. They will rest completely in the righteousness of Christ. And thus, John says, those who truly believe "may have boldness in the day of judgment" (*1 John* 2:17).

The Neo-Liberal Pseudo-Gospel

This is the Biblical way of salvation. There is, however, another "way" of salvation being preached in the OPC and elsewhere. It is the neo-liberal pseudo-gospel of justification by faith-plus-works. It teaches that justification is not a once-for-all judicial act of God, but unfinished business whose outcome depends on the believer's obedience. It teaches that justification is not brought about solely by the unilateral action of God. In this false gospel, the sinner does not come to God empty-handed, either at conversion or at the Judgment, because faith is not mere belief. Faith, according to this pseudo-gospel, is really *faithfulness*. Norman Shepherd and other neo-liberals say that the belief that Scripture declares to be the sole instrument of justification must be embellished by good works.

This false gospel teaches that God's "not guilty" verdict remains an open question until the Day of Judgment. On that day, say the neo-liberals, the Lord Jesus Christ does not at the outset openly acknowledge those who were declared not guilty at their conversion, by placing them at His right hand and giving them the inheritance of a kingdom that is rightfully theirs in Him. No, in the neo-liberal teaching Jesus evaluates men's works on the Last Day for the purpose of making the final decision as to their eternal destiny.

Despite repeated opportunities, neither the Orthodox Presbyterian Church nor Westminster Theological Seminary has repented and cleansed itself of these errors. Instead, during the past three decades the proclamation of this false gospel has moved from quiet protection to open endorsement, and its corrupting influence has spread beyond the OPC into other churches. And its proponents audaciously proclaim the false gospel as the one that is "truly Reformed."

In the long run, it is not simply a matter of the OPC *tolerating* the preaching of two gospels. The true Gospel is being *displaced*. Satan is quite content to fight a war of attrition. If the false gospel continues to be propagated at the seminary level as the one that is "truly Reformed," it will take only a generation for the preaching of the true Gospel to become rare or even die out entirely in the denomination. That is exactly what has happened in other denominations. The false gospel of justification by faith-plus-works will come to be the only "gospel" that the people of the OPC will know. And they will be so steeped in neo-liberal thinking concerning the nature of God and the authority of Scripture that they will be unable to discern the true Gospel, apart from a miraculous revival wrought by God the Holy Spirit.

The threat is not only to the OPC. It is a threat to the church at large. It is no exaggeration to say that the propagation of this false gospel threatens to plunge the church into a new Dark Age.

The Shepherd Controversy: Background

The history of the advance of another gospel in the OPC largely coincides with the history of its failure to condemn the false teachings of Norman Shepherd – and the OPC's conspiracy of silence on the matter, which has only begun to be broken in the past few years.

The facts of the Shepherd case are too little known and have often been suppressed. Mention of the controversy is conspicuously absent from official histories of the OPC. But in recent years the details of the Shepherd case have been brought to light in three books: *The Changing of the Guard* by Mark W. Karlberg, *The Current Justification Controversy* by O. Palmer Robertson, and *A Companion to The Current Justification Controversy* by John W. Robbins.[3]

I commend those books to readers of this one. They provide vital background on the material with which we are about to deal. In this chapter we shall review events that Karlberg, Robertson, and Robbins cover in much more detail.[4] Following that overview, and in succeeding chapters, we shall examine further developments in the accelerating propagation of another gospel that have occurred since their books were published.

Norman Shepherd received his theological training at Westminster Seminary, earning his master's degree in 1959. He became a minister in the Orthodox Presbyterian Church and a member of the Presbytery of Philadelphia. Shepherd

3. All three are available from The Trinity Foundation.

4. The author has also had the opportunity to examine presbytery and general assembly archives and to interview and correspond with several eyewitnesses, on both sides of the issue, to verify details of the events described in this chapter.

joined Westminster's systematic theology faculty in 1963.

In early 1975, the Seminary faculty began receiving disturbing reports about the doctrinal positions expressed by Westminster students and recent graduates when they were being examined for licensure and ordination in the OPC and other denominations. These young men were openly professing a doctrine of justification by faith-plus-works and other related errors. When asked where they had learned these heresies, the students named Norman Shepherd as the principal source.

Beginnings of the Conspiracy of Silence

These reports triggered what became an excruciatingly lengthy investigation and cover-up at the Seminary. Between April 1975 and November 1981, there were at least 46 meetings of the Westminster faculty, board of trustees, and four different committees appointed by the board to deal with the matter.[5] Norman Shepherd was present and given the opportunity to explain and defend his views in many of those meetings.[6]

Early on, it became clear that Shepherd taught the following heresies:

5. I base this number on a combination of sources: O. Palmer Robertson, *The Current Justification Controversy* (Unicoi, Tennessee: The Trinity Foundation, 2003); "Reasons and Specifications Supporting the Action of the Board of Trustees in Removing Professor Shepherd," a document approved by the Westminster Theological Seminary board of trustees which is reproduced in Robbins, *A Companion to The Current Justification Controversy* (Unicoi, Tennessee: The Trinity Foundation, 2003); plus conversations and correspondence with men who participated in many of those meetings.

6. Robertson, *The Current Justification Controversy*, 13-74.

- Justification is by both faith and works.

- Baptism is necessary for salvation, and salvation takes place at baptism.

- Good works are necessary for an individual to maintain his state of justification.

- Justification is not a single judicial act of God at conversion based solely on the imputed righteousness of Christ and received by faith alone, but rather is a process culminating in the evaluation of the individual's works at the Last Judgment.

- It is possible for a person to lose his justification.[7]

During six-and-a-half years of investigation and discussion, Shepherd defended these and related assertions, and continued to teach them in the Seminary. And during most of those years, members of the faculty, board, and the four board-appointed committees seemed to bend over backwards to find ways to conclude that Shepherd's teachings were somehow within the bounds of Scripture. The conspiracy of silence regarding the influence of the teachings of Norman Shepherd on the Seminary and the OPC has continued to the present day.

Members of the faculty and board, especially those who were ministers of the OPC, failed to do what they should have done unanimously as soon as it became evident that Shepherd would persist in wide-ranging error. They should have brought charges of heresy against him in the Presbytery of Philadelphia. They should have made the evidence in their possession freely available to the Presbytery so that

7. Robertson, 17, 22, 24, 34-35, 39.

it could perform its duties under the OPC *Book of Discipline*. They should have lent their unqualified support to the prosecution of those charges. The Presbytery had jurisdiction over Shepherd as an ordained minister, and the responsibility to ensure his ongoing fidelity to Scripture. His teachings were a matter of concern to the entire denomination and to the evangelical church at large. As ministers of the Presbytery they had, like Shepherd, vowed to "be zealous and faithful in maintaining the truths of the gospel and the purity, the peace, and the unity of the church, whatever persecution or opposition may arise unto you on that account."[8] But the OPC men on the Westminster faculty and board – with few exceptions[9] – were disturbingly unwilling to do their duty before God. They failed to make the Word of God their highest authority and priority.

Instead, for six-and-a-half years the faculty and board of Westminster Seminary sought to conceal the Shepherd controversy behind its walls, to obstruct the legitimate functions of the Presbytery, and to find ways to tolerate error. And all the while, they permitted Shepherd and his supporters to continue to poison the theological well by teaching a false gospel to the next generation of young Timothys in the Seminary.

No one who is loyal to the truths of authentic Biblical

8. *The Form of Government of the Orthodox Presbyterian Church*, Chapter XXIII, Section 8.

9. One faculty member, Arthur W. Kuschke, Jr., did bring charges against Shepherd in the Presbytery of Philadelphia in 1977, fighting for the truth of the Gospel and against the obstructionism of the majority of the faculty and board. He did this with little support from his faculty colleagues, the board, or members of his presbytery, most of whom either fiercely opposed him or simply sought peace at the sacrifice of sound doctrine.

Christianity can read the historical record or speak with eye-witnesses without being deeply troubled by the Seminary's attitudes and actions during those six-and-a-half years. Incredible as it may seem, the Seminary faculty and board were divided on the question of the orthodoxy of Shepherd's teachings. Among Shepherd's staunchest defenders were John Frame, Richard Gaffin, and Cornelius Van Til.[10] Over three years elapsed before anyone doing the investigating actually listened to tape recordings of Shepherd's classroom lectures.[11] A similar amount of time elapsed before the Seminary board gave any official indication to the church at large that serious error was being taught within its walls.

When the Seminary did make the matter "public" it did so in a whisper. It published, but with limited distribution and without condemnation, a 53-page paper by Shepherd in which he outlined and defended his heresies.[12] On four occasions Shepherd was exonerated by the faculty and board of trustees.[13] His teachings were "judged to fall within

10. Robbins, *A Companion to The Current Justification Controversy*, 14-15, 35-36, 42-46.

11. Robertson, 15, 67-68. John Frame at least took the initiative to hear what Shepherd was actually teaching in his classroom. In his Foreword to *Backbone of the Bible* (vii) Frame states, "After I myself had been teaching theology [at Westminster] for ten years or so [Frame arrived in 1968], I audited Shepherd's lectures in the Doctrine of God and the Doctrine of the Holy Spirit (salvation) – not just to get a direct line on the 'Shepherd Controversy,' but for my own edification. Anyone who knows Shepherd's work on the doctrine of God and has also read my own book on the subject will know how deep his influence on me has been." Frame was a minister in the OPC at the time and a member of the Presbytery of Philadelphia (*Minutes of the Presbytery of Philadelphia*, January 17, 1977, 112).

12. Robertson, 20.

13. Robertson, 26, 30, 66.

the limits tolerated by Scripture and the Confession."[14] Shepherd was even "commended for his fresh insights."[15] Such were, and still are, the doctrinal conditions at Westminster Seminary in Philadelphia.

Heresy Charges Against Shepherd

During these years of controversy the Presbytery of Philadelphia of the Orthodox Presbyterian Church also became involved, albeit reluctantly. It too bent over backwards to find ways to shoehorn Shepherd's teachings inside the boundaries of orthodoxy. Three times the Presbytery had the opportunity to condemn Shepherd's heresies, and three times it failed to do so.

On the first occasion, charges of heresy were filed against Shepherd in October 1977.[16] The principal evidence supporting the charges consisted of Shepherd's 53-page paper and the testimony of witnesses concerning it. Neo-liberals and their fellow travelers immediately began a fierce fight to protect Shepherd, and themselves. When the clerk attempted to publicly read the charges on the floor of the Presbytery as required by the OPC *Book of Discipline*, supporters of Shepherd interrupted the reading and sought to silence it through parliamentary maneuvers. After the charges were finally read, eight men associated with the Seminary, five of them on the faculty, entered a formal protest against the reading.[17] The president and faculty of

14. Robertson, 30.

15. Robertson, 30.

16. *Minutes of the Presbytery of Philadelphia*, October 1, 1977, 147.

17. *Minutes of the Presbytery of Philadelphia*, November 19, 1977, 157-160. The protesters from the faculty were Richard Gaffin, D. Clair

Westminster Seminary sought to block the use of the evidence in the case before the Presbytery. They argued that Shepherd's paper should not be admitted as evidence in order to protect his "academic freedom."

The Presbytery yielded to this pressure and ruled that the paper was inadmissible.[18] The squelching of the primary evidence of Shepherd's doctrinal position made the testimony surrounding the paper useless, and the charges were dropped because of the resulting lack of admissible evidence. Thus Norman Shepherd escaped exposure and discipline – and the Presbytery of Philadelphia escaped its responsibility – on a contrived technicality. In his history of these events O. Palmer Robertson comments that

> in effect, the Presbytery relinquished its right of supervision over one of its own ministers. In effect, the academic community of the Seminary was judged by Presbytery to possess a right of supervision over its ministers that was above its own.[19]

Robertson also observes that the Presbytery established the precedent of allowing the Seminary to decide when the Presbytery could or could not examine the teachings of one of its ministers who was also a member of the Seminary faculty. Worse yet, the governing principle facilitating that cloak of protection would be academic freedom, not Scripture. The Presbytery's decision effectively made the question

---

Davis, John Frame, Robert Strimple, and Shepherd himself. The others who signed the protest were W. David Leverell, James R. Payton, and George F. Morton.

18. *Minutes of the Presbytery of Philadelphia*, March 17-18, 1978, 190.

19. Robertson, 32.

of how well or poorly a professor's teachings conformed to Scripture irrelevant.[20]

Conservatives appealed the decision of the Presbytery of Philadelphia not to admit the evidence against Shepherd, but the 1979 General Assembly denied their appeal.[21] Thus the General Assembly also acquiesced to the false principles that academic freedom trumps Scripture and that the Seminary's authority supersedes the Presbytery's. And, it allowed the Presbytery to evade its Scriptural responsibilities for ministerial oversight.

Debate of Shepherd's Thirty-Four Theses

The Presbytery's second opportunity to declare Shepherd's teachings heretical came in 1979, after the Westminster Seminary board made Shepherd's 53-page paper public. This action opened the way for renewed charges of heresy against Shepherd, since the supporting evidence was now clearly on the public record. In order to deflect renewed heresy charges, Shepherd submitted his *Thirty-Four Theses on Justification in Relation to Faith, Repentance, and Good Works*[22] for the Presbytery's consideration.

Dr. Mark W. Karlberg describes this as "a shrewd and calculated move" since it permitted Shepherd to appear to be submitting to open inquiry, when in fact the *Theses* did not deal with the aspects of his theology that were at the root of his false teachings: his radical hermeneutics and his

20. Robertson, 33.

21. *Minutes of the Forty-Sixth General Assembly of the Orthodox Presbyterian Church*, 1979, 186-188. Robertson (34) has the year as 1978.

22. Shepherd's *Theses* have been reproduced with his permission at www.hornes.org/theologia/content/norman_shepherd/the_34_theses.htm

deconstruction of the Biblical covenants. Unfortunately, the Presbytery of Philadelphia went along with this ploy to restrict the scope of its inquiry. Richard Gaffin, frequently answering for Shepherd during the Presbytery's subsequent debate of the *Theses*, was able to advance the strategy Shepherd had begun, to "mislead the church court concerning the critical issues in the Seminary dispute."[23]

Still, it is both amazing and disturbing that the Presbytery was deceived. Shepherd's *Theses* were clear enough in denying justification by faith alone, asserting that justification is a process involving human works, asserting that good works are necessary for salvation, and teaching that believers can lose their justification if their works are deficient.[24]

Yet the Presbytery of Philadelphia found it necessary to debate the *Theses* for a full year in ten day-long meetings. Most of those meetings were held, fittingly, in the auditorium of Van Til Hall at Westminster Seminary. Frequently the sessions were packed with onlookers, many of them students. The Presbytery not only restricted its examination of Shepherd's teachings to the *Thirty-Four Theses*; it also chose to debate and to vote on the *Theses* one at a time, and to limit itself to voting on two questions about each thesis: "Is it in harmony with the teaching of Scripture and the Westminster Standards?" and "Are the views expressed consistent with the ordination vows of the Orthodox Presbyterian Church?" Attempts at various points to have the Presbytery vote on the more definitive statement that some

23. Mark W. Karlberg, *The Changing of the Guard: Westminster Seminary in Philadelphia* (Unicoi, Tennessee: The Trinity Foundation, 2001), 32.

24. Robertson, 34-35. See especially *Theses* 18 through 24.

of Shepherd's theses clearly denied the teachings of Scripture were rebuffed.[25]

It is clear, from the minutes of the meetings and from the subsequent comments of participants who stood on the side of the Gospel, that many members of the Presbytery did not think in terms of Scripture as setting forth a system of doctrine that must be considered and defended as a whole. Nor did they think of Shepherd's *Theses* as a system, but as a series of semi-independent assertions. Their approach was dialectical and pluralistic. Truth and falsehood could coexist under the same confessional tent, and within the same statement of doctrine. The Presbytery approved theses that stated that the exclusive ground of justification is the righteousness of Christ. But it approved other theses that also made the believer's works the ground of justification. It approved theses that spoke against Roman Catholic teaching that justification is a process and that good works merit eternal life. Yet it approved other theses that said that justification *is* a process and that good works *do* merit eternal life.

Perhaps the example *par excellence* of the Presbytery's confused thinking was its handling of Thesis 20, a keystone of Shepherd's heresy of justification by faith-plus-works – his radically wrong interpretation of *Romans* 2:13. Shepherd's Thesis 20 states:

> The Pauline affirmation in *Romans* 2:13, "the doers of the Law will be justified," is not to be understood hypothetically in the sense that there are no persons who fall into that class, but in the sense that faithful

25. *Minutes of the Committee of the Whole of the Presbytery of Philadelphia*, various dates, 229-298.

disciples of the Lord Jesus Christ will be justified (compare *Luke* 8:21; *James* 1:22-25).

On successive votes taken within the space of two hours, the Presbytery first declared that Thesis 20 was not in harmony with Scripture, and then declared that Thesis 20 was consistent with the OPC's ordination vows![26]

At the end of the debates, on January 22, 1980, the Presbytery took two votes. In the first vote, the Presbytery deadlocked on a motion to declare that Shepherd's teachings as a whole were in accord with the Scriptures. In the second vote, the Presbytery decisively defeated a motion to declare that Shepherd's teachings as a whole were *contrary* to the Scriptures. The Presbytery voted at a subsequent meeting to take no further action against Shepherd.[27]

Conservatives in the Presbytery appealed this decision to the 1981 General Assembly. The Assembly denied the appeal, saying that individuals could bring new charges before the Presbytery if they wished.[28] Thus the General Assembly placed the burden of trying to safeguard the denomination against Shepherd's heresies on the backs of the few conservatives in the Presbytery of Philadelphia who remained, in the words of their vows, truly "zealous and faithful in maintaining the truths of the gospel."

26. *Minutes of the Committee of the Whole*, January-February 1979, 248-253.

27. Robertson, 35-36.

28. Robertson, 36; *Minutes of the Forty-Eighth General Assembly of the Orthodox Presbyterian Church*, May 1981, 18-20, 140-141.

Shepherd's Dismissal from Westminster

The Presbytery's third opportunity to take a stand against Norman Shepherd's errors came after his dismissal from the faculty of Westminster Theological Seminary.

The sequence of events that led to the reluctant dismissal of Shepherd by the Westminster board began with a December 4, 1980, letter to the board.[29] Fifteen individuals, some of them Westminster faculty members, wrote a "letter of concern" to the board of trustees in which they outlined Shepherd's heresies by quoting directly from his own words in public lectures, books, magazine articles, and his *Theses*. The letter was written in anticipation of a board meeting that was to take place on December 10. The fifteen signers concluded with an exhortation:

> On December 10th the board should make a clear break with Mr. Shepherd's doctrinal position. The break should be unmistakable, so as to hold the Seminary to the historic testimony for which it was founded.[30]

But at that meeting the Westminster board of trustees voted to exonerate Norman Shepherd, to allow him to remain and teach, and to take no further action against him.

In his history of the controversy, O. Palmer Robertson reminds us that "to a remarkable degree," the entire matter had been kept inside the walls of the Seminary up to this point.[31] Few outside the Seminary and the Presbytery of Philadelphia knew or recognized that heresy was being taught at Westminster or had begun to spread in the OPC.

29. The full text of the letter appears in Robbins, 120-130.

30. Robbins, 130.

31. Robertson, 58.

After the board's December 10 exoneration of Shepherd, the signers of the letter believed the time had come – actually was long overdue after six years of cover-up – to alert the church at large concerning the crisis. On May 4, 1981, the original fifteen signers, joined by thirty other men, published the December 4 letter with a covering letter of explanation addressed to "Friends of the Reformed Faith."[32] The covering letter informed the church at large for the first time that there was serious division over the Gospel itself in both the OPC and Westminster Seminary. Signers of the covering letter included five conservative members of the Westminster faculty, seven of the twenty-five members of the Westminster board, faculty members of several other seminaries, and other respected ministers and theologians in the United States and the United Kingdom. The letter was widely circulated in the OPC, the PCA, and other churches "with the hope that Westminster Seminary might be called back to its clear commitment to justification by faith alone, and that the Gospel might be preserved in the church."[33]

A majority of the Seminary faculty – both neo-liberal supporters of Shepherd and fence-straddlers – were incensed by this action. Members of the board of trustees feared that these revelations would adversely affect financial contributions to the Seminary, and that prospective students (and congregations providing them financial aid) would think twice about enrollment at Westminster. Thus the board took steps to assure the OPC and the PCA, which at that time were considering union, that nothing was really

32. The full text appears in Robbins, 117-120.

33. Robertson, 63.

wrong.[34] But for those who had ears to hear and eyes to see, it was clear that something was radically wrong.[35]

A second development leading to Shepherd's ouster occurred during the summer and early fall of 1981. Westminster president Edmund Clowney, who up to that point had defended Shepherd both privately and publicly, finally listened to forty hours of tape recordings of Shepherd's classroom lectures. He at last concluded that Shepherd's views concerning justification and the covenants "differ from our Confessional standards."[36] Clowney reported his findings to the Seminary board.

The board, which had three times exonerated Shepherd and had maintained a cover-up for six-and-a-half years, now found its position exposed by these developments. Clowney found it difficult to convince the board to reverse its position, but the increasingly public nature of the controversy, and growing pressure from donors, helped him. Clowney's findings gave the Westminster board a rationale for removing Shepherd as a matter of expediency, while saving face.

Noting "certain ecclesiastical repercussions" as a result of the now-public controversy, and fearing their potential adverse effects on the Seminary's reputation, finances, and enrollment, the Westminster board at last took action to

34. Robertson, 64-65.

35. In 1982 the PCA – which today has its own serious problems with false teaching on the doctrine of justification as a result of the spread of Shepherdism – narrowly rejected a merger with the OPC. Dr. O. Palmer Robertson, a PCA minister who participated in General Assemblies where the merger was considered, states that "it is clear that the 'justification issue' played a decisive role" in the PCA's decision (Robertson, 66).

36. Robertson, 68.

remove Norman Shepherd from the faculty on November 20, 1981.[37] The action required a two-thirds majority, and it received exactly that support with no votes to spare.

But the board showed its true colors at the same meeting by reprimanding the faculty members who, as godly watchmen, had signed the May 4, 1981, letter making Shepherd's heresies – and Westminster's quiet protection of error – at last known to the church at large.[38] Shepherd was thrown overboard in a misguided effort to save the ship, but in the board's view the real villains were those who had sounded the alarm that the ship was sinking. They were reprimanded, but neo-liberal faculty members who had been busy alongside Shepherd drilling holes in the bottom of the Seminary ship were allowed to remain, and to keep drilling away.

The board authorized a statement of the reasons for Shepherd's dismissal.[39] The statement began by saying that Shepherd's ouster "was necessary for the best interests of the Seminary." But the board's statements regarding Shepherd's doctrines were contradictory. The board said it was making no judgment concerning Shepherd's teachings. It further stated that "the Board did not remove Mr. Shepherd on the ground of demonstrated errors in his teaching." But in the very next paragraph the board said that it had become "convinced" that Shepherd's teachings were not in accord with Scripture and the Westminster Standards. However it also noted that others were not convinced of that fact. The board vacillated, failing to judge Norman Shepherd's teachings – and those of his supporters – by the one infallible

37. Robbins, 146.

38. Robertson, 69.

39. The full text appears in Robbins, 131-161.

yardstick, the Scriptures. In the end, the board's basis for Shepherd's dismissal was not a conclusion that he taught heresy, but that Shepherd had caused a controversial situation from which the Seminary needed to distance itself in order to preserve its reputation, enrollment, and finances.

Shepherd's Escape to the CRC

At its May 1982 meeting the Presbytery of Philadelphia had its third opportunity to denounce Norman Shepherd's false teachings, and once again it failed.[40] Before the meeting, charges of heresy were once more filed against Shepherd, and Shepherd was made aware of the charges by his accusers. Shepherd then submitted a letter to the Presbytery requesting that he be dismissed to take up ministry in the Christian Reformed Church (CRC). The docket of the Presbytery's May meeting was engineered so that Shepherd's request for dismissal from the denomination would be considered before the charges of heresy.

While Shepherd's request for dismissal was being discussed, a motion to inform the Christian Reformed Church that heresy charges were pending against Shepherd was defeated. The Presbytery then formally dismissed Norman Shepherd to the CRC as a minister in good standing, with no indication of the fact that by leaving the OPC he was once more escaping heresy charges.

The Presbytery held an adjourned meeting in June 1982 to take up unfinished business from the May meeting. That business included a neo-liberal effort to instigate judicial charges against signers of the May 4, 1981, letter to "Friends

40. The account that follows is from Robertson, 82-86 and from the *Minutes of the Presbytery of Philadelphia,* May 7-8 and June 5, 1982.

of the Reformed Faith" which had pulled aside the cloak long covering the evil taking place at Westminster Seminary. Like the Seminary board, the Presbytery was poised to "shoot the messengers" – to discipline the godly watchmen who had sounded the alarm, rather than disciplining the heretics in their midst. The effort to bring charges against the conservatives was instigated by ruling elder John O. Kinnaird, and will be discussed in more detail in chapter seven. Although he had already been dismissed to the CRC and was no longer a member of the Presbytery, Norman Shepherd was allowed to return and participate in the Presbytery's deliberations, personally pressing for the censure of the conservative watchmen. After many months the effort to bring charges against these defenders of the faith was dropped, but not without unwarranted damage to their reputations.

Shepherd after Westminster

After Norman Shepherd's departure, the attitude in both Westminster Seminary and the OPC was, "Let's put this behind us and move on." But the controversy wasn't behind them, and under the circumstances there could be no moving on except moving downward doctrinally. Shepherd had been made a scapegoat, but his neo-liberal supporters remained, undisciplined by the church and now unencumbered by presbytery oversight, on the Westminster faculty. Their adherents in pulpits and sessions of the OPC, and their fellow travelers who prized a false peace above doctrinal purity, remained also. In the years that have followed, others have joined their ranks. During the two decades since Shepherd's departure, a false gospel of justification by faith-plus-works has moved from quiet protection to open endorsement at Westminster, in the OPC, and far beyond.[41]

In the intervening decades Shepherd's own theology has not changed, except perhaps for the worse. After years of quiet work within the increasingly neo-liberal Christian Reformed Church, Shepherd emerged once more into the public arena in 1999. In April of that year he gave a series of lectures at Erskine Theological Seminary (the denominational seminary of the Associate Reformed Presbyterian Church) in which he restated his heretical views to a friendly audience. Those lectures formed the basis of his book, *The Call of Grace,* which was published by Presbyterian & Reformed Publishing Company in 2000. His writings, lectures and sermons since then have confirmed that Norman Shepherd remains as committed to another gospel today as he was thirty years ago.

Yet Shepherd is still welcome today in many parts of the OPC. Many of Shepherd's former students and followers in the OPC and elsewhere maintain personal relationships with him. In chapter two we noted his participation in a 2003 conference for the purpose of spreading neo-liberal heresies, sponsored by the educational arm of an OPC congregation in Southern California and supported by other OP churches in that region. In the same year Shepherd conducted conferences promulgating his views in four Orthodox Presbyterian churches in the Pacific Northwest.[42] In

41. A visitor to Westminster Seminary today will be struck by its significant number of Asian students. Neo-liberalism is not only being spread from WTS to the churches of North America, but also to Japan, Korea, Taiwan, and the Chinese mainland.

42. The churches were: First OPC in Portland, Oregon; Grace Reformed OPC in Bend, Oregon; Faith OPC in Grants Pass, Oregon; and Trinity OPC in Newberg, Oregon.

2004 he participated in the installation service of an OPC minister who now serves as pastor of a PCA church in the Midwest.[43] Shepherd also preached at this church in September 2002.

Defenders of Norman Shepherd have become more open and aggressive. These words of John M. Frame, written in 2004, express the sentiments of many who have been blinded to the truth:

> I find it hard to credit the intelligence or spiritual perception of anyone who objects to [Shepherd's teachings on salvation]...no one, I think, can legitimately doubt that he has the gospel straight....
>
> I must here also use some harsh language with some of Shepherd's critics (including official statements of two small denominations) who have accused Shepherd of denying the gospel or of preaching "another gospel."
>
> ...[I]t should be plain that such criticisms are stupid, irresponsible, and divisive. Theological professors who make such comments, in my judgment, do not have the intellectual, theological, or spiritual maturity to prepare students for gospel ministry. Similar comments can be made against pastors, writers, and web gurus who try to turn this debate into some kind of new reformation.[44]

43. This is Dr. Peter J. Wallace, M. Div., Westminster Theological Seminary, 1996, Ph. D., University of Notre Dame, 2004; member of the OPC Committee to Study the Days of Creation that promoted the "hermeneutic of trust"; although he remains a minister of the OPC, he is now pastor of Michiana Covenant Church (PCA), Granger, Indiana.

44. Frame, Foreword to *Backbone of the Bible*, xi-xii.

OPC ministers, elders, and church members continue to attend inter-denominational conferences around the country where Shepherd is a featured speaker. Some who attend those meetings already possess a deep loyalty to Shepherd and his positions. But many others who come to them know little or nothing about the controversy during his tenure at Westminster Seminary, and they are deceived by his misuse of Biblical and confessional terminology. Because both the OPC and WTS have been deathly quiet regarding the Shepherd controversy during the past two decades, and because of the quiet spread of neo-liberal theology from seminary classrooms to the pulpits and on to the pews, many of these people are ill-prepared to understand that they are hearing another gospel whenever they hear Norman Shepherd.

Chapter 6

Richard Gaffin's New Perspective on Paul

Jesus Christ is the same yesterday, today, and forever.
Do not be carried about with various and strange doctrines.
Hebrews 13:8-9

One of the principal Shepherd supporters who remained on the Westminster Seminary faculty and in
the OPC after his departure was Richard B. Gaffin, Jr.[1]
Despite the fact that he held views similar to Shepherd's,
and openly defended him throughout the controversy, no
charges were brought against Gaffin. The OPC, in its negli-
gent handling of the 1977 charges against Shepherd, had
abandoned its responsibility to oversee its ordained ministers who served on the Seminary faculty. Thus Richard
Gaffin, undisciplined by church or seminary and unencumbered by presbyterial oversight, has been free to
perpetuate Shepherd's teachings down to the present day.

Eighteen years after Shepherd's 1982 departure, Gaffin's

1. Born 1936 in Beijing to missionary parents; undergraduate studies,
University of Southern California; B. A., Calvin College, 1958; B. D.,
Westminster Theological Seminary, 1961; Th. M., 1962; Th. D., 1969;
graduate studies at Georg-August Universität, Göttingen, Germany,
1962-1963; Professor of Biblical & Systematic Theology, Westminster
Theological Seminary, 1965-present; ordained minister, Orthodox Presbyterian Church, Presbytery of Philadelphia.

loyalty to him remained unchanged. In 2000 he glowingly endorsed Shepherd's proclamation of another gospel in *The Call of Grace*. Richard Gaffin continues today as the leading theologian of Westminster Theological Seminary and of the Orthodox Presbyterian Church. In his forty years at Westminster he has played a major role in the training of most of the ministers presently serving in the OPC, as well as those of many other churches in North America and overseas. It is from Richard Gaffin that they have learned much of their theology.

From his earliest days as a Westminster professor, Gaffin along with Shepherd championed what they termed "progress in theology." It is now clear that this was not merely their way of restating the venerable Protestant motto *Semper Reformanda* – "always reforming," that is, seeking an ever-deeper conformity to Scripture. Rather, it has meant the deconstruction of authentic Biblical Christianity. Richard Gaffin, like Norman Shepherd, proclaims a gospel that is not in accord with Scripture.

Gaffin's Own "New Perspective on Paul"

Gaffin first enumerated his views in his doctoral dissertation, for which Norman Shepherd was a faculty advisor, in 1969. Gaffin's dissertation was published in 1978 as *The Centrality of the Resurrection*, and was re-published under the title *Resurrection and Redemption* in 1987. The subtitle of the book is "A Study in Paul's Soteriology."

Richard Gaffin has stated publicly that he is opposed to the New Perspective on Paul of Wright, Dunn, and Sanders. But *Resurrection and Redemption* is Gaffin's own "new perspective on Paul," and it is just as heterodox. While Gaffin's doctrine of salvation is couched in the language of orthodoxy, it is in fact radically revisionist, since he deconstructs and redefines not only the key doctrines of salvation – including faith, redemption, justification, sanctification, and adoption – but also the *way* of salvation itself. Gaffin's most recent public statements, including his lectures at the Auburn Avenue Pastors Conference in January 2005, show no fundamental change in his views. In fact, the lectures Gaffin delivered at Auburn contained large sections lifted almost verbatim from his 1969 doctoral thesis. Gaffin and Wright (who also spoke at Auburn 2005) each presented his own New Perspective on Paul. Neither presented the authentic Gospel.

It is important to understand how Gaffin redefines the way of salvation. The main theme of *Resurrection and Redemption* is that people are saved, not through belief in Christ alone, but through an "existential" and "experiential" union through which believers achieve "solidarity" with Christ.[2] (He uses these three terms frequently.) Gaffin states plainly that the instrument of this saving union is water baptism. His statements regarding the nature of baptism echo those of Norman Shepherd, who writes that baptism "is the moment when we see the transition from death to life and a person is saved."[3] Gaffin writes:

> Baptism signifies and seals a *transition* in the experience of the recipient, a transition from being (existentially) apart from Christ to being (existentially) joined to him. *Galatians* 3:27 is even more graphic: "Those

2. Norman Shepherd also teaches union with Christ through baptism. See his "Justification by Works in Reformed Theology" in *Backbone of the Bible*, 118-119.

3. Shepherd, *The Call of Grace*, 94.

who have been baptized into Christ have put on Christ" (cf. I Cor. 12:13).[4]

Here Gaffin eliminates the distinction between the sign (baptism) and that which it signifies (salvation). Emphasizing his assertion that baptism marks the point of saving transition, Gaffin quotes the Irish theologian Ernest Best: "Those who are baptized into Christ are those who afterwards are *in* Christ." Gaffin continues:

> Consequently, the transition described in [*Ephesians* 2] verses 5f. as being made alive with Christ, etc. pivots on being joined to Christ in an existential sense.... The transition from being an object of God's wrath (v. 3) to experiencing his love (v. 4) takes place at the point of being joined (existentially) to Christ.[5]

A few pages later Gaffin calls this "union with Christ" commencing with water baptism "the inception of the individual Christian existence, the moment of being joined existentially to Christ."[6] In Gaffin's teaching, all of salvation – including redemption, justification, sanctification, adoption, and glorification – comes by means of this "union with Christ" through baptism.

In response to a question at the 2005 Auburn Avenue Pastors Conference, Gaffin admitted that his teaching implies a different method of salvation for Old Testament versus New Testament saints. He said that it would be "redemptive-

4. Richard B. Gaffin, Jr., *Resurrection and Redemption: A Study in Paul's Soteriology* (Phillipsburg, New Jersey: Presbyterian and Reformed Publishing Co., 1987), 50-51. Emphasis and parentheses in the original.

5. Gaffin, 51. Emphasis in the original.

6. Gaffin 58.

historically anachronistic to say that an old covenant believer like Abraham or David" was "united with Christ, because the Christ who is in view, and union with Christ, is specifically the exalted Christ, the redemptive-historical Christ if you will, the Christ who is what He is now by virtue of His death and resurrection, and He did not exist...in the situation of Abraham or David."[7] But Jesus says, "Before Abraham was, I AM" (*John* 8:58); He is the Word from the beginning (*John* 1:1); His "goings forth are from of old, from everlasting" (*Micah* 5:2); the Israelites "drank of that spiritual Rock that followed them, and that Rock was Christ" (*1 Corinthians* 10:4). Gaffin avoided the question of how he thinks saints were actually saved under the Old Covenant, and he does not address this critical issue at all in *Resurrection and Redemption.* However, he does say this:

> Only by virtue of the functional identity of the Spirit and Christ, effected redemptive-historically in his resurrection, is Christ the communicator of life. No principle in Paul's soteriology is more fundamental.[8]

Note carefully that Gaffin is saying that Christ was not the "communicator of life" before His resurrection. How (or if?) spiritual life *was* communicated to believers before Christ's resurrection, Gaffin does not say.

Redefining the *way* of salvation – perhaps we should say *ways* – involves redefining the *terms* of salvation, which Gaffin proceeds to do.

First, Gaffin redefines redemption. He claims that Christ

7. Auburn Avenue Pastors Conference 2005, transcript of Session 13, response to the fourth question from the audience. Audio tapes and CDs of the conference are available from the church.

8. Gaffin, 89.

Himself was redeemed, and that Christians are redeemed by participating in Christ's own personal redemption through union with Him in baptism.[9] Gaffin says plainly that when he calls the resurrection Christ's redemption, he means His "deliverance or salvation."[10] He says that the resurrection is "the point of his transition from wrath to grace"[11] and that "what characterizes the redemption of Christ holds true for the redemption of the believer."[12]

Second, Gaffin redefines justification. He claims that Christ Himself was justified, and that Christians are justified by participating in Christ's own justification through union with Him in baptism.[13] He insists that the word "justified" as applied to Christ in *1 Timothy* 3:16 (where we read that He was "justified in the Spirit") must have the same meaning that it does when applied to sinful men in passages such as *Romans* 4:25, where we read that Christ was "raised *for our* justification." Gaffin says that "to eliminate the usual forensic, declarative meaning" of "justified" when interpreting *1 Timothy* 3:16 "is wrong." "The constitutive, transforming action of the resurrection is specifically forensic in character. It is Christ's justification."[14]

What, then, is the nature of the "justification" that Gaffin has in mind? He makes it virtually synonymous with sanctification. Justification and sanctification, he says, cannot and

9. Gaffin, 114-117.

10. Gaffin, 114.

11. Gaffin, 116. Emphasis in the original.

12. Gaffin, 130.

13. Gaffin, 119-124.

14. Gaffin, 121. Note that "justification" is both "constitutive," "transforming," and "forensic." This is the view of both Roman Catholic theologians and Karl Barth, as Gaffin admits on page 131.

should not be distinguished as separate acts of God. To say that justification and sanctification are ever spoken of as distinct acts of God makes the words, Gaffin says, "permanently unintelligible." He rejects the idea that justification by faith alone is central to the epistles of Paul to the Roman and Galatian churches. In Gaffin's false gospel, justification is not a once-for-all distinct judicial act of God at the sinner's conversion, based on the merits of Christ and applied through the act of believing. Rather, it is an "existential" and "experiential" union with Christ through baptism. And in this union both justification and sanctification, Gaffin insists, "are future as well as present."[15] God's "not guilty" declaration is both "already" and "not yet."

Third, Gaffin redefines sanctification. He claims that Christ Himself was sanctified, and that Christians are sanctified by participating in Christ's own sanctification through union with Him in baptism.[16] Gaffin moves back and forth, at times almost without distinction, between discussions of the believer's *definitive* sanctification (that which Scripture describes as being constituted holy based on the merits of Christ) and the believer's *progressive* sanctification (that which Scripture describes as putting to death the deeds of the flesh and growing in grace and in the knowledge of the Lord, by the power of the Word and the indwelling Spirit).[17] However, Gaffin makes it clear that he sees both aspects of sanctification coming through "the solidarity factor" of

15. Gaffin, 133.

16. Gaffin, 124-126.

17. For a discussion of the nature and importance of the distinction between definitive and progressive sanctification, see Reymond, *New Systematic Theology of the Christian Faith*, 756-759 and 767-781.

union with Christ through baptism. This union, he says, "involves possession in the inner man of all that Christ is as resurrected"[18] including both definitive and progressive sanctification. This is a doctrine of infused righteousness, an error of Roman Catholicism.

In *Resurrection and Redemption* Gaffin's meaning in this last statement is unclear. But he gives a more definite indication of his position on sanctification in his unequivocal endorsement of the following theological statement, written by OPC ruling elder John O. Kinnaird:

> It is not possible that any could be a brother to Jesus Christ and enjoy with Christ, in the Kingdom of Heaven, the presence of God the Father except that one be fully conformed to the image of Christ in true and personal righteousness and holiness.... [T]he imputation of the righteousness of Christ, which all Christians receive at justification...can[not] suffice for that purpose. Christ does not have an imputed righteousness; His righteousness is real and personal. If we are to be conformed to his image, we too must have a real and personal righteousness.[19]

Of this statement – that believers must have a righteousness of their own in addition to the righteousness of Christ in order to inherit eternal life – Gaffin says:

> [W]e see nothing in the above...which would lead us in any way to question that Elder Kinnaird has continued faithfully before God in his sworn commit-

18. Gaffin, 138.

19. *Kinnaird Declaration and Theological Statement*, reproduced at www.trinityfoundation.org/KinnairdDeclarationTheologicalStatement.php.

ments to the Scriptures, to the System of Doctrine taught therein, and to the Reformed Faith.[20]

Fourth, Gaffin redefines adoption. He claims that Christ Himself was adopted, and that Christians are adopted by participating in Christ's own adoption through union with Him in baptism.[21] Gaffin says that this is what the Apostle Paul meant when he wrote that Jesus was "declared (from the Greek *horizo*) to be the Son of God...by the resurrection" (*Romans* 1:4). Gaffin asserts that "the resurrection of Jesus is his adoption (as the second Adam)." He offers no Scriptural support for this interpretation, despite the fact that the word translated adoption (Greek *huiothesia,* "to be placed as a son") is never used of Christ but only of believers (see *Romans* 8:15, 23, 9:4; *Galatians* 4:5; *Ephesians* 1:5).

Fifth, Gaffin does not merely redefine regeneration, but eliminates it from salvation. He claims that "Paul explicates the inception of the application of redemption without recourse to the terminology of regeneration or new birth understood as 'a communication of a new principle of life.'"[22] Gaffin alleges this despite Jesus' unequivocal statement to Nicodemus in *John* 3:3 – "Unless one is born again he cannot see the kingdom of God" – and Paul's repeated references to believers' having been made alive (*Romans* 6:11 and 13; *1 Corinthians* 15:22; *Ephesians* 2:1-5; *Colossians* 2:13). In Gaffin's "new perspective on Paul" there is really no need of regeneration as a unilateral act of God. As we have seen, Gaffin asserts that baptism, not regeneration apart from

20. Preface to *Kinnaird Declaration and Theological Statement.*
21. Gaffin, 117-119.
22. Gaffin, 140.

154

works by the power of the Holy Spirit, is the point of transition from death to life.[23]

Problems with Gaffin's "New Perspective"

What is wrong with these teachings? There are a number of serious problems, all of which strike at the heart of the Gospel.

First and most obviously, salvation by "existential" and "experiential" union with Christ through baptism is not the way of salvation that Scripture teaches. It is "another gospel." In *Resurrection and Redemption* Gaffin often (and misleadingly) speaks of "believers" but hardly ever speaks of faith. This is telling. "Belief," in his system, is not a matter of believing Biblical propositions but of experiential "uniting." In contrast, the Scriptures unambiguously teach that salvation is by the instrument of unadorned faith. Faith means believing that the Gospel of salvation by the merits of Christ alone is true. The *Westminster Confession of Faith* rightly calls faith itself "the act of believing"[24] and affirms that "the principal acts of saving faith are accepting, receiving, and resting upon Christ alone for justification, sanctification, and eternal life, by virtue of the covenant of grace."[25] Faith looks entirely away from human effort to the full sufficiency of Jesus Christ. Faith itself is the gift of God, and not of works. We have no reason to boast of our faith, much less of our baptism. Baptism *signifies* our relationship with Christ;

23. Gaffin, 51. Here he makes explicit reference to the opening verses of *Ephesians* 2.

24. *Westminster Confession of Faith* chapter 11, paragraph 1.

25. WCF chapter 14, paragraph 2.

it is neither the *instrument* by which we are united to Him, nor our relationship itself.

As we have already noted, Gaffin and Shepherd are on the same theological ground in viewing baptism as the "point of transition" from death to life. Their teaching on the way of salvation also finds its place in Federal Vision theology. Federal Visionist Steve Wilkins says of baptism:

> It's like a wedding. There is a transformation that takes place because of the ritual. A single man becomes a married man. He is transformed into a new man, with new blessings and privileges and responsibilities he didn't have before. A similar thing happens at baptism. The one who is baptized is transferred from the kingdom of darkness into the kingdom of light, from Adam into Christ, and given new privileges, blessings, and responsibilities he didn't have before.[26]

Gaffin's teaching also coincides to an alarming degree with the dogma of the Roman Catholic Church. Rome also teaches that union with Christ through baptism is the way of salvation, the means of redemption, and it condemns those who teach otherwise.[27] Rome teaches that baptism marks the transition from death to life, and that baptism effects union with Christ, "a permanent community of man with God."[28] Rome teaches that justification "cannot, according to Christ's precept, be effected except at the foun-

26. "The Monroe Four Speak Out," *Christian Renewal*, April 28, 2003.

27. "Baptism" in *The Catholic Encyclopedia* (New York: Robert Appleton, 1907; *2003 Online Edition* at www.newadvent.org/cathen/); Ludwig Ott, *Fundamentals of Catholic Dogma* (Rockford, Illinois: Tan Books and Publishers, 1974), 356.

28. *Fundamentals of Catholic Dogma*, 251.

tain of regeneration, that is, by the baptism of water." Rome says that baptism confers sanctification, and that no distinction can be made between justification and sanctification. The Vatican condemns those who teach such a distinction.[29] Rome teaches a "first justification" at baptism as well as a "final justification" at the Last Judgment in which believers lay claim to entry into the kingdom of Heaven based on their works plus Christ's.[30] Rome also teaches that adoption comes through union with Christ in baptism.[31]

Secondly, Gaffin makes Christ the recipient of the saving acts of God that only sinners need to receive. In this vein he speaks of the "passivity" of Christ and of His "solidarity with believers."[32] But Christ the Redeemer did not need to be redeemed. The Propitiation for our sins needed no propitiation of His own. The giver of grace, God coming in flesh in the ultimate act of grace, did not need to make a "transition from wrath to grace" Himself. Biblical redemption (Greek *apolytrosis*) speaks of the payment of a ransom. The sinless Christ needed no ransom to be paid on His behalf. In *Ephesians* 1:7 the Apostle Paul writes that it is believers in Christ who "have redemption through His blood, the forgiveness of sins, according to the riches of His grace." In *Romans* 3:24-25 we read that believers are "justified freely by His grace through the redemption that is in Christ Jesus, whom God set forth as a propitiation by His blood, through faith." Biblical redemption is tightly connected with the forgiveness of sins through the propitiation of the wrath of

29. "Justification" in *The Catholic Encyclopedia.*

30. *Fundamentals of Catholic Dogma,* 251, 264.

31. "Supernatural Adoption" in *The Catholic Encyclopedia.*

32. Gaffin, 65.

God by the blood of Christ. It has nothing to do with a supposed redemption of Christ Himself.

Likewise, Christ the Justifier did not need to be justified as sinners do. Jesus was declared to be the Righteous One, not because the righteousness of another was imputed to Him, but because He was the only man ever to possess a righteousness of His own. His sinless life, perfect atonement, and resurrection from the dead demonstrated that fact. Gaffin, contrary to this, bases his doctrine of justification largely on a wrong interpretation of 1 *Timothy* 3:16, where we read that Christ was "justified in the Spirit." Protestant exegetes, comparing Scripture with Scripture, have long understood that the usage of the word "justified" (*dikaioō*, "declared righteous") must of necessity be different when applied to the sinless Son of God than when it is applied to sinful men. In support of this they cite numerous passages which set forth the system of Bible doctrine concerning the person and work of Christ. These passages include *Matthew* 3:16 (where the Spirit testifies to the deity of Christ); *Romans* 1:4 (Christ is "declared to be the Son of God with power according to the Spirit of holiness"); and numerous passages, many in *Isaiah*, where Christ was declared to be the promised Holy One, the one who even the demons acknowledged (*Mark* 1:24, *Luke* 4:34) but the nation of Israel denied (*Acts* 3:14).

Because Jesus Christ is the Holy One of Israel, He did not need to be justified or thereafter be sanctified as sinners do. Jesus does say, in *John* 17:19, "for their sakes I sanctify Myself, that they also may be sanctified by the truth." But this is in the context of verse 17: "Sanctify them by Your truth. Your word is truth." It is also in the context of the Son of God being glorified (verses 1-2). As the Lord says through the prophet Ezekiel, "'And I will sanctify My great name, which has been profaned among the nations, which you [Israel] have profaned in their midst; and the nations shall know that I am the Lord,' says the Lord God" (36:23). The sanctification of the Son of God is not the same as the sanctification of sinners. Therefore sinners cannot be sanctified by union with Christ in His sanctification.

Likewise, the only begotten Son of God did not need to be adopted. Only those who are aliens from the household of God need to be adopted. The benefits of adoption – access to the throne of grace, God the Father's pity, protection, provision, and correction, and the sealing of the Holy Spirit for the day of redemption – are gifts of God that sinners need, not the only begotten Son.

Gaffin's doctrine of salvation reduces Jesus to little more than the first Christian. In an exposition of *Romans* 6:1-11, Gaffin not only echoes Shepherd's doctrine of "experiential" union with Christ through baptism,[33] but also demonstrates a faulty conception of Christ's person. He says that "the plain implication" of *Romans* 6:10 ("For the death that He died, He died to sin once for all")

> is that prior to his resurrection (*cf.* v. 9) Christ was alive to sin. The preceding verse confirms this by stating that death (which is the exponential of sin, *cf.* v. 23) *no longer* rules over him. It is likewise plain from verse 10 that his present life to God (subsequent to the resurrection) has its distinguishing character in contrast to his former life to sin. Further, this aspect of his resurrection, that is, his having died to sin and his living to

33. Shepherd, *The Call of Grace*, 101.

God, provides the pattern for the experience of believers in their having died to sin and their living to God.[34]

It is an incredible thing to say that Christ was ever "alive
to sin," that He had a "former life to sin," or that there was a
time when, as Gaffin implies, sin "rule[d] over him." These
things are true of sinners prior to their conversion, but were
never true of Christ. In fact, Scripture never speaks of
believers themselves as having been alive to sin. Believers
are *made* alive, having been "dead in trespasses and sins"
(*Ephesians* 2:1 and 5).

*Thirdly, but certainly not least, Gaffin's way of salvation
makes redemption depend on something other than the perfect
righteousness of Christ, the alien righteousness that is imputed
to, not infused into, those who believe the Gospel.* Instead,
Gaffin substitutes existential, experiential union with Christ
– "the solidarity factor" – a merger of sinners and Christ.

Our salvation is a legal matter – but not, as Gaffin
teaches, the cosmic equivalent of a corporate merger. Rather,
our salvation concerns a *criminal* case of universal propor-
tions. Mankind has been found guilty before the judgment
bar of God, and is under the sentence of eternal death. But
God's only Son has paid the death penalty for sinners as an
innocent substitute. The Apostle Paul's doctrinal exposition,
beginning in *Romans* 5 and continuing into chapter 6, is not
that believers are united "existentially" or "experientially"
with Christ, but *legally*. As John W. Robbins writes, believers
are united to Christ legally,

> because Jesus Christ is the legal representative of and
> substitute for his people, the federal head of his race....
> What Jesus Christ did in his life, death, and resur-

34. Gaffin, 125. Emphasis in the original.

160

rection is imputed to believers, as if they had done it, and their sins are imputed to him as if he had done them. Believers do not die with Christ "existentially" or "experientially," but legally. They do not possess Christ's perfect righteousness "in the inner man." Christ's righteousness is imputed, not infused. His act and righteousness are legally, not experientially, theirs. Their sins are legally, not experientially, his. Christ's suffering and death are imputed to believers, and we are freed from the penalty of death for our sins. By substituting "existential" and "experiential" union with Christ for the Biblical doctrines of intellectual and legal union, Gaffin has fabricated an entirely un-Biblical soteriology. Tragically, he has been indoctrinating future pastors in this heterodox nonsense for at least three decades.[35]

The Fault Lines Beneath Gaffin's "New Perspective"

One cannot arrive at such heterodox views without a faulty beginning. What are the fault lines running beneath Richard Gaffin's teachings? What leads him to un-Biblically redefine the way of salvation, and the terms of Scripture? The first section of *Resurrection and Redemption* is titled "Methodological Considerations" and deals primarily with Gaffin's approach to Scripture. Here we find three underlying problems that color Gaffin's handling of Scripture through the rest of the book.

The first factor is Gaffin's commitment to the alleged

---

35. John W. Robbins. "In Christ," *The Trinity Review*, September 2004, www.trinityfoundation.org/PDF/235-InChrist.pdf.

superiority of modern "Biblical Theology" (which is actually the postmodern counterfeit of a valid theological discipline) over systematic theology.[36] The Biblical Theology movement, also known in Reformed circles as the Redemptive-Historical movement, has many adherents among neo-liberals in the OPC and at Westminster Seminary, and even among conservatives.

The legitimate discipline of Biblical theology takes the Bible "as it comes" – book by book, chapter by chapter, verse by verse. The study of Biblical theology results in an understanding of each book of the Bible in terms of its divine and human authorship, setting, literary form (history, poetry, etc.), use of symbolism, outline, main messages, relationship to other books of the canon, and so on. The legitimate discipline of systematic theology looks at the Bible topically, collecting and organizing – not capriciously, but according to sound principles of interpretation – all the Scriptures pertaining to a particular question. What does all of Scripture say about the nature of God? What does all of Scripture say about the nature of Scripture itself? What does all of Scripture say about the way of salvation? What does all of Scripture say about the covenants? How are those doctrines progressively revealed? Systematic theology, legitimately practiced, does not impose a system upon Scripture but seeks to understand and articulate the system of doctrine that Scripture already contains.

Both Biblical theology and systematic theology require a proper approach to Scripture. This approach entails recognition of several facts that Scripture tells us about itself:

---

36. See chapter six for additional discussion of the pitfalls of the Biblical Theology movement.

- God the Holy Spirit is the Author of every word of the Book, and He infallibly employed human writers as His instruments.

- The Bible, as a divine Book, is therefore inerrant and internally consistent from beginning to end.

- The Bible, as the *only* divine Book, is therefore its only infallible interpreter. Traditions and the words of men are not.

- God's Word is intelligible. God intended to communicate truth to mankind at large, and to instruct His church specifically, through His Word and through the illumination of Scripture by the Holy Spirit.

- God did not communicate in an analogous or indirect manner. He communicated His own thoughts directly. Man can understand such direct communication of God's thoughts because he is created in God's image.

The approach to Scripture which recognizes these facts requires submission to God, an attitude of servanthood toward the Book.

In contrast, the modern Biblical Theology movement does not take the Bible "as it comes" nor does it adhere faithfully to these five principles. As a result, it builds from Scripture an artificial system, actually multiple systems. One of the principal dangers of the Biblical Theology movement is that it focuses on the study of "theologies" in the plural – a "theology of Moses" – a "theology of David" – of Isaiah – of Matthew – of Paul – of James – and so on. Thus we have, in the writings of Richard Gaffin, N. T. Wright, and the Federal Visionists, studies of the "theology of Paul" in semi-isolation from the rest of Scripture. This is a reflection of religious academia's embracing the postmodern concept of "truth" as the product of the individual functioning within a "historical community of interpretation." This leads quite naturally to the false notion that Paul's "truth" can be different from that of James or Matthew or John, or even Jesus.

A companion danger of the modern Biblical Theology movement is that it relegates the doctrine of the Holy Spirit's primary and comprehensive authorship of *all* of Scripture, through His supernatural inspiration of the words themselves, to secondary status. Though proponents of the movement deny it, their handling of Scripture constantly demonstrates that human rather than divine authorship has become their primary focus, and that they primarily view the Biblical writers as functioning within a "historical community of interpretation."

Gaffin revealed both dangers in a lecture at the 2005 Auburn Avenue Pastors Conference:

> Let me begin by saying [that] by Biblical Theology
> I have in mind giving attention to the *distinctive contributions* of each of the Biblical writers, *within his immediate historical circumstances or situatedness*, and as that involves taking into account the *fully occasional character* of their writings, as especially [is] the case with Paul. And I'm using the word "occasional" here in the sense that many if not all of us are familiar with, that is, these writings are addressed to *particular groups or individuals in specific situations* with concrete concerns or problems.[37]

37. Richard B. Gaffin "Paul's Perspective: The Apostle and His Theology," 2005 Auburn Avenue Pastors Conference, Session 2, January

This reflects Gaffin's thinking as he opens *Resurrection and Redemption* with a section describing his interpretive methodology:

> To approach Paul as a theologian means that no encyclopaedic [that is, comprehensive] structure or set of distinctions may be allowed to make the situation in which he developed the teaching of his epistles incommensurable in principle with the various contexts in which the later church has hammered out her doctrines.[38]

Unpacking this statement discloses a defective view of the inspiration of Scripture and of the system of doctrine it sets forth. Gaffin is asserting that the teachings given to us through Paul are not to be approached, first and foremost, as integral parts of a fixed and transcendent system of doctrine, revealed by one Divine Author in a comprehensive and structured ("encyclopaedic") manner across the whole of Scripture. Rather, in Gaffin's view, we must approach Paul's writings in semi-isolation. "Encyclopaedic" considerations must not be allowed to violate "the continuity between Paul and his interpreters."[39] The continuity between Paul's epistles and the rest of Scripture is less important than an alleged continuity between Paul's writings and subsequent church interpretation. In Gaffin's view, Bible doctrine continues to "develop" in the subsequent history of the church because of this "continuity." And thus we have the basis for the Shepherd-Gaffin motto of "progress in theology." It is thoroughly postmodern. But there is more.

3, 2005. Transcribed from the lecture video. Emphasis added.

38. Gaffin, *Resurrection and Redemption*, 26. Emphasis added.

39. Gaffin, 23.

The second and third factors influencing Gaffin's theology are interrelated: His implicit denial of the perspicuity (intelligibility) of Scripture, and the rejection of the principle that Scripture is its own interpreter.

These factors spring from a third danger of the Biblical Theology movement of which Gaffin is a leader. This is the movement's insistence that *revelation consists of events, not dogma*. To Gaffin and others, Scripture consists of stories or narratives, not systematic doctrine. This is exceedingly dangerous, because proponents of the Biblical Theology movement claim the right to engage in the "interpretation" of "redemptive events" just as (they claim) the New Testament writers "interpreted" them.

Gaffin, quoting Geerhardus Vos, says that "Paul's is 'the genius of the greatest constructive mind ever at work on the data of Christianity.'"[40] What are "the data of Christianity"? For Gaffin, Vos, and others of this school, the data are the events. And how, according to Gaffin, are we to interpret those events? He says this:

> [T]he exegete, despite every cultural and temporal dissimilarity, stands in principle...in the same situation as the writers of the New Testament and, therefore, is involved with Paul (and the other letter writers) in a common interpretive enterprise.[41]

Expanding on this statement, Gaffin uses an illustration from differential calculus:

> Redemptive events constitute a function (f), the authentication and interpretation of the New Testa-

40. Gaffin, 19.

41. Gaffin, 24.

ment its first derivative (f') and the interpretation of the later church its second derivative (f"). F', to be sure, is of a different order than f", since the former, the infallible verbal revelation (Scripture) which has God as its primary author, is the basis (principium) of the latter. But both, as derivatives, have a common interpretive reference to f. Indeed, it may be said that...f" "goes beyond" f' by seeking to make more explicit the structure implicit in the latter.[42]

Unpacking these statements, we find Gaffin saying that "the data of Christianity" consist of the "redemptive events." The writings of Paul, Peter, James, *et al* in the New Testament are the "first derivative" interpretations of those events – not the revelational events themselves, but "interpretations" of them. The commentaries, councils, creeds, and confessions of the church from the post-apostolic period to the present day are "second derivatives" – interpretations that are also based on the "redemptive events" themselves as well as on the "interpretations" of the New Testament writers.

Gaffin thus replaces an authoritative word from God with a series of "interpretations." All of them have a common reference to the redemptive-historical events themselves, which he alleges constitute the actual "revelation." These begin with the "interpretation" of those events by Paul and the other New Testament writers, and continue through the "interpretations" of the present-day church. Men of the church today, according to Gaffin, are engaged in a "common interpretive enterprise" with Paul and the other writers of Scripture.[43]

---

42. Gaffin, 25. Italics in the original.

43. Richard L. Pratt, chairman of the Old Testament Department at

What is sorely lacking in this line of thinking is any credible commitment to the doctrine of the verbal, plenary inspiration of Scripture. Richard Gaffin pays lip service to it, but he denies it in practice. In his view, Scripture is "interpretation." It is not in itself revelation, but one step removed from revelation.

But the Apostle Paul and the other writers of Scripture were not "interpreters" of events; they were penmen for the Holy Spirit. What Paul wrote was not an "interpretation" of a "revelation" consisting of "redemptive events." What Paul and the other penmen of Scripture wrote down *is* the revelation (*2 Peter* 1:20-21, *2 Timothy* 3:14-17).

Gaffin's line of thinking leads him to imagine great difficulties in the interpretation of the writings of Paul:

> The real difficulty for interpretation lies in the fact that in Paul's writings we encounter a thinker of constructive genius, with a dogmatic bent, but only as he directs himself to specific situations and questions, only as he expresses himself in "occasional" fashion.[44]

In other words, Gaffin is alleging that Paul himself is no more committed to a systematic view of Biblical revelation

---

Reformed Theological Seminary in Orlando, Florida and a former Westminster student, echoes this theme in his book, *He Gave Us Stories* (Phillipsburg, New Jersey: P & R Publishing, 1993). Pratt views the Old Testament as largely a collection of stories, and promotes what he calls an "authority-dialogue model" of Biblical interpretation that is less "like a lecture in which we simply listen to the text" and "more like a classroom discussion where both *we and Scripture make contributions to the final outcome*" (23, emphasis added). Vern S. Poythress and John M. Frame also echo this approach in their "perspectivalist" model of Biblical interpretation, which we shall discuss at length in chapter eight.

44. Gaffin, 28.

than Gaffin himself. For Gaffin, Paul's "theology" is really Paul's alleged situational "interpretation of events." Because of this, Gaffin insists that Paul is systematic only within the context of his own writings, and "only as he directs himself to specific situations and questions."[45] Gaffin continues:

> In short, the true problem in understanding Paul is that he is a theologian, a careful and systematic thinker, accessible only through pastoral letters and records of his sermons. His writings are obviously not doctrinal treatises; but neither do they consist in a variety of unrelated, ad hoc formulations or in an unsystematic multiplication of conceptions. They reflect a structure of thought. The Pauline epistles may be aptly compared to the visible portion of an iceberg. What juts above the surface is but a small fraction of what remains submerged. The true proportions of the whole lie hidden beneath the surface. The contours of what can be seen at a first glance may also prove deceptive. Put less pictorially, that conception or line of thought having relatively little explicit textual support, on reflection may prove to be of the most basic, constitutive [that is, essential or defining] significance. This state of affairs makes the interpretation of Paul, particularly a comprehensive attempt, an inherently difficult and precarious undertaking.[46]

45. The phrase used by Neo-orthodox theologians for this idea was *Sitz im Leben* (situation or setting in life). Gaffin avoids the phrase but makes the idea basic to his thought.

46. Gaffin, 28. Notice that the Reformation's emphasis on the clarity of Scripture plays no part in Gaffin's method of interpretation.

In Gaffin's approach to Biblical interpretation, since the writings of the New Testament are only "interpretation" of the "data of Christianity," and not the data themselves, human authorship is the primary consideration. Gaffin's alleged difficulty springs from his assumption that we only have "the tip of the iceberg" of Paul's "theology." The pages of the Bible only give us so much information to work with. Besides, Gaffin continues, Paul's writings "are obviously not doctrinal treatises" (an amazing and unsupportable assertion) although they do, he says, reflect a "structure." But according to Gaffin we only have so much of that structure, the tip of the iceberg. Therefore, he asserts, the writings of Paul that we do have in the Bible "may prove deceptive."

This is a deeply disturbing assertion. There is no thought here of God's purpose for humanity to have, in the pages of Scripture, just what He *intends* us to have – no more, no less. We know there was more material, because Scripture itself tells us so (*John* 20:30, 21:25). "But *these are written*," the Holy Spirit says through John, "that you may *believe* that Jesus is the Christ, the Son of God, and that *believing* you may have life in His name" (20:31). God has given us all we need, and calls upon us merely to believe in Him.

Not so, says Richard Gaffin. We have only "the tip of the iceberg" and that limited body of information in the pages of Scripture "may prove deceptive." How then shall we avoid being "deceived"? Gaffin offers the solution: The "conception or line of thought" that has "relatively little explicit textual support" becomes the consideration "of the most basic, constitutive significance" – that is, it becomes the controlling factor – in interpreting Paul's writings. In other words, we must interpret what we have of Paul's "theology" in light of what is least supported by the text. We must interpret what is there based on what is not there. This, says

Gaffin, makes the interpretation of these portions of the Word of God "an inherently difficult and precarious undertaking." Indeed it would be, if anything that Gaffin has just said were true.

If we are to believe Richard Gaffin, Christians have been ill-equipped by God to understand the epistles of Paul. The plain sense of the Apostle's writings is not enough, is not comprehensible, and "may prove deceptive" because we only have the "tip of the iceberg" of Paul's thinking. Paul's writings are unintelligible without expert help.

And who are the experts who will lead ill-equipped Christians through this interpretive minefield? Who will describe for them the great mass of Paul's "theology" that allegedly lies unseen below the tip of the iceberg, the hidden part that must govern the interpretation of the Pauline writings that we do have in our hands? According to Richard Gaffin we are to rely upon neo-liberal theologians like Norman Shepherd and himself, whose interpretive methodology has already disclosed thoroughly defective views of the inspiration, systematic nature, and comprehensibility of the Scriptures. If we rely on Shepherd, Gaffin, and their cohorts, we do so at the peril of our souls. By denying the perspicuity of Scripture, Gaffin here lays the foundation for a new priesthood – the academic theologians – and all that priestcraft implies.

A few paragraphs later Gaffin pays lip service to the principle that Scripture "by virtue of its divine origin is self-interpreting."[47] But he does this only after he has explicitly denied that principle by saying that we lack, in the Biblical text, most of what we need to interpret the epistles of Paul.

47. Gaffin, 30.

From this dubious starting point Richard Gaffin writes the rest of his book, which is hailed in some conservative circles as a classic treatise on the subject of how sinners are saved.

In marked contrast to Gaffin's assertions, the Psalmist writes, "The entrance of Your words gives light; it gives understanding to the simple" (*Psalm* 119:130). Paul himself by the Holy Spirit writes, "All Scripture is given by inspiration of God, and is profitable for doctrine, for reproof, for correction, for instruction in righteousness, that the man of God may be complete, thoroughly equipped for every good work" (2 *Timothy* 3:16-17). In contrast to Gaffin's methodology the Holy Spirit says, "Every word of God is pure [tested and proven true]; He is a shield to those who put their trust in Him. Do not add to His words, lest He rebuke you, and you be found a liar" (*Proverbs* 30:5-6).

Gaffin describes the Apostle Paul thus: "In his writing and teachings we encounter a mind of unusual constructive energy with an unparalleled capacity for synthetic thinking, in a word...a 'master-mind.'" But the Apostle himself debunks this view that his words are inaccessible and incomprehensible except to the theologically initiated. He tells the Corinthian church that he came to them, "not with wisdom of words, lest the cross of Christ should be made of no effect" (1 *Corinthians* 1:17). In fact, Paul is careful to emphasize that his words are not even his own. In *John* 7:16-17 even Jesus himself says the same: "My doctrine is not Mine, but His who sent Me. If anyone wills to do His will, he shall know concerning the doctrine, whether it is from God or whether I speak on My own authority." For the Apostle Paul the matter of first and greatest concern is not human authorship – not the "theology of Paul" – but the inspiration of his words by the Holy Spirit:

Now we have received, not the spirit of the world, but the Spirit who is from God, that we might know the things that have been freely given to us by God. These things we also speak, not in words which man's wisdom teaches but which the Holy Spirit teaches, comparing spiritual things with spiritual. But the natural man does not receive the things of the Spirit of God, for they are foolishness to him; nor can he know them, because they are spiritually discerned. But he who is spiritual judges all things, yet he himself is rightly judged by no one. For "who has known the mind of the Lord that he may instruct Him?" But we have the mind of Christ [1 Corinthians 2:12-16].

Richard Gaffin's theology is couched in the language of orthodoxy, but he employs a methodology that violates the most basic principles of sound Biblical interpretation. On that crumbling foundation Gaffin erects a counterfeit salvation through existential solidarity with a counterfeit Christ. While purporting to exalt Christ, his theology actually debases the Son of God. Gaffin depicts a Christ who is no better than the Levitical high priests, who had to repeatedly offer blood atonement for themselves as well as for the people (Hebrews 9:6-7, 23-27). It was they who needed and received redemption, justification, sanctification, and adoption, not Christ. If Gaffin's depiction of Christ and salvation were true, Reformation Christianity would be a monumental lie.

Richard Gaffin has taught this theology to Westminster Theological Seminary students for four decades. Those men occupy two-thirds of the OPC's pulpits, besides many pulpits and positions of influence in other denominations and institutions around the world. In addition to poisoning the theological well himself, Gaffin has also been a staunch supporter of other disseminators of Norman Shepherd's heresies such as ruling elder John O. Kinnaird, whose case we shall consider next.

Chapter 7

The Kinnaird Case and
Its Aftermath

For the time will come
when they will not endure sound doctrine...
they will heap up for themselves teachers;
and they will turn their ears away from the truth....
2 Timothy 4:3-4

The failure of the Orthodox Presbyterian Church and Westminster Theological Seminary to condemn the false teachings of Norman Shepherd and Richard Gaffin has permitted their adherents to preach another gospel with increasing boldness.

John O. Kinnaird, an OPC ruling elder who has held numerous leadership positions in the denomination, is one such adherent. In acts of spiritual vigilance and courage that have become all too rare, members of Kinnaird's own church formally charged him with heresy in two separate cases beginning in late 2001. They persevered in the face of intense, ungodly opposition. Kinnaird's subsequent trial and appeals helped reveal how much the cancer of neo-liberalism had grown within the OPC since the Shepherd controversy. The Kinnaird case also revealed the kinds of corrupt strategies neo-liberals have employed to protect and strengthen their hold on the church.

As in the Shepherd case, the denomination once again failed to defend the faith. Neo-liberals and those who cooperated with them sought to continue the long-standing conspiracy of silence in the OPC regarding Shepherdism. John Kinnaird was convicted of heresy, but his conviction was later overturned. And the denomination went even further than it had in the Shepherd case: Not only was Kinnaird acquitted, the General Assembly also declared that those who found him guilty were the ones in error.

When Kinnaird was charged with heresy, Richard Gaffin and other neo-liberals rallied to his defense. They were compelled to defend Kinnaird to protect themselves, since his doctrines are theirs. If Kinnaird's conviction had stood, conservatives might have been emboldened to bring charges against other neo-liberals. But neo-liberal leaders succeeded in gaining Kinnaird's acquittal. They did so with the aid of men in the indifferent middle, whom they were often able to mislead, confuse, or intimidate. More importantly, by gaining vindication for Kinnaird the neo-liberal leaders and their adherents maintained and strengthened the shield of protection for themselves. As a result, the teaching of another gospel – salvation by union with Christ through baptism, justification by faith-plus-works – has become more open and widespread in the OPC and elsewhere.

Events since the Kinnaird acquittal have both demonstrated and reinforced the strength of neo-liberalism's grip on the denomination. Neo-liberals and their supporters have successfully blocked repeated conservative efforts to have the OPC take a definitive stand against this false gospel.

John Kinnaird (born 1931) has been a ruling elder at Bethany OPC in Oxford, Pennsylvania, for nearly 40 years. He has served on a number of presbytery and denominational committees from the 1970s to the present. For

several years he was a member of the Presbytery of Philadelphia's Candidates and Credentials Committee, which
examines men for licensure and ordination to the ministry.
He also served for many years on the OPC's Foreign Missions Committee. He continues to serve on the denomination's Committee on Revisions to the Directory for Public
Worship. Kinnaird was moderator of the OPC General
Assembly in 1987.

Kinnaird publicly defended Norman Shepherd during
the controversy of the 1970s and early 1980s. He was a
member of the investigating committee appointed by the
Presbytery to look into the 1977 heresy charges against
Shepherd and make recommendations to the full body.
Kinnaird said the charges were baseless and recommended
that they be dropped.[1]

Kinnaird also sought to punish those who opposed
Shepherd's errors. In May 1982, he urged the Presbytery of
Philadelphia to institute judicial proceedings against men
who had brought heresy charges against Shepherd, as well
as those who had helped expose the long-hidden crisis by
signing the May 1981 letter alerting "Friends of the
Reformed Faith." As we already noted in chapter five, the
Presbytery of Philadelphia permitted Shepherd to return
and participate in its June 1982 meeting (even though it had
dismissed him a month earlier at his own request) so that he
could help John Kinnaird argue for the censure of those
defenders of the authentic Gospel.[2]

Kinnaird was also an instructor in Bethany Bible
Institute, a three-year evening school program conducted
under the auspices of his home church. He used Shepherd's

1. *Minutes of the Presbytery of Philadelphia*, March 17-18, 1977, 187-188.

2. *Minutes of the Presbytery of Philadelphia*, June 5, 1982, 174-177.

recorded Westminster Seminary lectures and written materials as the basis for his own classroom lectures.[3] He also taught Norman Shepherd's heresies from the Bethany pulpit while preaching on occasions when the pastor was absent. He incorporated Shepherdism into a theological statement that the Bethany session subsequently approved as the official doctrinal position of the church, in addition (and contrary) to the Westminster Standards, and over the vigorous objections of its pastor, Dr. Clinton S. Foraker. Kinnaird called this statement "my confession."

A Recurring Pattern in the Church

The situation that led to the Kinnaird trial at Bethany represents a recurring pattern in the OPC and elsewhere. During the past three years, a number of members and elders in the OPC (and PCA) who are concerned about the direction of their own churches have contacted this writer to discuss their situations. Often they describe developments in their churches that parallel what took place at Bethany. They describe a recurring four-part pattern.

First, the cancer of neo-liberalism grows subtly in the local church, over a period of years or even decades. Pastors and teachers often slowly change members' thinking by dispensing error in small doses over months and years (and this may be due to the fact that these men are imbibing error gradually themselves). These pastors and teachers often do not identify the sources of their ideas. If they do – by recommending books and other materials from neo-liberal

3. Including Shepherd's WTS course on the Doctrine of the Holy Spirit and his 1979 position paper *The Grace of Justification*, which appears at www.hornes.org/theologia/content/norman_shepherd/the_grace_of_jus tification.htm.

spokesmen, for example – members usually assume that the men being recommended to them are conservative in their theology.

Second, because the encroachment is so gradual, people in the pews often do not recognize that they are hearing another gospel, understand how it is entering the church, or realize the damage being done. Some are beguiled by what they see as (or are told is) a more sophisticated or nuanced approach to the Bible. Many fall prey to the "no-liberals-here" paradigm we described in chapter two, assuring themselves that they are in a conservative church in a conservative denomination, so by definition there can be nothing wrong.

Third, an awakening begins among at least some of the membership. Sometimes it results from exposure to books or sermons from men and organizations that are exposing the downgrade and its causes. Sometimes the awakening begins when new people come into the church. Their sudden exposure to false teaching makes a disquieting contrast with their own foundations in the true faith. Often, relative newcomers are the first to sound the alarm.

Fourth, the church session, having fallen prey to neo-liberal theology (or perhaps due to indifference, or wanting to avoid conflict in the name of unity) suppresses the efforts of church members who try to resist the teaching of error. Often the session will not even answer concerned members' questions about the false doctrines they are hearing. It is a common tactic to label these people as un-Reformed, un-Presbyterian, lacking in theological perception, or just plain troublemakers. Much of the time these concerned people simply leave the church. They are blocked from doing anything else, and do not wish to further risk their own spiritual well-being (and that of their household) by remaining.

What these people from other churches around the country have described to me is what happened at Bethany. There, the encroachment of another gospel began in the 1970s, during the original Shepherd controversy. Gradually, over a period of years, some Bethany members came to realize that false teaching was gaining a foothold in the church. Others in the congregation were indifferent. One long-time member, now in her 80s, who had also witnessed the encroachment of liberalism in the PCUSA in the 1930s, put it this way: "The problem is relativism. Then, as now, many people in the congregation simply said, 'So what?'" Coupled with these developments was the strong adverse reaction of newcomers to Bethany, who had not been previously exposed to neo-liberal theology. A critical development in the awakening at Bethany was the release of Mark W. Karlberg's *The Changing of the Guard* in 2001. Members of the church who read this book began to see the origins of the false teachings they were hearing from John Kinnaird: Westminster Seminary in Philadelphia, and two of its best known professors, Norman Shepherd and Richard Gaffin.

In Bethany's case the new blood included not only the members who eventually charged John Kinnaird with heresy but also a new pastor, Dr. Clinton S. Foraker. Foraker, who came to the Bethany pulpit in 1989, was true to the Gospel. When he came he was unaware of the growing doctrinal divide in the church. Because of the conspiracy of silence in the OPC regarding the Shepherd controversy, as a relative newcomer he was also unaware of the ongoing influences of neo-liberalism in the denomination at large and at Bethany specifically. Foraker's predecessors – Peter A. Lillback (1982-1988) and Jonathan F. Peters (1971-1981) – were influenced by Shepherd and Gaffin. Both former pastors publicly endorsed Kinnaird's teachings before and during his trial. Lillback, who also testified in Kinnaird's defense at the trial, is now president of Westminster Theological Seminary.

Events Leading to the Charges

Over a number of years, the fundamental differences between the Biblical teachings of Clinton Foraker and the errors of John Kinnaird became clear. At one point Foraker preached a series on the book of *Romans*, emphasizing the authentic Christian Gospel. But what Foraker would preach from the pulpit one week, Kinnaird would methodically counter with the teachings of Norman Shepherd the following week in his adult Sunday school class.

By the mid 1990s, some Bethany members had begun to recognize the growing doctrinal divide. By the early 2000s the division over the Gospel had deepened to the point where it was affecting personal relationships within the congregation as well as almost every other aspect of the church's life and ministry. But the source of the division was the encroachment of another gospel, not conflicts of personality.

The majority on the Bethany session, influenced by Kinnaird's neo-liberalism, was blocking efforts by Foraker and others to rid the church of the cancer. Foraker, along with one ruling elder, was fighting a losing battle against entrenched heresy – seven session members against two.

Worse yet, Foraker received little support within the Presbytery of Philadelphia, which in the end betrayed him, the Bethany congregation, and the Gospel. Because of the increasing tension over doctrinal divisions at Bethany, in the spring of 2001 Foraker requested the Presbytery's assistance in resolving the issues. In May of that year the Presbytery appointed a committee to work with Bethany. At its first meeting, members of the congregation gave the committee evidence that Kinnaird was teaching another gospel. But the committee refused to view the cause of the rift at Bethany as anything but a personality conflict between Foraker and members of the session, especially Kinnaird. In fact, the committee refused to discuss doctrinal matters with members of the congregation at all.

Members of the committee did not admit to the Presbytery that there were doctrinal issues until a year later. When John P. Galbraith closely questioned committee members at a May 2002 Presbytery meeting, they reluctantly admitted that there were issues at Bethany related to the doctrine of justification by faith alone. Members of the committee described these issues only in the most cryptic terms, alluding to "questions raised twenty years ago" – in other words, the Shepherd controversy. But this was as far as they would go in breaking the OPC's conspiracy of silence on the Shepherd-Gaffin heresies.

The committee's answer to the church's doctrine-rooted problems was not to inculcate sound teaching, not to assist those who were contending for the Gospel, not to deal Biblically with a session that was tolerating the propagation of error – but to schedule a seminar for the congregation and session on Presbyterian church government, with emphasis on the authority of the session.[4]

At its peak in 2002, Bethany was one of the twenty largest churches in the OPC. By the time John Kinnaird's

---

4. This "Presbyterian Polity Seminar" was conducted by OPC minister Stuart R. Jones, February 22-23, 2002. Jones would later be a member of the Advisory Committee that would recommend Kinnaird's acquittal at the 2003 General Assembly.

appeal of his heresy conviction reached the 2003 General Assembly, Bethany's Sunday morning attendance had plummeted by over 65 percent. The Presbytery had put Foraker out of the pulpit without judicial proceedings. The vast majority of members who were true to the Gospel had left, some joining other congregations and the rest forming a new one which later called Foraker as its pastor.

Kinnaird was charged with heresy twice within the space of a few months.[5] In October 2001, two members of the

5. For those unfamiliar with the judicial processes of the OPC, an overview of the steps in a heresy case involving a ruling elder may be helpful. All judicial cases are regulated by the OPC *Book of Discipline* (www.opc.org/BOCO/BOD.html). A charge against an elder must be brought by two or more individuals, with sufficient evidence. The local church Session reviews the charge and related documents for admissibility. Once it admits the case, the Session then meets as a trial judiciary to hear testimony and examine evidence on both sides, and delivers its verdict. In a heresy trial, the judiciary issues a separate verdict on each specification of error accompanying the charge. If it finds the defendant guilty on any of the specifications, the Session pronounces one of five degrees of censure based on the severity of the case: admonition, rebuke, suspension from office, deposition from office, or excommunication from the church.

The defendant may appeal the session's verdict to the Presbytery. The appeal must specify the alleged error(s) in the deliberations or judgments of the Session that tried the case. The Presbytery then convenes as an appellate judiciary. This proceeding is not a re-trial of the entire case but a hearing of arguments related only to the specification(s) of error in the appeal. The Presbytery then votes to sustain or deny the appeal, voting separately on each specification of error contained in the appeal. The Presbytery may also modify or reverse the Session's judgment, or send the case back to the Session for a new trial.

The defendant may also appeal the Presbytery's verdict to the General Assembly. When the Assembly convenes it assigns an Advisory Committee to conduct a preliminary investigation of the case and make recommendations to the full Assembly. The Assembly then meets as an appellate judiciary, hears arguments and evidence from both sides regarding

Bethany congregation, William and Janice Freeman, charged Kinnaird "with heresy in believing and teaching that water baptism and good works are required conditions for justification, while numerous portions of Scripture make faith the only instrument of justification and salvation."[6] In March 2002 two other Bethany members, Arlyn and Wanda Wilkening, charged Kinnaird with "teaching a doctrine of justification by faith plus works, contrary to the Word of God and the Westminster Standards."[7] The two charges were based on separate bodies of evidence.

The Freeman Charge

The Freeman charge was backed by six items of evidence, including a sermon Kinnaird had preached at Bethany while Dr. Foraker was on vacation, and a book review he had written for the OPC's *New Horizons* magazine.

---

the points of the appeal, and votes on each specification of error in the appeal. The Assembly, like the Presbytery, may affirm or deny the appeal, modify or reverse the Session's judgment, or send the case back for a new trial. The General Assembly is the final court of appeal in the OPC.

In a fallen world no body of man-made rules can guarantee righteous judgments, even in the church. Under the *Book of Discipline* any member of the OPC may file a formal complaint against a decision of any judicatory, citing violations of the Scriptures, the OPC's secondary doctrinal standards, or its *Form of Government*, and seeking specific remedies.

6. William Freeman and Janice Freeman, *Judicial Charge Against Ruling Elder John Kinnaird*, October 14, 2001. Reproduced at www.trinity foundation.org/kinnaird.php.

7. Arlyn A. Wilkening and Wanda J. Wilkening, *Judicial Charge Against Ruling Elder John Kinnaird*, March 18, 2002. Reproduced at www. trinityfoundation.org/KinnairdCharge.php.

In the sermon, Kinnaird echoed Shepherd and Gaffin by proclaiming union with Christ through water baptism as the way of salvation. Preaching from *Mark* 16:14-16, he asserted that the passage "goes against the teaching that one is saved by faith alone, without baptism." He also stated the content of the "gospel" thus:

> Namely, that [Christ] died for sin and that He will send the Holy Ghost into the lives of those who are united to Him through baptism, to deliver them from the power of sin, and that those who are thus united with Him are now justified and will be justified on the Great Day of Judgment.

In the same sermon Kinnaird asserted that

> adults who hear the gospel, properly presented, and who believe the gospel, will always seek to be baptized in order to be united to Christ, and when they believe and are baptized they will be saved.[8]

In November 1999, *New Horizons* published Kinnaird's review of the book *Not by Faith Alone* by Robert A. Sungenis, a Westminster Seminary graduate. Sungenis was a one-time Roman Catholic who converted back to Romanism after he left Westminster. His book is subtitled "A Biblical Study of the Catholic Doctrine of Justification." The *New Horizons* editors substantially revised and condensed Kinnaird's review before publication, eliminating questionable statements. In the original manuscript, Kinnaird stated that "Mr. Sungenis is right when he says" that salvation is "not by

---

8. John O. Kinnaird, Sermon on Baptism, Bethany Orthodox Presbyterian Church, Oxford, Pennsylvania, September 1, 1996. From transcript of tape recording.

faith alone." In another passage deleted by the magazine's editors, Kinnaird continued: "[T]here are those in the Reformed camp who do hold the view that works only demonstrate the sincerity of 'saving faith.' However, that is not the position of the Reformed confessional documents."[9]

Because the OPC editors removed these and other passages supporting a doctrine of salvation by faith-plus-works, the published version of Kinnaird's book review appeared to have been written by someone committed to the true Gospel when in fact he was not. The editors did, however, retain this glaring doctrinal error from Kinnaird's original manuscript: "Those who repent and believe in Jesus *and are baptized* [emphasis added] 'will receive the gift of the Holy Spirit'...."

The Wilkening Charge

The Wilkening charge was supported by four items of evidence, including Kinnaird's own written statements and a September 2000 sermon. At the trial, the Wilkenings submitted eighteen additional exhibits. In this body of evidence, John Kinnaird asserts several things that are diametrically opposed to the Gospel, echoing the teachings of Norman Shepherd and Richard Gaffin.

Kinnaird begins by asserting that believers are justified by faith at conversion. But Kinnaird's "justification by faith" is not the Bible's justification by faith. He redefines justification in four steps.

9. From the original manuscript of his review of *Not by Faith Alone* by Robert A. Sungenis, provided to members of the church by Mr. Kinnaird, available online at www.trinityfoundation.org/nbfa_Sungenis review_unedited.php. The edited version appeared in *New Horizons*, November 1999, 24.

1. He states, "It is those who obey the law who will be declared righteous at the day of Judgment."

2. He says that this must be the case because the righteousness of Christ is not sufficient for believers to inherit the Kingdom of Heaven.

3. He asserts, therefore, that believers must add a righteousness of their own to Christ's.

4. This is necessary, he says, because the Last Judgment is a "forensic act of God." Christ the Judge will evaluate believers' works to see if they have indeed added a righteousness of their own to His. Admission to the Kingdom of Heaven is based upon that added righteousness, not the merits of Jesus Christ alone.

Kinnaird's teaching, though he denies it, is the false doctrine of justification by the infusion of righteousness into the believer, one of the principal errors of Roman Catholicism.

Kinnaird wrote a theological statement which the Bethany session (over the strenuous objections of Pastor Foraker) subsequently adopted as the official position of the church, though it clearly contravened Scripture and the affirmations of the Westminster Standards.[10] In it he said:

> It is not possible that any could be a brother to Jesus Christ and enjoy with Christ, in the Kingdom of Heaven, the presence of God the Father except that one be fully conformed to the image of Christ in true and personal righteousness and holiness. Neither the imputation of the righteousness of Christ which all Christians

10. *Kinnaird Declaration and Theological Statement*, reproduced at www.trinityfoundation.org/KinnairdDeclarationTheologicalStatement.php.

receive at justification, nor the infusion of the righteousness of Christ (a false and non-existent concept
taught by the Roman Catholic Church) can suffice for
that purpose. Christ does not have an imputed righteousness; His righteousness is real and personal. If we
are to be conformed to his image, we too must have a
real and personal righteousness. [11]

But in another written statement Kinnaird spoke of an
infused righteousness through sanctification:

Whereas in justification we receive credit for the
righteousness of Christ, here [in sanctification] we
receive, through the work of the Holy Spirit, a righteousness that is really and personally our very own,
not just that of another credited to us, but our very
personal own.[12]

In his teachings, Kinnaird repeatedly states that *Romans*
2:13 teaches that "it is those who obey the law who will be
declared righteous *on that Day of Judgement.*"[13] Kinnaird
consistently adds the last five words to the text of this verse.
He has done it so often that his hearers often forget that
those words are not part of inspired Scripture. Adding them
changes the meaning of the verse entirely. In context the
Apostle Paul is arguing that no one but Christ was capable
of keeping the law, and that His perfect law-keeping righteousness is imputed to believers. Kinnaird, by adding five

11. *Kinnaird Declaration and Theological Statement.*

12. John O. Kinnaird, message 7846 titled "Justification," posted on the
Presbyterians-OPC Yahoo® forum December 24, 2001. Reproduced at
www.trinityfoundation.org/OPCListPosting12-24-01.php.

13. *Kinnaird Declaration and Theological Statement.* Emphasis added. Use
of the British spelling *judgement* in the trial evidence is Kinnaird's.

words to the end of the verse almost every time he mentions it, changes *Romans* 2:13 to mean that law-keeping is required of believers themselves in order to be declared righteous (that is, justified) on the Last Day.

Developing this theme, Kinnaird says:

> *Romans* 2 puts it this way: "God will give to each person according to what he has done. To those who by persistence in doing good seek glory, honor and immortality, He will give eternal life. But for those who are self seeking and who reject the truth and follow evil there will be wrath and anger." Now by this we know the decision, the judgment as to who enters the city and who stays outside for eternity will be made on that great Day of Judgement in accordance with what you have done in this life.[14]

Regarding the Day of Judgment and the qualifications for entry into the heavenly city of *Revelation* 22, Kinnaird teaches the following:

> God has provided not only justification from the guilt of sin, he has also, for all those begotten from above by the seed of God, provided that holiness without which no one will see the Lord. *Hebrews* 12:14. These good works are a required condition if we would stand in the Day of Judgement and they are supplied by God to all His people.
>
> Every description of the Judgement events speak of these good works. Without them, no one will see God.

14. Kinnaird, "Though the Waters Roar and the Mountains Quake," sermon preached at Bethany OPC, Oxford, Pennsylvania, September 22, 2000. Transcript reproduced at www.trinityfoundation.org/Revelation sermon.php.

Our God is not unjust. His judgements are always righteous and in accordance with the facts of the case. On the past two Lord's Days I shared over 25 texts and passages of Scripture with my Sunday School class on just these two concepts. They were about evenly divided between the concept that our God's judgements are always righteous and in accord with the facts of the case and the concept that the final judgement will be in accord with what we have done in this life....

There will be glory, honor, and peace on the Day of Judgement for everyone who does good. [*Romans* 2] verse 10. Who are these people who thus benefit – who stand on the Day of Judgement? They are those who obey the law who will be declared righteous, verse 13. When God declares them righteous, that is a forensic declaration of righteousness.... This is a judicial scene, the Day of Judgement. It is an act of God sitting as Judge. It is justification – a forensic act of God whereby he declares a person righteous. God is able to make this declaration on That Day because it is a truth. Something has happened to change those who were once sinful. What is it?... Paul says, verses 14 and 15, these are those who by nature, a new nature, do the things required by the law.[15]

Thus we rightly conclude that those inside the city [of *Revelation* 22] are those who have kept the law of God and those only. So, a pretty simple answer to our last two questions. Inside the city are those who do righteousness and outside are those who do evil.[16]

15. John O. Kinnaird, message 8014 titled "Justification," posted on the Presbyterians-OPC Yahoo® forum January 6, 2002. Reproduced at www.trinityfoundation.org/OPCListPosting1.php.

16. Kinnaird, "Though the Waters Roar and the Mountains Quake."

Eight present and former leaders of the Orthodox Presbyterian Church and Westminster Theological Seminary signed a statement publicly endorsing John Kinnaird's heresies:

- Donald J. Duff, long-time Stated Clerk of the OPC General Assembly

- Dr. Richard B. Gaffin, Jr., Professor of Biblical and Systematic Theology, Westminster Theological Seminary

- Ross W. Graham, General Secretary, OPC Committee on Home Missions

- Barry Hofstetter, OPC licentiate; doctoral candidate, Westminster Theological Seminary; member of the adjunct faculty, Center for Urban Theological Studies, Philadelphia; member of the visiting faculty, Reformed Theological Seminary

- Dr. Peter Lillback, former pastor of Bethany OPC, Oxford, Pennsylvania; pastor of Proclamation Presbyterian Church (PCA), Bryn Mawr, Pennsylvania; now President and Professor of Historical Theology, Westminster Theological Seminary

- Dr. Samuel T. Logan, at the time President and Professor of Church History, Westminster Theological Seminary; now Chancellor of the Seminary

- Jonathan F. Peters, former pastor of Bethany OPC, Oxford, Pennsylvania

- Thomas E. Tyson, OPC minister; Regional Home Missionary, Presbytery of Philadelphia; former editor (1989-2000), *New Horizons*.

Thomas Tyson was Kinnaird's defense counsel during the trial and appeals. Peter Lillback and Richard Gaffin testified in defense of Kinnaird at his trial. Gaffin later led the effort to overturn Kinnaird's conviction in the Presbytery of Philadelphia and at the 2003 General Assembly. The eight leaders' endorsement of Kinnaird's theology was unequivocal:

> As ordained ministers of the Word and licentiates in the Orthodox Presbyterian Church or in the Presbyterian Church in America, *we see nothing* in the above Declaration or in the Theological Statements which would lead us *in any way* to question that Elder Kinnaird has continued faithfully before God in his sworn commitments to the Scriptures, to the system of doctrine taught therein, and to the Reformed faith.[17]

Arthur W. Kuschke, former member of the Westminster Seminary faculty and one of Norman Shepherd's chief opponents during the controversy of the 1970s and 1980s, refuted Kinnaird and his supporters with Biblical precision:

> Elder Kinnaird teaches "a doctrine of justification by faith and works." He does not use the phrase, "justification by faith and works." He says that believers are justified by faith at their conversion. He also says, "It is those who obey the law who will be declared righteous" at the Day of Judgment, "according to what they have done in the body." To be "declared righteous" is, precisely, to be justified. Thus he affirms justification by faith, and also justification by obedience to the law.
>
> After justification at conversion, why does he speak of justification at the Judgment? He says that the im-

17. *Kinnaird Declaration and Theological Statement*, section titled "Appraisal by Others." Emphasis added.

192

puted righteousness of Christ, which all Christians receive at conversion, "cannot suffice" to bring us into full conformity to the image of Christ in true and personal holiness.... Obedience to the law, in this life, is therefore still necessary for eternal life. The justification at conversion, by "the imputed righteousness of Christ," "cannot suffice" to supply this need; there must still be a justification at the Judgment according to our obedience to the law. This is a doctrine of justification by faith and works.

...Elder Kinnaird has suggested two reasons why the imputed righteousness of Christ "cannot suffice." The first is that sanctification is also given [to] us, and that the obedience wrought by sanctification *does* provide the real and personal righteousness and holiness required; we reply, that even our best sanctification and obedience *in this life* cannot suffice for this purpose....

His second reason why the imputed righteousness of Christ "cannot suffice" is that by the very nature of *imputation*, Christ's righteousness is the righteousness of *another*, and therefore cannot be truly and personally *our own*. He says that real and personal righteousness must be "our own, our very own, not just that of another credited to us".... Here he challenges the imputation of the righteousness of Christ as *not* providing us with real and personal righteousness. But if the righteousness of another is truly credited to us, is not that righteousness then *ours*, really and personally? Is imputation empty? Is it a legal fiction? Christ died for particular persons. By his death he paid our full penalty. And by his righteousness he gained our full righteousness. Justification at conversion is complete justi-

fication, not limited justification, and not partial justification.

It is of the very essence of the Scriptural doctrine of
justification that as sinners we *cannot* be redeemed in
any other way, by any righteousness of our own, but
must have an imputed righteousness that is *not our own,*
an alien righteousness, the righteousness of *another,*
credited to us, if it is to be real and personal *and our very*
own. This righteousness Christ gives us, by His grace,
through faith alone.[18]

However, Kuschke's statement – delivered on the opening day of Kinnaird's trial – was many months in the future.
What lay immediately ahead were efforts by Kinnaird and
his supporters on the Bethany session and in the Presbytery
of Philadelphia to suppress the charges against him.

Conspiracy to Suppress the Charges

Employing tactics that can only be described as ungodly,
Kinnaird and his supporters sought to put the lid on both the
Freeman and Wilkening charges. But for God's providential
hand, neither charge would have ever seen the light of day.

Kinnaird and his allies, who constituted a 7-2 majority on
the Bethany session, blocked the Freeman charge. But they
were not successful in blocking the Wilkening charge.

In December 2001 the session voted 7-2 to reject the Freeman charge, claiming that some of the evidence was inadmissible because it was over two years old. This decision violated the OPC *Book of Discipline,* which specifically prohibits

18. Arthur W. Kuschke, *Opening Statement for the Prosecution at the*
Trial of John O. Kinnaird, November 23, 2002, reproduced at www.trinity
foundation.org/KuschkeOpeningStatement.php.

dismissal of a serious charge on a technicality.[19] The decision also ignored the fact that Kinnaird's false teaching was not a one-time event in the past, but an ongoing heresy.

In January 2002 the Freemans filed a formal complaint against the session's dismissal of their charge. At the same time Dr. Clinton Foraker, Bethany's senior pastor, and ruling elder Mark Whiteman, moderator of the session, filed a separate complaint of their own.[20] In March 2002 the Bethany session denied both complaints.

---

19. "The judicatory...should it be persuaded that the charge and specifications, if proved true, would constitute an offense serious enough to warrant a trial, shall not dismiss the case on technical grounds but shall require that the charge and specifications be put in proper form. If the person bringing the charge fails to do this, it shall become the responsibility of the judicatory" (*Book of Discipline of the Orthodox Presbyterian Church*, chapter 3, section 7.b).

20. Foraker had been told of Kinnaird's September 1996 sermon on baptism by concerned members of the congregation when he returned from vacation. He listened to a recording, had it transcribed, and confronted Kinnaird in a session meeting about his teaching. Kinnaird denied that he taught anything contrary to the *Confession of Faith*. At this point Foraker, who as yet had no knowledge of the Shepherd heresy because of the OPC's conspiracy of silence, asked the session to reaffirm its belief in the doctrine of justification by faith alone. All gave consent.

Foraker also contacted other ministers in the OPC and PCA for advice. Though they recognized the seriousness of the error, they advised him not to bring a charge against Kinnaird. None of the OPC men Foraker contacted made any mention of the teachings of Norman Shepherd, though they had personal knowledge of the Shepherd controversy.

The Freemans prepared their charge without involving Foraker (since he was a member of the session that would hear the case) after further evidence of Kinnaird's belief in salvation through baptism surfaced. Clinton Foraker, who steadfastly opposed the preaching of another gospel, was subsequently forced to resign his pastorate by the Presbytery of Philadelphia because of his stand, although he was never charged with any offense under the OPC *Book of Discipline*.

In April 2002 the Freemans, Foraker, and Whiteman appealed both decisions to the Presbytery of Philadelphia. However, the Presbytery delayed action on their appeals for nearly a year. The Freemans' complaint did not come before the Presbytery until February 1, 2003. By that time they had already left the OPC to seek the fellowship of a church that would be unequivocal regarding the Gospel. Therefore the Presbytery dismissed their appeal without a hearing.[21] The Foraker-Whiteman complaint did not come before the Presbytery until February 22, 2003. By that time Whiteman had also left the OPC, and Foraker had been forced out of his pulpit by the Presbytery – without being charged with any offense under the *Book of Discipline* – because of his stand for the Gospel. Foraker, who was still a member of the Presbytery at that point, withdrew the complaint,[22] and soon afterward renounced the OPC's jurisdiction and left the denomination.[23] Thus the neo-liberals, aided by their supporters, killed the Freeman heresy charge against John Kinnaird.

The Bethany session employed even more egregious tactics to block the Wilkening charge. Members of the ses-

21. *Minutes of the Presbytery of Philadelphia*, February 1, 2003, item 16.

22. *Minutes of the Presbytery of Philadelphia*, February 22, 2003, item 4.

23. In an April 2, 2003, letter to the Presbytery of Philadelphia, Foraker wrote: "The serious doctrinal division within the Bethany session, and the manner in which it was consequently handled by the Philadelphia Presbytery during the last few years, has made me conscious of deep and serious divisions within this denomination regarding the *Westminster Confession of Faith* and the *Catechism* as containing the system of doctrine taught in the Holy Scriptures, and going to the very heart of the Gospel. I cannot, in good conscience, remain in subjection to fellow ministers when there no longer exists unity regarding the essentials of the faith; therefore, I must renounce the jurisdiction of the OPC." Foraker is now pastor of Calvert Reformed Presbyterian Church, Calvert, Maryland.

sion participated in a detailed plan, drafted by John Kinnaird himself, to obstruct justice. But in the providence of
God their conspiracy was discovered.

The Wilkenings submitted their charge against Kinnaird
to the Bethany session on March 18, 2002. Four days later, a
member of the congregation discovered a memorandum
written by Kinnaird that had been left behind on the church
photocopier. The memo, from Kinnaird to the rest of the
seven-man session majority, outlined a detailed strategy to
engineer his acquittal. Kinnaird's plan stated two purposes:
to have the session adopt his heresy-laced theological statement as the official position of the church, and to dismiss
the Wilkenings' charge against him without a trial. The
memo detailed two alternative versions of the scheme,
which Kinnaird had labeled "Plan One – Safe" and "Plan
Two – Risky."[24]

Kinnaird's memo instructed his allies on the session to
sequence the dockets of upcoming meetings to achieve his
stated goals. They were to use specific parliamentary maneuvers to orchestrate proceedings to his benefit, such as
moving from open session into executive (closed) session at
one critical juncture, and moving into a committee of the
whole to permit off-the-record discussions during open session at another point. He instructed his allies to make motions on his behalf at critical moments in those meetings –
motions he would not be permitted by the OPC *Book of Discipline* to make himself because he was a potential heresy
defendant. And, John Kinnaird instructed his fellow elders
to vote to dismiss the Wilkening charge against him.

When confronted, Kinnaird admitted that he had written

24. This document, which was later distributed to the entire Bethany
congregation, is reproduced in full in Appendix B.

the document but denied wrongdoing. But the document spoke for itself. These actions clearly violated the OPC *Book of Discipline*,[25] to say nothing of Scripture's condemnation of wicked conspiracies (*e.g.*, *Psalm* 10:2, 64:2; *Proverbs* 6:16-19).

Foraker and Whiteman – the two members of the session who were faithful to the Gospel and therefore had not received the Kinnaird memo – were made aware of its existence the day it was found. They informed the session and the special Presbytery committee of this discovery by letter on March 25, 2002. At a meeting on that date, the session refused to permit the letter to be read. At a meeting on April 1, the session permitted the letter to be read but refused to take action on it, because it was addressed to "Brothers" and not to "The Session" and therefore was not an "official communication." Nevertheless, members of the Presbytery special committee who were attending the meeting urged the session to recuse itself from further consideration of the Wilkening charge. Kinnaird's supporters refused. The special Presbytery committee, though it was tasked with helping to heal divisions in the church that were clearly rooted in a conflict over the Gospel, did not inform the Presbytery of the existence of the Kinnaird memo, or the compromised position of the session in ruling on the charge.

In the meantime, Kinnaird and his allies on the session had been seeking to oust Foraker. In February 2002 they had begun circulating a petition to request a congregational meeting on the question, "Shall we ask Rev. Clinton S. Foraker to resign from the pastorate of Bethany Orthodox Presbyterian Church?" On March 9, Kinnaird and his six

25. "The accused may not sit in judgment on his own case at any stage thereof, including the preliminary investigation" (*Book of Discipline* chapter 4, section 3.a).

allies on the session signed a letter to the full congregation recommending that it vote to ask Foraker to resign. On March 13 a congregational meeting was held, with the cooperation of the special Presbytery committee, to seek Foraker's ouster. But to the surprise of his adversaries Foraker was sustained as pastor with 59 percent of the vote.

Another petition, circulated by members concerned for the Gospel, asked for a congregational meeting to "inform the congregation and discuss with them the doctrinal position of the *Westminster Confession of Faith* regarding the doctrine of salvation versus the position on the doctrine of salvation as expounded in Elder John O. Kinnaird's proposal." OPC minister John W. Mallin III, who was now serving as moderator of the Bethany session as part of the Presbytery's peace-keeping efforts, ruled the second petition out of order because it dealt with doctrinal matters.

In a series of votes at its April 29, 2002, meeting, the Bethany session followed the party line prescribed in Kinnaird's plan. It first determined that the evidence (cited earlier in this chapter) did not support the Wilkening charge. It then voted to dismiss the charge itself. Later in the meeting it voted to adopt Kinnaird's error-laden theological statement as the official position of the church. Foraker and Whiteman dissented vigorously in all of these decisions. On June 17 the Wilkenings brought a formal complaint against the session's decision to dismiss their case.[26]

The Presbytery of Philadelphia scheduled a special meeting at Bethany for July 8, 2002, to deal with the deteriorating situation. On July 3, Foraker wrote a letter to the congregation. It said in part:

26. The Wilkening complaint is reproduced at www.trinityfoundation. org/wilkening_complaint.php.

I will be unable to serve communion this Sunday, July 7, 2002, at the Bethany services. The Session is being informed of my decision.

As a minister charged with administering the Lord's Supper, it is my duty to issue a warning to those present at the service that they should not partake of the sacrament if they are not true believers in the Lord Jesus Christ, according to the Holy Scriptures.

In the Directory of Worship, a believer is described as one confessing his dependence for pardon and cleansing upon the perfect sacrifice of Christ, basing his hope of eternal life upon Christ's perfect obedience and righteousness, resolving to deny himself, crucify his old nature and follow Christ as becomes one who bears His name. In other words, we are to rely on Christ's merits alone for our salvation. Herein lies the conflict. The Session, on April 29, approved and adopted a series of theological statements by Elder Kinnaird, some of which are in direct contradiction to the clear teaching of Scripture, the Westminster Standards, and our Directory for Worship. This set of theological statements declares that, "It is those who obey the law who will be declared righteous on that Day of Judgement." This is not the teaching of the Scripture or our Reformation forefathers (*Gal.* 2:16, *Rom.* 3:19, 20, 28.) Here we have two conflicting statements regarding those who are saved. It is my concern that individuals partaking of the Lord's Supper may incorrectly understand that either of these beliefs is acceptable. Since I do not believe this to be true, I have a conflict of conscience which prevents me from administering the Lord's Supper until the Orthodox Presbyterian Church can rule on the validity of the action of the Bethany Session.

The members of Bethany Session who approved the motion concerning Elder Kinnaird's theological statements have denied that they have approved a theological standard in addition to the Westminster Standards for our church. Yet on May 28, 2002, the Session passed a motion demanding that I detail, in writing, at what points the theological statements are not in agreement with the Word of God and the Westminster Standards. Consequently, contrary to their public statement I am being held "officially" accountable to these statements as a standard of doctrine....

As long as there are two standards of doctrine and two versions of the Gospel at Bethany church there will be no unity or peace. While there is no greater privilege for me than to serve you Holy Communion, I am fearful that at this moment in our church's history, for me to serve in the light of conflicting doctrinal standards would breed confusion which could jeopardize the immortal souls of some. "Here I stand, I can do no other...."

Foraker also wrote a letter to be read at the July 8 Presbytery meeting, which he was unable to attend because of serious health problems:

The problem at Bethany is that we have two gospels, two conflicting views as to how a man is saved. As long as there are two standards of doctrine and two versions of the gospel, there can be no unity or peace. As a minister of the OPC, I subscribe to the Holy Scriptures and the Westminster Standards. When I joined the OPC and became the pastor of Bethany, I was never told that I would be required to subscribe to the theology of John Kinnaird, or the theology of Norman Shepherd, or the theology of anything or anyone else. If I had thought that this would be the case, I would never have joined this denomination.

When I was received into the OPC, I did not know, as many of you did, about the New Perspective, the Norman Shepherd teachings, Neo-Covenantalism, etc. I had never heard of Norman Shepherd, but I now see (from the list of those who endorse Mr. Kinnaird's theology) that the Shepherd teaching, or variations thereof, have shadowed my ministry at Bethany from the beginning. If I had known that this teaching was accepted, permitted, or even tolerated unofficially, I would never have accepted the call to this church.

When I took my vows, I took them in the clear, historic, traditional sense. There was no equivocation, no law of mental reservation employed. I came to the Reformed Faith joyfully by fire. I crossed the Rubicon and burned bridges behind me as I stood for the truth of the Gospel. Now I find that I am called upon once again to stand for the Gospel. Make no mistake, the battle at Bethany is the battle for the Gospel, and I ask the [members of the] Philadelphia Presbytery to declare themselves. Failure to do so has split our beloved church, and could result in the loss of many precious souls from the OPC. On the other hand, if you reaffirm the historic position, you must strike down Elder Kinnaird's statements and require the immediate resignation of all those who voted in favor of them. All of heaven awaits your decision.

And with Heaven watching, at the July 8 special meeting the Bethany session asked the Presbytery to request both Foraker and Kinnaird to resign their offices. Instead, the Presbytery voted to suspend Foraker and the entire session from office, without judicial proceedings.

The Presbytery's action was based on a wrong focus. Reports from the special committee had said that there were irreconcilable personality conflicts within the church. The special committee largely turned a blind eye to the doctrinal issues that were the true cause of the conflict. The full Presbytery now followed suit. It instructed the special committee to continue to seek reconciliation by "counseling" the deposed pastor and session. The Presbytery was attempting to promote "peace and unity," but without acknowledging that neither is possible without doctrinal purity.

The Presbytery also appointed an interim session comprising five of its ministers from other churches. One of the appointees was Thomas Tyson, who was already serving as Kinnaird's defense counsel and thus had a clear conflict of interest. Tyson soon resigned from the interim session and was replaced by a ruling elder from another church. After Tyson's resignation, the makeup of the interim session was essentially conservative and Confessional.

On July 21 the Bethany congregation voted to approve the Presbytery's arrangements for the interim session. On August 26 the interim session sustained the Wilkening's June 17 complaint regarding the suspended session's April 29 decision to dismiss their charge. This at last opened the way for John Kinnaird to be tried for heresy. The interim session scheduled those proceedings to begin on September 16.

On that date, in accordance with the *Book of Discipline*, only three actions were permitted: the reading of the charge, submission of evidence, and arrangements for the summoning of witnesses. The trial itself began on November 23, 2002, and concluded on January 25, 2003.

The Trial: Prosecution Case

Kinnaird was charged with "teaching a doctrine of justification by faith and works, contrary to the Word of God and the Westminster Standards." There were three specifications of error associated with the charge, and the interim session found him guilty on all counts.[27]

Carl W. Hayes, a Bethany member and former PCA ruling elder who was part of the prosecution team,[28] recognized the marks of neo-liberalism that we described in chapter two: its unsound principles for interpreting Scripture, arbitrary redefinition of key doctrinal terms, and tendency to admit multiple perspectives as to what constitutes Biblical truth. Hayes warned of the need to guard against these abuses during the trial. In his opening statement he said:

> We intend to apply the following basic principles and ask that the accused and his counsel and witnesses do likewise:
>
> 1. Define key words, terms, and phrases at the outset.
>
> 2. Traditional theological words, terms, and phrases must be used.
>
> 3. The words, terms, and phrases must be taken in their plain and ordinary meaning unless otherwise stated.
>
> 4. Their meaning must never change during the proceedings in a given context.

27. The full record of the trial is available on The Trinity Foundation's website at www.trinityfoundation.org/kinnaird.php.

28. The other members were Foraker, Kuschke, and Arlyn Wilkening.

5. The main ideas must be demonstrably derived from the Word of God.

6. The phrase, "That's your interpretation," is not a satisfactory conclusion for deciding the validity of a theological position.

7. Any intended playing on words, ambiguities, sophistry, or other techniques intended to mislead are a violation of the ninth commandment.

Many theological controversies could have been averted by the careful and consistent use of these basic principles.[29]

Also speaking for the prosecution, Arthur W. Kuschke presented the opening statement we quoted earlier. Later in that statement he delivered a precise summary of authentic Biblical doctrine regarding the issues of the case, and a compelling summation of Kinnaird's principal errors:

Justification is a central doctrine of the gospel. It must be clearly stated, clearly defined, clearly guarded, clearly preached. Many have stumbled at it, but it is clearly revealed in God's Word.

Justification is God's declaration *that we are righteous*. How can this be? How can God justify *the ungodly*?

Only because *God has imputed to us* the righteousness of Christ. On that ground alone He declares what is now the case: we *are* righteous, for he has given us "the gift of righteousness" (*Romans* 5:17). So justification is the key doctrine that makes the difference between the lost and the redeemed, according to God's eternal law. And justi-

29. www.trinityfoundation.org/HayesOpeningStatement.php.

fication is complete and thorough, once for all; it is perfect in this life and forever, so that we can never fall into condemnation. And it is entirely by God's grace, not by any righteousness that we have done. And it is by faith alone without any works of any kind on our part: it must be by faith alone if it is to be by grace alone.

There are other great central doctrines of the faith, and they are necessarily interlocked together in Scripture, to reveal the system of doctrine which Scripture teaches. Such other great central doctrines are, God's law; sin; God's wrath; God's grace; the person and work of our Redeemer and Perfect Substitute, the Lord Jesus Christ; His substitutionary death, whereby He paid the penalty for our sins; His resurrection and His resurrection power to save; the Holy Spirit's grace of regeneration; repentance and faith; sanctification; perseverance; glorification after this life; judgment. All are necessarily interlocking truths within the one system. They move together. They are interdependent. If one is changed or diminished from its true force, the others are also influenced. As one system they give us the pure Gospel, which is the only true Gospel.[30]

These truths are linked together not only because it is given to us to understand their interrelatedness. They are explicitly linked together in Scripture. For example, in *Romans* 4:16, faith is necessarily tied to grace, and then

30. To this list of great interlocking truths, which was not meant to be comprehensive, we would add these: the doctrine of Adamic probation, the doctrine of the Covenant of Works, the Biblical antithesis between Law and Gospel, the distinction between the Old and New Covenants, and the federal headship of Adam (over sinners) and Christ (over the redeemed). We mention these doctrines specifically because they are also under attack in neo-liberal theology.

both faith and grace are necessarily tied to the surety of God's promise. The Greek is very explicit, not employing as many words as our English translations. It focuses on great principles:

> For this reason through faith,
>
> in order that by grace,
>
> to the end that the promise might be sure
>
> to all the seed.

This inescapable logic demands our attention. Faith, grace and surety not only belong together but they *must* go together.

Other examples of such explicit linkage are numerous: *Romans* 3:20, "Therefore by the deeds of the law shall no flesh be justified in his sight, for by the law is the knowledge of sin." *John* 3:16. *1 Peter* 3:18. *1 John* 5:10. *Galatians* 3:13. *2 Corinthians* 5:21. *Isaiah* 53:4-6. *Ephesians* 2:4. *Romans* 7:12-17. *Romans* 8:28-30.

We see the integrity of many other truths involved with the integrity of the doctrine of justification especially. One principle that is repeated, and insisted upon many times, is that "the deeds of the law" are excluded from justification: *Acts* 13:38-39, *Romans* 3:20, and *Romans* 3:28 – "Therefore we conclude that a man is justified by faith without the deeds of the law." *Romans* 4:5. *Romans* 4:6. *Romans* 4:13. *Romans* 9:30-32. *Galatians* 2:16. *Galatians* 3:10. *Galatians* 3:20. *Galatians* 3:21-24. *Galatians* 5:4. *Ephesians* 2:8-9. *Philippians* 3:9. *2 Timothy* 1:9.

Justification is also linked necessarily to the *atonement* by the common principle of *substitution*. In Question 33 of the *Shorter Catechism*, the *pardon* spoken of in the first part of the answer ("Justification is an act of

God's free grace, wherein he pardoneth all our sins") comes to us only through the *substitutionary atonement*. We can have no pardon without that substitutionary sacrifice. Likewise the second part of question 33 ("and accepteth us as righteous in his sight, only for the righteousness of Christ imputed to us, and received by faith alone") also depends entirely on substitution. There is full substitution in each. Our guilt was imputed to Christ our Substitute; He paid the full penalty of God's eternal wrath in our place, the just for the unjust. And His righteousness is imputed to us, *an alien righteousness* that comes from *another*, who is our *Substitute, even Christ our Righteousness (Jeremiah 33:15-16)*.

It appears to be a flaw in Elder Kinnaird's teaching that he fails to relate together the great central doctrines of the Biblical system in the same way that the Scriptures and our Standards relate them. Nor does he identify correctly those doctrines, in the system, that are especially related to justification.

To sum up: Elder Kinnaird has re-defined justification by faith, to *limit* its fullness, completeness, and efficacious character so that after justification we do not yet have enough righteousness, or even the right *kind* of righteousness that is required at the Judgment; and he seeks to provide a *further* "personal" righteousness, expressed in *our obedience to the law*, for a final declaration of righteousness at the Judgment. He has tried to combine both *faith*, and *the works of the law*, for justification. This, Scripture and our Standards forbid.[31]

---

31. Kuschke, *Opening Statement for the Prosecution at the Trial of John O. Kinnaird*. Emphases in the original.

The Trial: Defense Case

The defense strategy in the Kinnaird case consisted of two main elements. First, the defense attempted to put the prosecution and the judicatory on trial. In his opening statement Thomas Tyson employed the kind of legal sophistry – use of an invalid but skillful argument in the hope of deceiving one's hearers – that Carl Hayes had warned against in the prosecution's opening statement. Tyson began by objecting to the entire proceeding.[32] He argued that the Wilkening charge was "ambiguous" and therefore must be either modified (to be agreeable to the defense) or thrown out. He based his argument on the placement of a comma in the charge. This kind of ploy is common among defense lawyers in civil and criminal courts: If you cannot refute the charge, attack the charge itself.

The judicatory denied Tyson's objection, but he and Kinnaird's defense witnesses continued to raise it to the very end of the trial. The judicatory was remarkably patient with these tactics. After the guilty verdict, Tyson would continue to raise the "ambiguous charge" objection during subsequent appeals before the Presbytery of Philadelphia and the OPC General Assembly.

The second major element of the defense strategy was the testimony of two "expert" witnesses, Drs. Peter A. Lillback and Richard B. Gaffin, Jr. The defense rested principally on the opinions of these two men. The testimony of both bore the marks of neo-liberalism we described in chapter two.

Lillback contributed four doctrinal errors to the defense

---

32. Thomas Tyson, *Defense Objections to the Trial Proceeding*, www.trinity foundation.org/DefenseObjectionsProceeding.php.

presentation.[33] First, he supported Kinnaird's teaching of a final justification according to works. In defense of this false doctrine, Lillback reiterated the revisionist history of the Reformation that he first published in his book, *The Binding of God*.[34] He argued that Calvin and Luther had two different doctrines of justification, the difference being that for Calvin and the framers of the *Westminster Confession* works are "in" but for Luther works are "out." Lillback repeated his position during cross-examination by Arthur Kuschke.

Second, Lillback supported Kinnaird's statement that the righteousness of Christ is "not sufficient" for the believer on the Day of Judgment. Tyson, referring directly to that statement, asked Lillback: "Do you find any teaching of justifycation by faith and works anywhere in these statements?" Lillback evaded the question for the next five minutes, making several postmodernist what-this-means-to-me statements ("What I read here"..."as I read this"..."I don't see him saying"). At one point Lillback added, with a note of seeming desperation, "I would ask Mr. Kinnaird if he would want to testify" on this question. But Lillback ended his answer to Tyson by saying, "I would argue that [Kinnaird's statement] seems to be well within the boundaries of our *Confession*."

Third, Lillback claimed that it is possible to interpret the same crucial statement of the Word of God about the nature of justification in two polar opposite ways, but still be within the bounds of orthodoxy. The passage in question was *Romans* 2:13 ("For not the hearers of the law are just

33. Lillback's testimony appears at www.trinityfoundation.org/day2_session_2B.php.

34. Peter A. Lillback, *The Binding of God* (Grand Rapids, Michigan: Baker Academic Books, 2001). For a critique of Lillback's arguments see www.trinityfoundation.org/PDF/194a-TheBindingGod.pdf.

in the sight of God, but the doers of the law will be justified"). It can, Lillback asserted, be interpreted as saying that keeping the law is *necessary* in order to be justified. (This is Lillback's view, and Kinnaird's.) Or, Lillback said, the passage can be interpreted to mean that it is *impossible* to be justified by keeping the law. (This is the only interpretation supported by the context and by other Scriptures, *e.g.*, *Romans* 3:20: "By the deeds of the law no flesh will be justified in His sight.") Lillback dismissed the plain statement of *Romans* 3:28 – "Therefore we conclude that a man is justified by faith apart from the deeds of the law" – as "incomplete."

In the neo-liberal world of analogy, paradox, and multiple perspectives on doctrine, polar opposites can be true. But not in authentic Biblical Christianity. The Apostle Paul told the Corinthian church that the Word of God is not "Yes and No." It is not filled with paradox and the possibility of conflicting but equally valid interpretations. The Word of God is "Yes" in Christ (*2 Corinthians* 1:18-20).

Fourth, Lillback invoked the tenets of the modern Biblical Theology movement to argue that one's interpretation of *Revelation* 22:14-15, as to why people are inside or outside the eternal city, is a matter of perspective. He then constructed two straw-man "perspectives." The first he called, disparagingly, a "justification alone paradigm of salvation." The second he called "a Reformed system of theology that is not justification-centered, it's salvation covenantally-centered and it's telling us *what all God requires of us* to be saved from His wrath and curse for sin" [emphasis added]. Lillback rightly understood, at least, that the "justification alone paradigm" excludes works from justification. But Lillback rejected this position. Instead he embraced his own straw-man "Reformed system of theology" which teaches

211

justification by faith *and* works ("what all God requires of us to be saved").

The truly Reformed, Biblical "perspective" of salvation *is* justification, once for all at conversion, by faith alone. This is *God's* perspective, which is the only one that matters. Good works resulting from the grace of sanctification are the fruits and evidences of a believer's having been justified by faith alone and indwelt by the Holy Spirit. They are not the basis of justification or of the believer's entry into the kingdom of Heaven.

On the next day of the trial, Richard Gaffin testified in Kinnaird's defense.[35] At the outset of his testimony he said that he saw "no reason to" amend his unqualified written endorsement of Kinnaird's theological statement. Gaffin also trotted out the defense's "ambiguous charge" accusation once more. Gaffin's testimony repeated many themes from *Resurrection and Redemption*, which we discussed in the preceding chapter.

In response to a question from a member of the judicatory, Gaffin denied that the "real and personal righteousness" of the believer is the *imputed* righteousness of Christ. "What *saves me*," Gaffin asserted, "is not an isolated imputative act" of God.[36] Sanctification, he said, must be added.

Developing this theme, Gaffin gave an explanation of the doctrines of justification and sanctification which made justification a life-long process, after the manner of Roman Catholicism. He did this in much the same way that John Kinnaird had, in twisting the meaning of *Romans* 2:13 by

35. Gaffin's testimony appears at www.trinityfoundation.org/day3_session_1.php.

36. Emphasis is in the recorded testimony.

misquoting it. Gaffin misquoted the beginning of the *Westminster Confession's* chapter on sanctification, and then based his argument on this counterfeit of sound doctrine. In the *Confession*, the sentence actually reads thus:

> They, who are once effectually called, and regenerated, having a new heart, and a new spirit created in them, are further sanctified, really and personally, through the virtue of Christ's death and resurrection, by his Word and Spirit dwelling in them: the dominion of the whole body of sin is destroyed, and the several lusts thereof are more and more weakened and mortified; and they more and more quickened and strengthened in all saving graces, to the practice of true holiness, without which no man shall see the Lord [13:1].

Gaffin's counterfeit version changed the meaning entirely. He reduced the *Confession's* affirmation quoted above to this:

> Our *Confession* also says, chapter 13, section 1, [that] our sanctification consists in being made, as the Confession says, "really and personally" – that's quoting – holy or righteous.

By this sleight-of-hand Gaffin redefined sanctification as a *process* involving the *infusion* of righteousness into the believer. This is neither Biblical justification nor sanctification, and is completely unsupported by Scripture. It is the Roman Catholic doctrine of justification.

The *imputed* righteousness of Christ is the basis of our justification, and nothing else. His righteousness becomes ours. It is not, as Paul says, "my own righteousness, which is from the law, but that which is through faith in Christ, the righteousness which is from God by faith" (*Philippians* 2:9). In contrast to justification, sanctification is the process of the justified believer's being conformed more and more to the image of Christ (*Romans* 8:29, *Colossians* 3:10). Sanctification is not justification, nor is it *how* we are justified.

When Gaffin says that we are *made* righteous by sanctification – that justification and sanctification are indistinguishable – he is asserting that being justified is a *process* involving works and not total reliance on the imputed righteousness of Christ.

One of the great breakthroughs of the Protestant Reformation was a renewed recognition of the Bible's clear distinction between justification and sanctification. Justification is *forensic*, involving a change in sinners' legal status before God based on the merits of Christ. Sanctification is *renovative*, involving the believer's becoming more and more conformed to the image of Christ by the work of the Holy Spirit. Justification is a one-time act of God. Sanctification is a process. Roman Catholicism had obliterated these distinctions. The Protestant Reformers reclaimed them. But in his testimony, as in his writings,[37] Gaffin obliterated them once again.[38]

Kinnaird himself, when called as a witness, denied the Biblical doctrine of sanctification in similar terms. During cross-examination by Carl Hayes, Kinnaird stated that the work of the Holy Spirit in sanctification (resulting in believers' good works) is *not* the fruit and evidence that we are justified, but is part of how we are saved. [39]

---

37. Gaffin, *Resurrection and Redemption*, 133.

38. This obliteration was not lost upon the trial judicatory. Moderator Douglas Winward remarked on this in his own questions to Gaffin, noting that "you talked about justification as [both] forensic and renovative."

39. Kinnaird's testimony appears at www.trinityfoundation.org/day3_session_2A.php. His cross-examination by Carl Hayes and the judicatory appears at www.trinityfoundation.org/day4_session_1B.php.

In his closing statement[40] Thomas Tyson did not focus on defending his client against the charge, but reverted once more to an attack on the charge itself:

> The defense objected to the form of the Charge, and that objection was denied. Consequently all of us – Prosecution, Defense, Court – have labored throughout this trial under that grievous impediment. Under these circumstances, we were forced to treat the Charge without the comma *and* without any clear statement of what it is about Mr. Kinnaird's teaching on the subject of justification that is contrary to our Standards. But then we have never been sure with what offense he is charged *in the Charge.* [Emphasis in the original.]

Tyson then resumed his attack on the prosecution:

> What are his accusers to do? The accusers' quarrel appears to us to be with the teaching of the Westminster Standards. The Defense contends that it has demonstrated, particularly from the testimony of Dr. Lillback and Dr. Gaffin, that Mr. Kinnaird's position is precisely that of the Westminster Standards.

Tyson delivered a final sophistry to the judicatory itself:

> Mr. Wilkening remarked, early in this trial, to the effect that we are here to determine whose view is correct. In saying *that*, he is not correct. It is not a judicatory's task to judge between the views expressed by the accusers and the views expressed by the accused, as to who has the correct view. It is this Judicatory's task to determine this question: are these Specifications, which we stipulate accurately set forth Mr. Kinnaird's words, sufficient to

40. www.trinityfoundation.org/DefenseClosingStatement.php.

support the weight of this Charge, that he "teaches a doctrine of justification by faith and works, contrary to the Word of God and the Westminster Standards."

Wilkening had in fact said no such thing. By putting words in the mouth of the prosecution, Tyson implied that there was a difference between the prosecution's position and the Gospel. There was none. The real difference was the great chasm between the teachings of John Kinnaird and his "expert" witnesses, and the teachings of the Word of God.

Guilty on All Counts

On January 25, 2003, the Bethany interim session, acting as a trial judicatory, found John Kinnaird guilty on all three specifications of error supporting the charge. The votes were decisive: 4 to 1 on the first specification, 5 to 0 on the second, and 4 to 0 (with one present but not voting) on the third. The vote on the manner of censure – indefinite suspension from the office of ruling elder – was unanimous.

Presbytery of Philadelphia Sustains Verdict

Kinnaird immediately notified the Bethany interim session of his intention to appeal the verdict to the Presbytery of Philadelphia. The Presbytery convened to hear the appeal on February 22, 2003.

An appeal hearing is not a re-hearing of an entire case, but a proceeding to consider specifications of error in the original trial, alleged by the appellant. Kinnaird based his appeal on a single allegation of error: that the Bethany interim session had erred in failing to dismiss the charge, and in finding him guilty of serious doctrinal error.

In the appeal document Kinnaird also raised procedural

points including the "ambiguous charge" allegation. But he stated that the defense "asks only that Presbytery address the doctrinal issue that lies at the heart of the case: *is the appellant's teaching...contrary to, or in conformity with, the Bible and the Westminster Standards?*"[41]

Thirty-two ministers and ruling elders convened for the appeal hearing. Members of the trial judicatory presented the reasons for their guilty verdict on each of the three specifications of error in the Wilkening charge.[42] Tyson and Kinnaird answered for the defense. Members of the Presbytery asked questions of both sides. In the schedule of proceedings the Presbytery had also allotted time for debate after these presentations and the question period, and prior to a vote. Only one minister rose to speak during that debate period, and then the floor was silent. The moderator continued to hold the floor open for several minutes in case someone else wished to speak.

After three calls for anyone else who wished to speak were met with silence, the moderator put the question to the Presbytery: "Shall the specification of error be sustained?" On a voice vote, the Presbytery denied John Kinnaird's appeal. The defense realized that the vote was not close enough to warrant a division of the house (having those on each side stand for a head count) and it did not call for one. The Presbytery had upheld the guilty verdict against John Kinnaird.

Six members of the Presbytery requested that their votes in favor of Kinnaird be recorded in the minutes: Luke

41. Appeal document distributed by the Kinnaird defense at his hearing before the Presbytery of Philadelphia, February 22, 2003. Emphasis in the original.

42. The trial judicatory's document *Reasons for Verdict* is reproduced at www.trinityfoundation.org/ReasonsfortheVerdictbytheInterimSession.php.

CHRISTIANITY & NEO-LIBERALISM

Brown, George Cottenden (a member of the Westminster Seminary board of trustees), Donald Duff (stated clerk of the General Assembly), Richard Gaffin, Harold A. McKenzie, and George F. Morton (who had also supported Shepherd in 1977 – see chapter five).

Presbytery of Philadelphia Reverses Itself

Kinnaird immediately notified the Presbytery of his intention to appeal his case to the General Assembly, which would convene on June 25, 2003. Kinnaird's defenders also went into action to hijack the lawful process and reverse the Presbytery's decision before the General Assembly would meet.

Richard Gaffin launched this effort on March 20, 2003, by submitting a complaint against the Presbytery's February 22 decision. Gaffin clearly wanted the decision reversed, but he opened his complaint by saying that it was "against the *process followed* in reaching its decision, not the decision itself."[43] Gaffin could cite no error on the part of the Presbytery – no violation of due process, the *Book of Discipline*, or any other standard of authority in the church. In hearing the Kinnaird appeal, the Presbytery had followed the process laid down in the *Book of Discipline* to the letter. The basis of Gaffin's complaint was not what the *Book of Discipline* prescribed, but what he and his supporters *wanted* the process to be, regardless of the rules.

His complaint, he said, was "a series of laments." The Presbytery, he claimed, had not spent enough time in debate. (But debate could continue only as long as men took

43. *Minutes of the Presbytery of Philadelphia*, May 2003, 515-517. Emphasis in the original.

218

the floor to speak.) The Presbytery, he protested, had not conducted a re-hearing of the entire case followed by a separate vote on each of the specifications on which Kinnaird was found guilty. (But that would have clearly violated the process mandated by the *Book of Discipline*, usurping the session's authority and responsibility.) As restitution for these alleged infractions of rules created out of thin air, Gaffin demanded that the Presbytery rescind its verdict on the Kinnaird appeal and conduct a full re-hearing of the case.

The Gaffin complaint came before the Presbytery of Philadelphia at its May 3, 2003, meeting. After sometimes heated debate, the Presbytery voted in Gaffin's favor, effectively reversing its February 22 decision. In addition, the Presbytery voted to usurp the rightful role of the Bethany interim session by re-hearing the entire case, and issuing its own verdict on each specification of error in the Wilkening charge.[44] The Presbytery scheduled an adjourned meeting for May 10 to begin the illegal re-trial of John Kinnaird.

With only one week to act, opponents of this abuse had little choice but to file their own complaint against the Presbytery's actions. This writer and John P. Galbraith filed separate but similar complaints in time for the May 10 meeting.

Both complaints argued that Gaffin had cited no violation of due process, of the *Book of Discipline*, or any other standard of the church. His complaint was against alleged violations of fabricated "rules." By agreeing to his complaint and reversing its judicial decision, the Presbytery had set dangerous precedents for the future. The Elliott complaint[45] said in part:

44. *Minutes*, 518.

45. *Minutes of the Presbytery of Philadelphia*, May 10, 2003, 523-526.

In doing these things the Presbytery has acted in a manner that resembles the dissolute state of many of our civil courts, where laws and rules of procedure are arbitrarily re-written from the bench and in the jury room, much more than it resembles the righteous dealings to which we are called by the Judge before whom we shall stand.

The Presbytery broke for lunch before voting on the Elliott complaint. During the recess, in the presence of witnesses, three individuals informed this writer that they agreed with my complaint on its merits. But they said they intended to vote against it because they wished to see the Kinnaird case re-tried by the Presbytery and his guilty verdict overturned. One of these men, a long-time member of the Presbytery and himself a former moderator of the General Assembly, told me in the presence of others, "I have my differences with John Kinnaird, but he can't possibly be a heretic. Why, he was once moderator of our General Assembly!"

The Presbytery voted 16 to 14 against the Elliott complaint. Had these three men voted on the merits of the complaint instead of cooperating with the neo-liberal leaders to hijack a court of the church for their own ends, the result would have been 17 to 13 in favor of the complaint. Later that day the Galbraith complaint was also defeated. But the Gaffin-led effort to illegally vindicate John Kinnaird and protect his neo-liberal mentors had been delayed if not stopped. There would not be enough time for an illicit re-trial by the Presbytery before the General Assembly met. The Kinnaird case was on its way to the full Assembly. Conservatives in the Presbytery of Philadelphia sanguinely assured one another that, once the case got beyond the shadow of Westminster Seminary, the full Assembly would "do the right thing" and sustain the original guilty verdict against Kinnaird. They were to be sorely disappointed.

General Assembly Acquits Kinnaird

The General Assembly began on June 25. An Advisory Committee was appointed to consider the Kinnaird case, and make recommendations to the full Assembly.[46] The committee, chaired by Dr. James Gidley, voted 8 to 1 to recommend Kinnaird's acquittal.[47] In its report to the Assembly, the committee used Kinnaird's theological statement as its main grounds for recommending acquittal, but cited only portions where he simply quoted the Westminster Standards' affirmations of justification by faith alone. The report made no mention of the many times that Kinnaird and his defense team had plainly un-said the affirmations of the *Confession* during his trial. Ignoring the weight of evidence, the committee reported that "Mr. Kinnaird affirms his belief in the doctrine of justification by faith alone on the ground of the righteousness of Christ alone and received by faith alone."

The committee's report also backed the neo-liberal view that two polar opposite interpretations of *Romans* 2:13 are

46. Under the *Standing Rules of the OPC General Assembly* (www.opc. org/GA/standingrules.html) the stated clerk (in this case Donald Duff, a vocal Kinnaird supporter and signer of his theological statement) determines who will sit on advisory committees. In addition to Dr. Gidley those named to the committee were: Ministers Randall A. Berquist, Stuart R. Jones, Daniel L. Korzep, Ronald E. Pearce, and William Shishko; and Ruling Elders Newman deHaas, Lars R. Johnson, and David Winslow, Jr.

47. Its full report appears in *Minutes of the 70th General Assembly of the Orthodox Presbyterian Church*, 32-36.

both within the bounds of orthodoxy: "There is strong evidence that it is allowable *in the OPC* to interpret *Romans* 2:13 (as Mr. Kinnaird does) as a description of something that will be done to the righteous at the day of judgment."[48] The only "strong evidence" the committee offered was the fact that the 2001 General Assembly had adopted a neo-liberal-backed recommendation to add *Romans* 2:13 as a proof text for *Westminster Larger Catechism* question 90.[49] (The 2004 General Assembly reversed that proof-text change as the result of an overture by the Presbytery of Connecticut and Southern New York.)

Using this wrong interpretation of *Romans* 2:13 as its starting point, the committee also agreed with Kinnaird that there is a final justification at the Last Judgment and that "both...are forensic."[50]

On the floor of the Assembly, Richard Gaffin continued to lead the effort to overturn Kinnaird's conviction. On July

48. *Minutes*, 35. Emphasis added. This statement implies that such diametrically opposite views on salvation are allowable *in the OPC* but might not be allowable elsewhere. This raises the question: Is there one authentic Gospel, or not?

49. "Q. 90: What shall be done to the righteous at the day of judgment? A: At the day of judgment, the righteous, being caught up to Christ in the clouds, shall be set on his right hand, and there openly acknowledged and acquitted, shall join with him in the judging of reprobate angels and men, and shall be received into heaven, where they shall be fully and forever freed from all sin and misery; filled with inconceivable joys, made perfectly holy and happy both in body and soul, in the company of innumerable saints and holy angels, but especially in the immediate vision and fruition of God the Father, of our Lord Jesus Christ, and of the Holy Spirit, to all eternity. And this is the perfect and full communion, which the members of the invisible church shall enjoy with Christ in glory, at the resurrection and day of judgment."

50. *Minutes*, 36.

1, 2003, the General Assembly ruled that "the Session and Presbytery erred in finding the Appellant's teaching to be contrary to the Church's Standards."[51] By this ruling, the Assembly not only found Kinnaird not guilty, but also said that *those who had found him guilty had erred*. Such a statement could only mean one of two things: that it was their doctrine, not Kinnaird's, that was faulty; or that Kinnaird's false teaching was acceptable alongside the authentic Gospel.

A protest, filed at the General Assembly and signed by ten commissioners, stated:

> The decision of the Assembly to sustain the appeal opens the gate, in the judgment of the undersigned, to the use throughout the Orthodox Presbyterian Church of a hermeneutic that allows interpretations of Scripture that are out of accord with the whole body of the Word.[52]

Was Kinnaird Merely Unclear?

Immediately after the General Assembly's decision and down to the present time, neo-liberals and their supporters, as well as some who claim to be conservatives, have employed two lines of argument to defend that decision.

Some claim that John Kinnaird's teachings were within the bounds of Scripture and the Westminster Standards. But Kinnaird's own words, the prosecution's presentation at his trial, and even the testimony of his defense witnesses, combine to present a mountain of irrefutable evidence against

51. *Minutes,* 38-39.

52. *Minutes,* 44. The protest was signed by ministers P. Michael DeLozier, John P. Galbraith (its author), Steven F. Miller, Mark C. Mueller, Marcus J. Serven, and Larry E. Wilson; and ruling elders John P. Jambura, Jack W. Pluister, Murali Rao, and William G. Swink.

that claim. The only way John Kinnaird's doctrine can be given standing in the church is by saying that the passages of Scripture he used to support his teachings can mean two mutually exclusive things.

But other defenders of the decision employ a different argument. They claim that John Kinnaird did not really mean what he said, but was simply "unclear" and therefore not culpable. They frequently cite a passage from the Advisory Committee report: "While Mr. Kinnaird's teaching should not be judged to be out of accord with the Church's Standards, his teaching has not been as clear as should be expected from an elder."[53]

But that argument falls apart completely when one examines the Advisory Committee's stated grounds for recommending Kinnaird's acquittal. That section of the report demonstrates that the committee not only understood Kinnaird's line of argumentation but also agreed with it.

In the evidence that the committee had examined, Kinnaird had stated that God's "not guilty" verdict is based *not only* on the imputed righteousness of Christ at conversion *but also* on His forensic, analytical judgment of the individual's personal righteousness on the Last Day. This is, by definition, justification by faith-plus-works.

In stating its grounds for recommending Kinnaird's acquittal, the Advisory Committee agreed with him on these points. As we saw earlier, the committee supported Kinnaird's misinterpretation of *Romans* 2:13 as saying that personal righteousness through law-keeping is required in order to stand in the Last Judgment. The committee also agreed that it is admissible to teach that there is a second

53. *Minutes*, 35.

justification at the Judgment. They further agreed that "both...are forensic."[54] Some of the committee members have subsequently attempted to revise this history in comments on Internet discussion forums and elsewhere. But their own report to the General Assembly – approved by a vote of 8 to 1 – contradicts them.

Other General Assembly commissioners who were not on the Advisory Committee have attempted to defend their votes to acquit Kinnaird by saying that they simply agreed with the Advisory Committee's statements that the main lines of his teaching were acceptable. Still others have said that they did not have the opportunity to read the volumenous record of the Kinnaird case for themselves, and that if they had, they might have voted to sustain his conviction rather than to acquit. That may be. But the Advisory Committee presented its report to the full Assembly. It was read in their hearing. Every commissioner who was present knew what it said: the recommendation to acquit, and the reasons why. Every commissioner who was present should have recognized that the teaching the committee called admissible was contrary to the Word of God. If commissioners *did not* recognize that, shame on them (and shame on the OPC and WTS for inducing such blindness). If they *did* recognize it and yet voted to acquit, *greater* shame on them.

And if there could be any remaining doubt that John Kinnaird indeed meant exactly what he said, his public statements since his acquittal erase it. He is still saying the same things he said in the evidence presented at his trial, and just as clearly as ever. In May 2005 Kinnaird wrote:

54. *Minutes*, 35-36.

The Father of our Lord Jesus Christ has promised that He will prepare His saints for that Great Day and for an eternity in the very presence of our holy God by conforming them to the image of His Son in righteousness in order that He (Jesus, the Christ) might be the first born of many brethren and that we might share with Him the enjoyment of being in the Father's presence. By reason of this conformance to His image in righteousness He will not be ashamed to call us brothers.... The final judgment will be in accord with what He has done for His people when He makes us really and personally righteous through regeneration, sanctification, and glorification.[55]

This statement encapsulates John Kinnaird's long-standing error yet again. He asserts that God *makes the believer ready* to stand before Christ at the Last Judgment through sanctification and glorification, as though the believer is not immediately fit to stand based on the imputed righteousness of Christ alone when he is converted. By saying that something more is required, he once again negates faith as the sole instrument of justification. He denies that it is faith alone that places the believer in right standing with God, making the believer acceptable based on the merits of Christ alone – in other words, that it is the *ungodly* whom God justifies (*Romans* 5:1-6). He denies the definition of saving faith – a *belief* that has the person and work of Christ alone as its object. He makes justification rest not on Christ's merits through His active and passive obedience alone, but *also* on the renewal of sinners through sanctification and

55. John O. Kinnaird, Message 28404 published on the Yahoo® Presbyterians-OPC discussion forum, May 18, 2005, groups. yahoo.com/group/presbyterians-opc/message/28404.

glorification. Like Richard Gaffin, he confuses justification, sanctification, and glorification; John Kinnaird always has, and continues to do so.

Kinnaird also misrepresents Biblical teaching regarding the relationship between Jesus and His brethren. God does not, as Kinnaird claims, *conform* us "to the image of His Son in righteousness *in order that* He (Jesus, the Christ) might be the first born of many brethren." The focus in *Romans* 8:29 (as in *Ephesians* 1:5) is on *predestination*. The New Testament tells us that our being made *brethren* to Christ is the result of *adoption*. Like justification, adoption is a once-for-all legal act of God; and like justification, adoption is based solely on the great redeeming transaction between God the Son and God the Father (*Galatians* 4:4, *Ephesians* 1:3-7, *John* 1:12).

Furthermore, Jesus openly and unashamedly called the disciples His brethren early in His ministry (*Matthew* 12:49, recorded also in *Mark* 3:34, *Luke* 8:21) and again even more emphatically immediately after His resurrection (*John* 20:17). He did this despite their many, many failings, including Peter's open denial of Him.

Kinnaird also misrepresents the relationship between sanctification, glorification and adoption in order to paint a false picture of the Last Judgment. Sanctification and glorification are the promised inheritance *by right of adoption* to those who are *already sons through faith* (*Galatians* 3:26-4:7, 1 *John* 3:1-3). But Kinnaird perverts the meaning of *Hebrews* 2:11 ("for which reason He is not ashamed to call them brethren") to say that it speaks of believers' likeness to Christ. He also distorts it, as he does *Romans* 2:13, into a picture of something that takes place *at the Judgment*. He says it is there that Jesus "will not be ashamed to call us brothers" because of our being "really and personally righteous."

That is not what *Hebrews* 2 says at all. The focus, in context, is on *Christ's likeness to believers*, not *believers' likeness to Him*. It is for this reason, the passage says, that Christ "is not [present tense] ashamed to call them brethren" – now, not merely in the future. Furthermore, it is the focus of the passage that *Christ's likeness to believers* – His becoming a man, the seed of Abraham, born under the law – made it possible for Him to earn a righteousness that could be imputed to them and to be the propitiation for their sins:

> But we see Jesus, who was made a little lower than the angels, for the suffering of death crowned with glory and honor, *that He, by the grace of God, might taste death* for everyone.
>
> For it was fitting for Him, for whom are all things and by whom are all things, in bringing many sons to glory, to make the captain of their salvation perfect [complete] through sufferings. For both He who sanctifies and those who are being sanctified are *all of one, for which reason* He is not ashamed to call them brethren, saying: "I will declare Your name to My brethren; in the midst of the assembly I will sing praise to You." And again: "I will put My trust in Him." And again: "Here am I and the children whom God has given Me."
>
> Inasmuch then as the children have partaken of flesh and blood, *He Himself likewise shared in the same, that through death* He might destroy him who had the power of death, that is, the devil, and release those who through fear of death were all their lifetime subject to bondage.
>
> For indeed He does not give aid to angels, but He does give aid to the seed of Abraham. *Therefore, in all things He had to be made like His brethren,* that He might be

a merciful and faithful High Priest in things pertaining
to God, to make propitiation for the sins of the people.
For in that He Himself has suffered, being tempted, He
is able to aid those who are tempted [*Hebrews* 2:9-18,
emphases added].

It is this all-sufficient righteousness of Christ that John
Kinnaird continues to deny. It is tragic enough that neo-
liberals like Norman Shepherd and Richard Gaffin have
promulgated these teachings at Westminster Seminary and
in the OPC. It is more tragic that leaders in the denomination like John Kinnaird have bought into their heresies. But
more tragic still is the fact that many other ordained men in
the OPC have accepted this teaching of justification by faith-
plus-works, or stand idly by as it proliferates. John Kinnaird
posted his May 2005 statement quoted above on the Yahoo®
Presbyterians-OPC discussion forum. This is not an official
forum of the OPC, but over 500 forum members, many of
them OPC ministers and ruling elders, read it regularly. All
forum members have the privilege of contributing to the online discussions and rebutting others' statements when they
disagree. But Kinnaird's recent statements, like many similar ones he has made over the years, went unchallenged by
any of those hundreds of OPC men. His statements were
treated as just another of many possible *perspectives* – a key
point on which we shall focus in the next chapter.

After the 2003 Assembly adjourned a victorious John
Kinnaird e-mailed his supporters:

I praise the Lord that once again the OPC has stood
firmly for the faith once delivered to the saints. I know
it has been difficult being patient as all this slowly un-
folded. I thank you for your prayers; now I commend
the OPC to you. Please give her all your support as

229

you did me. She is solid as a rock as she continues to proclaim the Faith that is founded on THE ROCK. The rock may have wobbled a little bit for just a short period of time, but she held. That is what counts. Now please pray for those who are less than satisfied with the decision of the Church.[56]

It is perhaps telling that the "Rock" of which Kinnaird speaks is not Christ, but the visible church. Kinnaird was wrong in implying that the "rock" (the church cannot Biblically be called that, but we will borrow Kinnaird's misnomer for the moment) had "wobbled a little bit" from the "faith once delivered to the saints" but renewed its commitment in the end. The church had not been on solid ground to begin with. The OPC had been sliding downhill for decades before the Kinnaird decision – away from the true Rock, the Lord Jesus Christ, and away from the unequivocal confession of the Gospel of His cross. And now that slide had accelerated.

When Kinnaird was convicted of heresy, the denomination had briefly "wobbled" – not from the truth, but from its accommodation of another gospel. For a short time, to the horror of the neo-liberal leaders, the church was in "danger" of taking a stand for the true Gospel of justifycation by faith alone. The church was briefly in "danger" of calling the Shepherd-Gaffin pseudo-gospel by its right name: *heresy*. But Richard Gaffin and his allies saw to it that such "wobbling" was short-lived. The General Assembly's decision showed how strong neo-liberalism's grip on the denomination had become in the last thirty years.

---

56. From a copy forwarded to the author at the time. This message was widely disseminated on the Internet.

Efforts to Right the Wrong Defeated

The Kinnaird decision emboldened neo-liberals and their followers. The teaching of false gospels has become more open in the OPC and elsewhere since the Kinnaird acquittal. Neo-liberals are less and less fearful that they will be called to account for their doctrinal positions.

But the Kinnaird decision also helped begin the mobilization of conservatives. The Kinnaird case was eye-opening for many of them, who began to ask, "How could this have happened?" As they sought answers to that question, their paths led them back to Richard Gaffin, Norman Shepherd, and Westminster Seminary in Philadelphia. They began to realize how widespread and pervasive the neo-liberals' influence had been. But others thought the Kinnaird verdict was either an anomaly or the result of a misunderstanding, and not the reliable indicator of the church's condition that it really was.

In the fall of 2003, many conservatives thought it would still be possible to turn the OPC around. But their efforts focused on the immediate past, the Kinnaird decision itself, and not on the decades-old root causes that created the environment for that decision. Furthermore, most of these efforts were based on the faulty assumption that the General Assembly had merely been "unclear" in its decision. But the evidence in the Kinnaird case had been very clear. The teachings of Norman Shepherd and Richard Gaffin, upon which Kinnaird's teachings were based, were also clear. And, the General Assembly had not been unclear: It had said that those who found John Kinnaird guilty of heresy were the ones in error.

The first public action in response to the General Assembly's decision was taken by the session of Grace Presbyterian Church in Hanover, Pennsylvania.[57] In September 2003 that session passed a *Resolution on Justification by Faith Alone*[58] which read in part:

> 1. The session of Grace Presbyterian Church shall withhold all financial support from the Orthodox Presbyterian Church and its agencies until this issue is resolved. Withholding funds is not a mere matter of protest. It is a matter of conscience in defense of the Gospel, and in bearing clear testimony to it.

> 2. The session shall work together with those of like mind within our denomination in seeking resolution of this matter by having the Orthodox Presbyterian Church:

> - Declare expressly its adherence to the historic Protestant Gospel fundamental of the faith which is taught in the Scriptures and affirmed in the subordinate Standards of the Church, namely, justification by grace through faith in the meritorious work and atoning death of Jesus Christ alone, apart from any works of men; and

> - Likewise declare that all deviations from this fundamental of the faith, including those cited in the Kinnaird case, are contrary to the Gospel of grace, are serious errors, and are therefore unacceptable for preaching and teaching in the Church.

57. Dr. Jeffery A. Sheely is pastor. The author is a member of the session.

58. Available online at www.gracehanover.org/resources_pages/justifica tion_controversy/justification_01.htm.

The Grace session sent this resolution to all OPC presbyteries, and published it widely on the Internet.

Simultaneous efforts began, in the Presbytery of Philadelphia and elsewhere, to submit overtures to the 2004 General Assembly to redress the wrongs of the Kinnaird decision. All of these efforts were either blocked or defeated, through the efforts of neo-liberals and their supporters.

In December 2003 the Presbytery of New Jersey began consideration of an overture asking the General Assembly to "restore the Protestant, fundamental, confessional witness of the church by resolving to uphold Justification by grace through faith alone, wherein the required righteousness in Justification and at the final judgment is precisely and only the righteousness of Christ imputed to true believers, apart from any works of men." The New Jersey Presbytery subsequently defeated this overture.

In the fall of 2003 a group of concerned men in the Presbytery of Philadelphia drafted an overture asking the 2004 General Assembly to not only affirm the authentic Gospel doctrine of justification by faith alone, but also to condemn counterfeits, in keeping with *Galatians* 1:6-12.[59] This overture met fierce opposition, led by Richard Gaffin, Donald Duff, and Thomas Tyson. Their efforts to have the overture ruled out of order because it would "re-open the Kinnaird case" were defeated. (Such an argument is ironic, since "reopening the Kinnaird case" is exactly what they had tried to do through the Gaffin complaint several months earlier.)

After this vote, the neo-liberals shifted their tactics to defeat the overture by talking it to death and preventing a final vote. Gaffin, Duff, Tyson, and others who made it clear

---

59. This overture is reproduced in full in Appendix C.

they would vote against the overture in any form, nevertheless began wordsmithing it on the floor of the Presbytery. They made motion after motion to change detailed wording, sentence by sentence, paragraph by paragraph, consuming the Presbytery's time by the hour and delaying a vote on the overture on its merits. Dr. Craig Troxel,[60] who signed the original overture,[61] brought a series of motions to enfeeble it by removing large portions of the text, including the section requesting the General Assembly to condemn specific teachings that many could readily recognize as those of Norman Shepherd and Richard Gaffin.

Neo-liberals and their allies stretched out the proceedings over several meetings and through fourteen hours of debate, so that the overture died a slow death.

Plans to bring a similar overture in the Presbytery of the Mid-Atlantic were abandoned when it became apparent there was little chance of passage.

A session in the Presbytery of the Midwest proposed a virtual duplicate of the overture that had been proposed in the Presbytery of Philadelphia. The moderator of the Midwest Presbytery, Alan D. Strange, told that session that he would rule the overture out of order because it would effectively re-open the Kinnaird case. In response the session drafted a weaker overture, but Strange made it known that he would rule this one out of order on the same basis.

60. Senior pastor, Calvary OPC, Glenside, Pennsylvania.

61. Troxel signed, but noted an exception to the overture's statements that *Romans* 2:13 is part of the Apostle Paul's inspired argument that no man can keep the law, and therefore Christ's perfect law-keeping must be imputed to believers in order for them to be justified before God. Troxel was of the opinion that Kinnaird's polar opposite view of *Romans* 2:13 was also within the bounds of orthodoxy.

Strange then arranged for a committee to be appointed, chaired by Dr. David Van Drunen (a member of the Presbytery and professor at Westminster Seminary in California), to draft a compromise overture that would be acceptable. The resulting overture merely asked the General Assembly to pass a resolution giving a rote recitation of portions of the *Westminster Confession of Faith* and *Catechisms*, many of them the same portions that John Kinnaird had mingled into his own false teachings.[62] The compromise overture called for no condemnation of false gospels. It also requested that the General Assembly erect a study committee

> to critique the teaching of the "New Perspective" on Paul, the Federal Vision, and other like teachings by the Word of God and our Church standards; and to give a clear statement to the Presbyteries and Sessions on these matters.

The Presbytery of the Midwest passed this weak overture, and the 2004 General Assembly acted favorably on it. Van Drunen was named convener (chairman) of the study committee, and Alan Strange (a professor at Mid-America Reformed Seminary) was named one of its members. Richard Gaffin was also named to it, along with Dr. William B. Barcley (of Reformed Theological Seminary), Drs. Anthony L. Curto and Sidney D. Dyer (both of Greenville Presbyterian Theological Seminary), and Dr. John V. Fesko (also of Reformed Theological Seminary). The committee is scheduled to deliver its final report in June 2006.

Some conservatives have great hopes for this committee. One OP church member told the author that his pastor, after

---

62. *Minutes of the Presbytery of the Midwest*, March 19, 2004, 11-13.

returning from the 2004 General Assembly, asked him to hold on and not leave the church because a "blue ribbon comittee" had been appointed and "is going to save the day."

But what exactly has the OPC done? *It has appointed a committee to spend two years studying errors that were the first to be officially condemned by the church, over 1900 years ago.* The Holy Spirit did not leave the matter open to question. God recorded those condemnations in the pages of the New Testament itself. We have God's own judgment of these errors in the account of the Council of Jerusalem in *Acts* 15, and in the first chapter of Paul's epistle to the Galatians, among other passages.

The OPC does not need to give these errors the dignity of two years of study by a committee of scholars. That kind of "scholarship" is not the need of the hour. Submission to the Word of God is. Pastoral concern for the spiritual well-being of the church is. The OPC needs to condemn these errors as God's Word condemns them, on His authority, and in terms that leave no room for misunderstanding or obfuscation. It needs to call upon those who hold those positions to repent, leave, or expect to be tried for heresy. But since those who hold these errors now hold sway in the denomination, and many others have long demonstrated their willingness to compromise with them, such an outcome is highly unlikely.

Instead, the OPC has erected a committee that will likely broker a compromise, if the denomination's most recent study committee is any indication.[63] When the Gospel is at

63. In 2004 the OPC's Committee to Study the Views of Creation delivered a single "big-tent" *Report* saying that any of several conflicting positions on the days of creation, ranging from literal days to billions of years, are acceptable for teaching in the church. We will discuss this committee's report, and the philosophy behind it, in the next chapter.

stake, God's Word is plain: There can be no compromise. There is only one true Gospel. All others are false and must be repudiated.

The OPC has had over thirty years to purge itself of these errors, and has repeatedly refused to do so. Instead of removing the cancer it has stimulated its growth. In 2004 it showed once again that it has no stomach for the hard choices it needs to make.

If the leaders of the present-day OPC had been the men convening the Council of Jerusalem 1900 years ago, that council would have announced to the church at large that those who preached another gospel were doing nothing amiss. The legalists of that day would have continued promulgating the heresy of salvation by faith-plus-works with impunity. And the Council of Jerusalem would have declared that those who opposed them and called for their censure – the Apostle Paul among them – were the ones in the wrong.

Chapter 8

The Hermeneutic of Trust: Prescription for Doctrinal Anarchy

If you believed Moses,
you would believe Me;
for he wrote about Me.
But if you do not believe his writings,
how will you believe My words?
John 5:46-47

Imagine for a moment that you own a house, and have been living in it happily for many years. But something strange has happened to the house. From time to time through the years, cracks have appeared in the basement floor and walls. Perhaps you've had to patch them because water came in through the cracks when it rained. You've also noticed cracks from time to time in your living room walls. Perhaps you've had to plaster them and re-paint the room to keep those fissures from becoming unsightly. Or, perhaps you've gotten tired of patching and painting and decided to cover the whole problem with wallpaper instead.

But then, you begin to notice that some of the windows and doors aren't opening or closing as easily as they once did because the frames aren't quite straight anymore. Pictures that once hung perfectly have developed an annoying tendency to hang askew. And, new cracks have appeared in the basement and in the living room. One day you look across your living room and see that one wall is noticeably crooked. You decide it's time to find out what is causing all this.

You call a home repair company and they send someone out to investigate. After checking things carefully, the comany representative comes to you with alarming news: Your foundation has been severely damaged by water seepage, and the wood inside the walls of your house has been badly eaten by termites. Your house, although it appears to be sound, is actually in danger of collapse. It is no longer safe for you to live there.

Sound Hermeneutics

What, you may be asking, does this have to do with a "hermeneutic of trust"? To answer that question we must first answer another: What is this thing called hermeneutics? Theologians have written thousands of pages on the subject and have offered much more involved definitions, but for purposes of our discussion a shorthand version will suffice: The discipline of hermeneutics consists of the principles that one employs, and the science of applying those principles, to correctly understand the meaning of the Scriptures.

What does hermeneutics have to do with our house illustation? The principles and methodology of hermeneutics are like the unseen supports of a house – the foundation under the basement, the wood inside the walls. The house – the part that we see – is the interpretation of the Scriptures, and the system of doctrine we derive from that interpretation.

If the interpretive principles and methodology we emloy are sound, and we employ them carefully and conistently, our system of doctrine will be sound. Our system of doctrine will be correctly derived from the words of Scripture. We will believe the right things, because we will believe what God really says. Spiritually speaking, our doctrine will be a house that is safe for us to live in.

But if sound interpretive principles and methodology are being gradually undermined, our system of doctrine will be increasingly unsound. It will not be correctly derived from the words of Scripture. We will believe the wrong things, because we are being deceived. Spiritually speaking, we will be living in a house that is increasingly in danger of collapse. If we go on living in that house, we will do so at the peril of our souls.

What are sound principles of interpretation? One of the great truths reclaimed at the Reformation was the principle of *sola scriptura* – "Scripture alone." The issue before the Reformers was this: Shall Christians interpret Scripture on the basis of the often-conflicting pronouncements and tradiions of the fallible (and often corrupt) rulers of the Roman Catholic Church, or shall we interpret the Scriptures based solely on the only infallible authority – the Word of God itself? The Reformers rightly concluded that Scripture alone can be trusted to serve as its own interpreter. Our attitude toward Scripture will drive our principles of interpretation.

The principle of *sola scriptura* is essential to sound hermeneutics. Employment of this principle led to the further development of what theologians call the grammatical-historical method for interpreting Scripture.

Use of the grammatical-historical method is not confined to Scripture. Its principles apply to any kind of literature. In the nineteenth century, Methodist Episcopalian theologian Milton S. Terry stated the most fundamental elements:

> The grammatico-historical sense of a writer is such
> an interpretation of his language as is required by the

laws of grammar and the facts of history. Sometimes we speak of the literal sense, by which we mean the most simple, direct, and ordinary meaning of phrases and sentnces. By this term we usually denote a meaning opposed to the figurative or metaphorical. The grammatical sense is essentially the same as the literal, the one expression being derived from the Greek, the other from the Latin. But in English usage the word grammatical is applied rather to the arrangement and construction of words and sentences. By the historical sense we designate, rather, the meaning of an author's words that is required by historical considerations. It demands that we consider carefully the time of the author, and the circumstances under which he wrote....

A fundamental principle in grammatico-historical exposition is that words and sentences can have but one significance in one and the same connection. The moment we neglect this principle we drift out upon a sea of uncertainty and conjecture.[1]

These principles apply, whether one is reading the Bible, Dickens' *A Tale of Two Cities*, or the editorial page of today's newspaper. But when we are dealing with Scripture, our use of grammatical-historical principles is governed by an additional, overriding principle: that Scripture alone is the Word of God. This leads us to apply grammatical-historical principles in Scripture-directed ways:

1.) Because Scripture alone is the inspired Word of God, every word having been authored by the Holy Spirit, Scripture is its only infallible and authoritative interpreter.

1. Milton S. Terry, *Biblical Hermeneutics* (Hunt & Eason, 1890; reprinted by Wipf & Stock, Eugene, Oregon, 1999), 101, 103.

No word of fallible man can stand in authority over the infallible Word.

2.) Scripture is intelligible. God meant to communicate truth to man through the words of the Bible, in a manner that man can understand. God did not communicate in an analogous or indirect fashion. God communicated His own thoughts directly, and man can understand them because he is made in God's image.

3.) Because it is the infallible Word of God, Scripture is internally consistent. God is consistent. With Him there are no contradictions or paradoxes. If we think we see paradox or inconsistency in Scripture, we are looking at God's Word improperly. God cannot lie.

4.) Because God meant to communicate truth, and because Scripture is internally consistent, the words of Scripture have only one meaning in context. There may be multiple legitimate *applications* of a passage of Scripture, but a passage has only one *meaning in context*. This is what it means to interpret Scripture according to its *literal*, or normal, sense. Literal interpretation is not a "wooden" interpretation of words without regard to their surroundings. In literature of all kinds, the literal sense is the grammatical-historical sense; in other words, the meaning the writer actually expressed. In the case of the Bible, the grammatical-historical sense is the meaning that *God* intended to express, communicating through human writers. Interpretation according to the literal sense takes into account the Holy Spirit's use of figures of speech and literary forms (narrative, history, poetry, instruction, etc.) found in the text and the ways in which the same words and phrases are used in various portions of Scripture.

5.) We are to employ passages in Scripture that are more clear on a particular subject to interpret those that are less clear, never vice versa.

6.) We must always remember that the Bible we hold in our hands is a translation. It is important for ministers of the church to examine the words of Scripture in the original languages (Hebrew and Greek) and in their historical and cultural setting in order to accurately understand their meaning in context and to properly translate them into other languages, thus accurately communicating God's truth.

7.) Extra-Biblical resources, such as language helps, commentaries, the writings of the so-called church fathers, and archaeological and scientific evidences, can be useful resources in correctly interpreting Scripture. But since they are the words and works of fallible men they are not authoritative. These resources and evidences must never be placed in a position of authority over Scripture itself, nor allowed to obscure the fact that God is the author of every word of the Bible. And, where Scripture and human scholarship come into conflict, our attitude must always be, "Let God's truth be inviolate, though *every* man becomes thereby a liar" (*Romans* 3:20).[2]

The "Hermeneutic of Trust"

As neo-liberalism has infiltrated Westminster Theological Seminary and the Orthodox Presbyterian Church, both the seminary and the denomination have gradually abandoned their commitment to these principles. The most recent and disturbing example is the OPC's Committee to

2. Robert Reymond gives this translation of the verse in his *New Systematic Theology,* 754.

Study the Views of Creation, which delivered its *Report* to the 2004 General Assembly. After a three-year effort, the committee drew no definite conclusion about the meaning of the word "day" in the *Genesis* creation account. This result was not surprising, given the makeup of the committee, which included advocates of a literal day, days of unspecified length, the day-age view, the framework view, and the analogical view. According to this spectrum of opinion, the *Genesis* day may have been twenty-four hours long or it may have been billions of years.

While the result was not surprising, it is deeply disturbing. The committee not only abandoned sound principles for the interpretation of Scripture, but embraced a radically revisionist hermeneutic instead. The committee said that a wide range of views are acceptable, because what is important is not the *word* "day" in the book of *Genesis* but the *doctrine* of creation "in the space of six days" in the *Westminster Confession of Faith* (chapter 4, part 1).[3] "Rightly understood," the committee asserted, "Confessions encourage *theological creativity* by establishing the conditions under which exegetical and theological investigation can take place."[4] Therefore, the committee said, "we believe that the *doctrine* of six-day creation can be preserved through different permissible understandings of the word, 'day'.... It is the judgment of the Committee that none of the five different views expressed in this report necessarily entails a denial of the integrity of the system of doctrine of our

3. *Report of the Committee to Study the Views of Creation*, 1606. Emphasis in the original. The full report is available online at www.opc.org/GA/CreationReport.pdf.

4. *Report*, 1605. Emphasis added.

standards."[5] There was no acknowledgement of the fact that only one interpretation can possibly be right.

Note carefully the principle of Biblical interpretation that this official committee of the OPC has endorsed: *Men of the church can all be said to embrace the same "doctrine," even if they differ radically on the meaning of its words, even if they differ radically on the principles and methods of interpretation used to arrive at the meaning of those words, and even if they arrive at conclusions that are mutually exclusive. Furthermore, no one has the right to say that the position he holds is the truth, to the exclusion of all others. Men holding widely varying views about the meaning of the words of Scripture – as we have seen throughout this book, even diametrically opposing views – can all fit under the same "big tent" as long as they can recite the words of the Confession together.*

The OPC *Report* calls this radical departure from sound principles of interpretation a "hermeneutic of trust."[6]

Origins of the Hermeneutic of Trust

The term "hermeneutic of trust" is not new, and the concept originated not in the field of theology but in the secular field of language philosophy. The "hermeneutic of trust" was popularized by the German philosopher Hans-Georg Gadamer (1900-2002) in his books *Truth and Method* and *Philosophical Hermeneutics*. Gadamer, though not a theologian himself, was a close associate of the existentialist theologian Rudolf Bultmann (1884-1976), a main spokesman for modern liberal/skeptical methods of Biblical interpretation.

Gadamer asserted that the hermeneutic of trust applies to

5. *Report*, 1606. Emphasis in the original.

6. *Report*, 1607.

any area of society, not just theology. Gadamer denied the existence of objective truth. Correctly interpreting a text, he asserted, does not mean correctly understanding the original intention of its author. Rather, Gadamer argued, interpreting any text – whether it is a piece of literature, a nation's constitution, or the Bible – involves what he termed a "fusion of horizons." In this "fusion," a "community of interpretation" made up of scholars and other so-called experts decides what that community's view of the "truth" will be. Each participant contributes his perspectives to this mix. According to this bankrupt philosophy, a community standard of "truth" is the best that men can hope for.[7] There is no objective truth.

The false principle of the hermeneutic of trust has been widely taught for many years in liberal mainstream academia, and has influenced many elements of society – none for the better. In the field of law, this hermeneutic underpins the pernicious practice of "legislating from the bench" – interpreting constitutions and laws in ways that ignore the framers' intent and run roughshod over the plain meanings of words to suit any agenda. The hermeneutic of trust facilitates the proliferation of nebulous (and ever looser) "community standards" of morality that vary from one jurisdiction to another and have no basis in a transcendent moral code. In the field of medical ethics, the hermeneutic of trust is behind treatment protocols based on "community standards" that permit the denial of medical treatment to the elderly and handicapped, euthanasia, and the administration of behavior-altering drugs to school-age children without parental consent.

7. See Hans-Georg Gadamer, *Truth and Method* (New York: Continuum International Publishing Group, [1960] 2005) and *Philosophical Hermeneutics* (Berkeley, California: University of California Press, 1977).

Prescription for Doctrinal Anarchy

In addition to its pernicious secular influences, the hermeneutic of trust has also become a buzzword of heterodox Biblical interpretation in liberal Protestant, Jewish, and Roman Catholic circles. Interpretation of Scripture is governed by the multiple perspectives of the participants in various "communities of interpretation" rather than by fixed principles derived from Scripture itself. Each "community" develops its own interpretation of Scripture, and each interpretation is to be considered valid in principle. This is the hermeneutic of trust endorsed by the Orthodox Presbyterian Church. The 2004 General Assembly commended the creation committee's *Report,* which is based on this radically revisionist hermeneutic, to its presbyteries and sessions. The hermeneutic of trust is a prescription for doctrinal anarchy.

The creation committee *Report* is the OPC's most public endorsement of the hermeneutic of trust by that name. But this no-rules method of interpreting the Bible while twisting the words of the secondary doctrinal standards is not new to the Reformed church. The OPC committee observes that the hermeneutic of trust has helped keep peace in the denomination for many years:

> The OPC has experienced doctrinal controversies through its history, and some of them have been serious enough to prompt individuals and churches to leave. But none of them escalated into a confessional crisis. The OPC...has cultivated a community of interpretation that has sustained confessional integrity among its ministerial membership without imposing over-exacting standards of confessional subscription....

Moreover, the *Report* credits Westminster Theological Seminary with a vital role in maintaining this artificial unity:

> The most important factor in establishing and maintaining this community of interpretation has been the function of Westminster Theological Seminary in Philadelphia as the OPC's *de facto* denominational seminary. In training the vast majority of the early ministerial membership of the OPC, Westminster Seminary did not devote excessive attention to the days of creation nor to the Westminster Standards. But what WTS accomplished that averted a creation or confessional crisis was *inducting Orthodox Presbyterian ministerial candidates into a culture of interpretation.* The effect was to cultivate a hermeneutic of trust within the church, as ministers had confidence in the training of their colleagues, even if they differed in their views. Westminster performed that function ably....[8]

Notice two important things about the hermeneutic of trust. First, it is not a fixed set of principles or a defined methodology for the interpretation of Scripture. It is postmodern. As we noted in an earlier chapter, in postmodern thinking there are as many legitimate interpretations of Scripture as there are communities of interpreters. The only absolute, certain, or fixed principle is that *there are no absolute, certain, or fixed principles* – only varying but allegedly equally legitimate interpretations.

As the creation *Report* says, the OPC with the aid of Westminster Seminary "has cultivated a community of interpretation" in which the restraints of grammatical-histor-

---

8. *Report of the Committee to Study the Views of Creation,* 1607. Emphasis in the original.

ical interpretation (what the OPC *Report* calls "over-exacting standards") are cast off. In such a self-contradictory and irrational atmosphere, whatever "principles" of Biblical interpretation one may choose to hold are in fact merely the *preferences* of the community of interpreters in which one chooses to participate. There are no fixed rules having their sure foundation in the Word of God. The result is artificial confessional unity without fidelity to the Word of God.

Second, notice that the primary focus of the hermeneutic of trust is not on correctly interpreting the *words of Scripture* at all. It focuses instead on interpreting the *words of the church's confessional standards*, and on construing them in ways that are elastic enough to permit the OPC to fit diverging doctrinal views under one big confessional tent.

The hermeneutic of trust employs a clever sleight-of-hand to take the focus off inspired Scripture. In the case of the creation committee *Report*, the focus is not really on understanding what God meant by the word "day" in *Genesis* 1 at all. The focus is on what the framers of the *Westminster Confession* and *Catechisms* and the so-called church fathers may or may not have meant by the words, "in the space of six days." So the hermeneutic of trust is at least one step removed from Scripture. It focuses not on Scripture itself but on human *perspectives* on Scripture. This is key, as we shall see later in this chapter.

It is not only significant that the hermeneutic of trust draws attention *away from* Scripture, but also that it draws attention *to* something called the *animus imponentis*, or "the intention of the imposing body."[9] The *animus imponentis* is

9. Men of religious academia often use Latin phrases when plain English would both suffice and make what they are saying much more intelligible to church members. Unfortunately, the use of the Latin may

CHRISTIANITY & NEO-LIBERALISM

not a new term. Speaking of it, nineteenth-century Princeton theologian Charles Hodge wrote:

> The question put to every candidate for ordination in our Church, is in these words: "Do you sincerely receive and adopt the Confession of Faith of this Church, as containing the system of doctrine taught in the Holy Scriptures?" It is plain that a very serious responsibility before God and man is assumed by those who return an affirmative answer to that question. It is something more than ordinary falsehood, if our inward convictions do not correspond with a profession made in [the] presence of the Church, and as the condition of our receiving authority to preach the Gospel. In such a case we lie not only unto man, but unto God...such professions are of the nature of a vow, that is, a promise or profession made to God.
>
> It is no less plain that the candidate has no right to put his own sense upon the words propounded to him. He has no right to select from all possible meanings which the words may bear, that particular sense which suits his purpose, or which, he thinks, will save his conscience.

All of this is worthy and true, and the reader hopes that Hodge will now direct our attention to the authority of Scripture. But he does not. He directs our attention instead to the authority of the visible church:

> The two principles which, by the common consent of all honest men, determine the interpretation of oaths and

---

also impart an aura of special authority and significance to words of human wisdom, elevating them to something approaching the status of holy writ when they are nothing of the sort.

professions of faith, are, first, the plain, historical mean-ing of the words; and secondly, the *animus imponentis*, that is, the intention of the party imposing the oath or re-quiring the profession. The words, therefore, "system of doctrine taught in the Holy Scriptures," are to be taken in their plain, historical sense. A man is not at liberty to understand the words "Holy Scriptures," to mean all books written by holy men, because although that inter-pretation might consist with the signification of the words, it is inconsistent with the historical meaning of the phrase. Nor can he understand them, as they would be understood by Romanists, as including the Apocry-pha, because the words being used by a Protestant Church, must be taken in a Protestant sense....

The Confession must be adopted in the sense of the Church, into the service of which the minister, in virtue of that adoption, is received. These are simple principles of honesty, and we presume they are universally ad-mitted, at least so far as our Church is concerned.[10]

In the essay quoted above, Hodge argues for the use of the *animus imponentis* as a means to prevent theological pluralism within a denomination. But with all due respect to Hodge, to use the *animus imponentis* as the *fundamental guiding principle* in establishing conformity to sound doc-trine is to adopt a fatally flawed benchmark. Hodge himself indirectly admits this when he implies that the Roman Cath-olic Church has every right to establish its own doctrinal standards and its own *animus imponentis*, and to require its

10. Charles Hodge, "What Is the 'System of Doctrine?'" in *The Presbyterian Guardian*, Volume 2, Number 9, August 1936. Reproduced at www.pcanet.org/history/documents/subscription/hodge.html.

priests to swear allegiance. The words of a confession must, according to Hodge (and the OPC committee) be adopted in the sense that a visible church body chooses, Protestants as Protestants, Romanists as Romanists. By this logic, Rome's doctrine of justification and the Protestant doctrine of justifycation have equal standing. In fact, any competing doctrines that bear the stamp of approval of their respective "imposing bodies" would have equal standing. Each imposing body is, after all, its own "community of interpretation."

Furthermore, in the case of the Reformed church, Hodge calls the *Westminster Confession of Faith* "the system which, as the granite formation of the earth, underlies and sustains the whole scheme of truth as revealed in the Scriptures." That assertion is fundamentally wrong. The doctrinal standards of the church do not "underlie and sustain" the Scriptures. Quite the opposite! Scripture *must* underlie and sustain the doctrinal standards of *any* body that calls itself a church of Jesus Christ. The Church is built, not on the words of fallible men, but on the foundation of the Spirit-inspired words of the apostles and prophets, Jesus Christ Himself being the chief cornerstone (*Ephesians* 2:20). To make the words of men the foundation of the Reformed faith is to say in essence the same thing Rome says about its traditions.

This writer does not believe for a moment that this is what Hodge intended, but there it is, in his own words. Let us not hold the opinions of our fathers in the faith in such high regard that we are blind to their inconsistencies. To be sure, the *Westminster Confession* is far closer to the truth of Scripture than the pronouncements of popes and their councils. But that is not the issue. The issue is the crux of the Reformation: Will the fundamental authority in the true church of Christ be the words of men, or the Word of God? If it is the former, a church is well on the road to becoming no true church of

Christ at all. The principle by which we must "determine the interpretation...of confessions of faith" is not, as Hodge and the OPC say, the intentions of men, but rather the intention of Almighty God as revealed in His Word. The intentions of men of the church must be in subjection to God's.

The OPC committee *Report* adopts the principle of the *animus imponentis* and merely carries it to its logical ends. What is important, according to the OPC, is not what Scripture says, and not even what the *Confession* plainly says, but the "intention of the imposing body," in this case the Orthodox Presbyterian Church. Those intentions may change over time; even in the most faithful bodies they *do* change over time. The creation committee *Report* itself admits this:

> For the Orthodox Presbyterian Church, this communal understanding of the church's constitution involves the sense in which it was adopted by the church in the second General Assembly in 1936 as well as *subsequent developments* in its corporate understanding of the phrase ["in the space of six days"].[11]

Those intentions are not only unsettled, they are also fallible. Those intentions, in the history of the church, have often become corrupted. What does *not* change is the Word of God. What is *alone* infallible is Holy Scripture.

Another logical end of the *animus imponentis* is that individual presbyteries, even sessions, can give their own "intention of the imposing body" to the oath that men take as ministers and ruling elders of the church. Each body can decide what it means by the words of Scripture and the Westminster Standards. The spread of neo-liberalism has

11. *Report of the Committee to Study the Views of Creation*, 1605. Emphasis added.

made this the *de facto* standard in both the OPC and the PCA. The PCA has taken the further step of formalizing the *de facto* standard. Its 31ˢᵗ General Assembly (2003) approved an amendment to the PCA *Book of Church Order* permitting each of its seventy-three[12] presbyteries to decide what constitutes the "fundamentals of the system of doctrine" when examining the doctrinal positions of men who are to be ordained to the ministry.[13]

What is neglected in the entire discussion in both the OPC and PCA is (using another Latin phrase only to draw a parallel) the *animus auctoris divini* – the intention of the Divine Author. At the end of the day, what is important is not what men say the Bible says, but what the Bible *actually says*. For that reason our starting point in sound doctrine must never be the secondary standards of the church, but always Scripture. It is Scripture that gives meaning to the words of the confessional standards, not *vice versa*. The hermeneutic of trust perverts this fundamental order.

History Repeated

A similar state of mind was at work in the PCUSA and its seminaries three generations ago. That hermeneutic gave rise to the *Auburn Affirmation* in 1924, signed by men who denied the inerrancy of Scripture and other fundamentals of the faith with impunity, yet claimed that they were true to the *Westminster Confession of Faith*. That same hermeneutic also gave rise to the PCUSA's later adoption of an entirely

12. As of this writing (2005).

13. This was enacted by an amendment to PCA *Book of Church Order* chapter 21, section 4. The full text of the amendment, and the overture that brought it about, appears at the PCA Historical Center web site, www.pcanet.org/history/documents/BCO21-4.htm.

different so-called confession of faith "alongside" the Westminster Standards – the *Confession of 1967*.[14] Manifesting in fuller form the false gospel we now see at work in the OPC and elsewhere, the *Confession of 1967* redefined salvation in terms of becoming part of the *church community*, with *baptism* as the means of entering that community. It said that the Scriptures were principally the words of men, and that the New Testament in particular contained the various writers' *perspectives* on the events of redemptive history. Calls for such a new confession in the PCUSA began just thirty years after the *Auburn Affirmation*, and less than twenty years after conservatives left to form the OPC. Actual work on the liberalized PCUSA confession began in 1958, and it was ratified just nine years later, with over ninety percent of its presbyteries approving.

History is being repeated. Less than fifty years after the formation of the Orthodox Presbyterian Church, the hermeneutic of trust facilitated the cave-in and cover-up during the Shepherd controversy at Westminster Seminary and in the OPC, which we discussed in chapter five. The hermeneutic of trust has given impetus to the conspiracy of silence that has facilitated the spread of another gospel in the OPC during the past thirty years. The hermeneutic of trust has provided fertile ground for the Federal Vision; the New Perspective on Paul of Dunn, Sanders, and Wright; and Richard Gaffin's own new perspective on Paul. The hermeneutic of trust gave the OPC General Assembly license to say that the teachings of John Kinnaird were in agreement with the doctrinal standards of the church when in fact they are clearly another gospel. And no wonder, because where

14. The text of the *Confession of 1967*, which is only nine pages long, is available online at www.pcusa.org/oga/publications/boc.pdf.

the hermeneutic of trust is at work, it is almost absurd to speak of doctrinal *standards* at all.

The *animus imponentis* of the Orthodox Presbyterian Church – the intention of the body imposing vows upon its ordained men – has indeed changed. It has moved from subjection to the Word of God to subjection to the words of men, just as it did in the PCUSA.

The hermeneutic of trust is a spiritual carcinogen. It has been a major factor in the development and spread of the cancer of neo-liberalism at Westminster Seminary, in the OPC, and beyond.

Perspectivalism

Two popular promoters of this kind of hermeneutic are Vern S. Poythress and John M. Frame. Poythress has been Professor of New Testament Interpretation at Westminster since 1976. Frame, a Westminster professor and member of the OPC Presbytery of Philadelphia in the 1970s and 80s, is now Professor of Systematic Theology and Philosophy at Reformed Theological Seminary in Orlando. These two theologians have trained many of the men now in the pulpits of the OPC, or have influenced them through their writings. Both Poythress and Frame are advocates of "perspectivalism" in the interpretation of Scripture. They are both self-described disciples of Cornelius Van Til whose view of Scripture, as we shall see, is an essential influence on their thinking.

Perspectivalism is not new, nor is it limited to theology. It has its roots in the writings of the German Antichristian philosopher Friedrich Nietzsche (1844-1900). In the secular world, perspectivalism is the enabling force behind the growth of culture- and gender-specific studies programs on college campuses – feminist studies, ethnic studies, Marxist studies, Islamic studies, gay and lesbian studies, and so on. Those unfamiliar with the radically relativistic agenda being carried out on most campuses may think that these are programs of study *about* feminism, Marxism, Islam, etc.

But that is not the case. In these programs, all disciplines – history, anthropology, sociology, politics, economics, and even mathematics and science – are studied from the *perspective* of one's gender, ethnicity, religion, or sexual perversion as "communities of interpretation." The motivation for this is the radical educators' drive to suppress what they refer to as the perspectives of the "power elite" – European males, capitalists, Christians, and "straight" people.[15] The results are often absurd: textbooks and courses on "feminist re-conceptions of knowledge" – "Marxist anthropology" – "gay and lesbian mathematics" and other forms of what are called "non-traditional studies," *ad nauseum.*[16]

15. This liberal college professor's glee over the perspectivalist perversion of American academia is typical: "Women's studies, African-American studies, gay and lesbian studies programs, and the moving of non-western and non-"traditional" studies in general out of the anthropology and sociology departments and into the academy on their own terms is the great success story of contemporary higher education.... Perspectivalism succeeds at making all viewpoints equally cogent" (Steven Jay Gimbel, "If I Had a Hammer: Why Logical Positivism Better Accounts for the Need for Gender and Cultural Studies" in *Studies in Practical Philosophy*: 2000, Volume 2, Number 2).

16. These examples, I am ashamed to say, are from the university system in my home state of Maryland. And in the so-called divinity schools of universities such as Harvard, Yale, and Princeton one finds "feminist theology," "black theology," even "Marxist theology." Neo-evangelical seminaries such as Fuller are not far behind. Fuller's courses in the Old Testament are based on books such as *A Feminist Companion to Genesis* and *A Feminist Companion to the Wisdom Literature*, and its systematic theology program uses books such as *She Who Is: The Mystery of God in Feminist Theological Discourse* and *Freeing Theology: The*

"All Perspectives Are Valid in Principle"

In Reformed seminaries, the promotion of perspectivalism is much more subtle, the element of gross immorality is absent, and the academic results are not so overtly absurd. But there are parallels with secular academia. Perspectivalism in the seminaries and the church destroys respect for the authority of Scripture and paves the way for advancement of the neo-liberal agenda.

The stated motivation for perspectivalism in the seminaries and the church is to displace what men like Poythress and Frame, echoing their secular counterparts, pejoratively refer to as the "traditional," "conventional," and "prosaic" interpretation of Scripture with "imaginative" and "fresh" interpretations.[17] What they refer to as the traditional, conventional, prosaic interpretation of Scripture is the grammatical-historical interpretation that underpins Protestant orthodoxy.

The effect of perspectivalism in the seminaries is to raise a cacophony of human perspectives and permit them to compete on an equal footing with what Poythress, Frame, Gaffin, and others claim are the individual Biblical writers' "perspectivalism" on "redemptive-historical events." These, they allege, form much of the content of Scripture. The focus is on human authorship of Scripture and human perspectives on Scripture. Divine inspiration is acknowledged, but only in a passing and superficial way. By this flawed

---

Essentials of Theology in Feminist Perspective.

17. The Westminster Theological Seminary board, when exonerating Norman Shepherd, commended him for his "fresh insights" which were, in fact, heresy (see chapter five).

procedure, the voice of the divine Author, God the Holy Spirit, is often drowned out or simply ignored.

Perspectivalism is a philosophy of interpretation that values vagueness over precision. It values "diversity" over a clearly defined, carefully derived, and God-unified system of doctrine. It values giving free rein to any and all human perspectives on Scripture as governing factors in interpretation, rather than "bringing every thought into captivity to the obedience of Christ" (2 *Corinthians* 10:5). John Frame states that "Scripture does not demand absolute precision of us" in interpretation, and says that it is a principle of Scripture itself that "vagueness is often preferable to precision.... Nor is theology an attempt to state truth without any subjective influence [*i.e.*, the interpreter's imposing his own opinions] on the formulation."[18] These statements contradict the Biblical admonitions not to add to or subtract from Scripture (*e.g.*, *Revelation* 22:18-19), and passages where the Bible itself tells us that correct interpretation hinges on the precise meaning of even a single word (*e.g.*, *Galatians* 3:16).

Poythress promotes perspectivalism under the name *Symphonic Theology*, and in 1987 he published a book by that title. Poythress' book makes it clear that the perspectivalist approach to Scripture is decidedly postmodern. "Truth" is man-centered, communal, and relative – not God-centered, God-authored, and unalterable. Poythress asserts that the way we know truth is by assembling various individuals' perspectives on it:

18. John M. Frame, *The Doctrine of the Knowledge of God* (Phillipsburg, New Jersey: Presbyterian and Reformed Publishing Co., 1987), 226, 307.

I call this procedure *symphonic theology* because it is analogous to the blending of various musical instruments to express the variations of a symphonic theme.[19]

How is this "symphonic theme" to be assembled?

[I]magination and creativity often work best when people allow themselves to juxtapose unlikely parallels or analogies or to develop apparently fanciful or absurd ideas. This freedom is one of the ideas behind so-called brainstorming. Research on the processes involved in creativity shows how, in an advanced and sophisticated form of brainstorming, good and workable plans often evolve from some core idea that pops up using "wild" analogies.[20]

Who may we invite to help us thus assemble the "truth"? Poythress says that in the interpretation of Scripture "*all perspectives are valid in principle,*"[21] even "wild" ones, even "apparently fanciful and absurd ideas" – even the perspectives of the unregenerate. The non-Christian's perspective on Scripture, Poythress says,

has "grains of truth" in it. Any such grain of truth *can* be used as the starting point for developing a perspective on a much larger field of truth. Sometimes the non-Christian system as a whole is based on a "root-

19. Vern S. Poythress, *Symphonic Theology: The Validity of Multiple Perspectives in Theology* (Grand Rapids, Michigan: Zondervan, 1987; reprinted by P & R Publishing Company, 2001), 43.

20. Poythress, 52.

21. Poythress, 43.

metaphor" of some kind, such as the world as mechanism or the world as organism.[22]

"[I]f we recognize such an analogy and detach it from its context in the non-Christian system," Poythress continues, "it can be used as a perspective" to interpret the Bible.

This climate of man-centered interpretive disorder is far removed from the Christ-centered discipline that Scripture demands of believers, and its warnings concerning the carnal mind:

> For those who live according to the flesh set their minds on the things of the flesh, but those who live according to the Spirit, the things of the Spirit. For to be carnally minded is death, but to be spiritually minded is life and peace. Because the carnal mind is enmity against God; for it is not subject to the law of God, nor indeed can be. So then, those who are in the flesh cannot please God. But you are not in the flesh but in the Spirit, if indeed the Spirit of God dwells in you. Now if anyone does not have the Spirit of Christ, he is not His [*Romans* 8:5-9].
>
> For though we walk in the flesh, we do not war according to the flesh. For the weapons of our warfare are not carnal but mighty in God for pulling down strongholds, casting down arguments and every high thing that exalts itself against the knowledge of God, bringing every thought into captivity to the obedience of Christ [2 *Corinthians* 10:3-5].

Where does the perspectivalist interpretive procedure lead? Poythress does not hesitate to tell us:

22. Poythress, 44-45. Emphasis in the original.

Our ability to use a number of different flexible perspectives is based partly on the fact that terms such as "ethics" or "adultery" or "covenant" or "prophet" can be stretched. We can use words [of Scripture] in a conventional, prosaic way. But we can also stretch them in an imaginative, almost playful way until they give us a perspective on the whole of the Bible.

This flexibility is, in fact, closely related to the flexibility that occurs in the meaning of words. A key area in our exegesis and our understanding of the Bible is the area of word meanings and the use of words in the Bible.... Some people have imagined that words in the Bible all have a special technical precision and give us automatically fixed, rigid categories. These fixed categories are then thought to exclude any kind of flexibility in the use of perspectives. In fact, I believe that the opposite is the case.[23]

Thus Poythress openly opposes grammatical-historical interpretation governed by the Scripture-derived principles discussed earlier in this chapter. He is saying that the words of Scripture need not be interpreted according to their meaning in context. To interpret Scripture by such principles is, Poythress says, "conventional" and "prosaic" – dull and unimaginative. This, Poythress says, is wrong. "My rule of thumb is to question profound conclusions in...theology that depend largely on key technical terms or systems of terms."[24] Those "technical terms," according to Poythress, include regeneration, saving faith, justification,

23. Poythress, 55.
24. Poythress, 61.

adoption, sanctification, and glorification.[25] In other words, he rejects systematic theology in principle. And it is telling that he would make it his "rule of thumb...to question profound conclusions" about the very doctrinal terms that neo-liberals radically redefine in preaching another gospel.

Poythress insists that we need to free ourselves of the constraints of "traditional," "conventional," "prosaic" Protestant theology. We need to be "imaginative," to "stretch" meanings of words in the Bible so that they will give us new "perspective[s] on the whole Bible."

This no-rules-but-yours-and-mine method for interpreting the Bible is based on the Van Tilian premise we have discussed in earlier chapters: Scripture is an analogy which at no point coincides with the truth in the divine mind.

> Finally, we may observe that *all human knowledge whatsoever* is analogically related to God's knowledge.... We are made in the image of God, which implies that our knowledge is an image of God's knowledge. In addition, I would claim that all growth in knowledge exploits analogy in one way or another.... General understanding of human experiences is achieved by moving by analogy from our own experience to other people's stories of their experiences. The use of perspectives is a way of becoming self-conscious and deliberate about the use of analogies and in this way promises a systematic way of searching to advance knowledge.[26]

The perspectivalist interpretive method – if it can be dignified by the term – facilitates the Biblical Theology of Richard Gaffin. Poythress writes:

25. Poythress, 74-75.

26. Poythress, 54. Emphasis added.

Finally, advances in the study of biblical themes challenge us to study the Bible in ways that cut across previous lines of separation between topics. "Biblical theology," as practiced by Geerhardus Vos and Richard B. Gaffin, studies main themes of the Bible in their historical development.... Gaffin appropriately challenges us to reorganize our systematic theology on the basis of this advance.[27]

In earlier chapters we saw the result of such "advances," or what Shepherd and Gaffin called "progress in theology." Shepherd's and Gaffin's efforts to "cut across previous lines of separation between topics" have yielded, among other things, thorough confusion of the Biblical doctrines of justification and sanctification. The "lines of separation" between the two doctrines, long obscured by the traditions of Rome, were re-established in bold strokes by the Reformers using Scripture alone. Shepherd, Gaffin, Frame, Poythress and their followers are erasing them once again.

Gaffin and Poythress both subscribe to the so-called "redemptive-historical perspective" of the modern Biblical Theology movement. For Poythress, like Gaffin, revelation consists of events, not doctrine.[28] The writings of the different human authors in Scripture are merely their different perspectives on those events.[29] In fact, Poythress views "redemptive history as *perspectives*."[30] What is hardly in view at all in his thinking is the doctrine of the Holy Spirit as the author of every word of Scripture.

27. Poythress, 122-123.

28. Poythress, 48.

29. Poythress, 85-86.

30. Poythress, 99. Emphasis in the original.

The perspectivalist approach of the redemptive-historical school facilitates Gaffin's radical reconstruction of the Gospel in *Resurrection and Redemption*. It allows Gaffin, as he himself admits, to take "the concept or line of thought" that has "relatively little explicit textual support" and make it the controlling factor in interpreting Paul's writings.[31] If, as Poythress asserts, "*all perspectives are valid in principle*" for the interpretation of Scripture – even "wild" ones, even "apparently fanciful and absurd ideas," even the perspectives of the unregenerate – then it is no problem to come up with an interpretation that lacks support in the sacred text. And since perspectivalism is so much a part of our postmodern, inclusivist culture, it is no problem for many of Gaffin's readers either.

Poythress also adopts a bizarre (but these days not uncommon) view of reality. He asserts that no "*particular event or reality as a whole exists prior to and independent of any perspective on it, any knowledge or interpretation of it.*"[32] For such interpretation, he says, "[a]ny motif of the Bible can be used as the single organizing motif."[33] "We see what our tools enable us to see."[34] In other words, according to Poythress, *human perspectives create reality*. That makes man and his subjective experiences – rather than God's objective, propositional revelation in Scripture – the measure of all things. It is dangerous nonsense.

What is missing in perspectivalism's no-rules hermeneutic is any basis on an authoritative Word from God, for

31. Gaffin, *Resurrection and Redemption*, 28.

32. Poythress, 49. Emphasis added.

33. Poythress, 86.

34. Poythress, 89.

which human writers served as the penmen of the Holy Spirit. Gone is the doctrine of a clearly communicated Divine revelation. Gone is the slightest acknowledgment that the words of the Book have a definite, God-fixed meaning. Gone is the doctrine of Scripture as its own interpreter. In place of these sound principles, perspectivalism gives us a purported vagueness from God and an interpretive Babel among men. In place of the apostles' and prophets' "Thus says the Lord," perspectivalism gives us the serpent's "Has God indeed said?"

As we have seen in the OPC creation committee *Report*, such thinking produces interpretations of the word "day" in *Genesis* 1 that oppose the meaning of the word which Scripture itself makes clear: *a literal day*. Day-age theories, days of unspecified length, analogical-day theories, and framework theories have become admissible because the anti-Biblical "perspectives" of the unregenerate are being viewed as "valid in principle" for the interpretation of Scripture. Perspectivalism forgets that there is only one "perspective" that matters – that of God the Holy Spirit, the Author of the words of Scripture. Perspectivalism forgets that it is the business of the believer to seek *that* perspective, and submit to *it*, and to no other. We shall do it imperfectly in this life to be sure, but it is what we are commanded to do.

Poythress' own employment of perspectivalism yields telling results. In *Symphonic Theology* he redefines many Biblical terms in the same ways as Norman Shepherd and Richard Gaffin. At various points he un-Biblically redefines key doctrinal terms such as regeneration,[35] righteousness,[36] and

35. Poythress, 58.
36. Poythress, 37.

266

saving faith[37] as they do. He says that it "appears from biblical revelation" that Adam is the federal head of the fallen race and Christ the federal Head of the redeemed.[38] But in keeping with the perspectivalist philosophy of vagueness and inclusivism, apparently it is not something he can say with the same certainty that Scripture says it, nor can he exclude other "perspectives" that might contradict it.

The hermeneutic of trust and perspectivalism go together hand-in-glove. We should, the OPC creation committee *Report* says, use the *Confession* as a vehicle to "encourage theological creativity." The report commends Westminster Seminary in Philadelphia for "inducting Orthodox Presbyterian ministerial candidates into" such a "culture of interpretation." The effect, the report says, has been to "cultivate a hermeneutic of trust within the church, as ministers had confidence in the training of their colleagues, even if they differed in their views." As Poythress says, "all perspectives are valid in principle" – even if they "stretch" the meanings of the words of Scripture beyond rationality.

Is Creation a Litmus Test?

In the providence of God, the controversy over the doctrine of creation has helped focus attention on the OPC's commitment to the hermeneutic of trust. The title of the 2004 General Assembly *Report* is telling: "Report of the Committee to Study the *Views* of Creation." It is a study of the conflicting views of men, not a study of the doctrine of creation in Scripture. In recent years, the PCA has also had its own controversy over the doctrine of creation, and it

37. Poythress, 63, 76, 94.

38. Poythress, 60.

"resolved" it in much the same way: by surrendering to a perspectivalist-inclusivist paradigm. These leading Reformed denominations have judged that stretching the confessional tent to cover every position short of atheistic evolution in order to keep peace is more important than faithful interpretation of Scripture.[39]

However, many people in both denominations wonder why – or if – the meaning of the word "day" in *Genesis* 1 should be a matter of such deep controversy. Are there not, they ask, far more vital issues at stake? Can we not overlook this one to keep the peace?

It is true that the hermeneutic of trust endangers much more than the doctrine of creation. It endangers the proclamation of the Gospel itself, as well as many other doctrines – in fact, the entire system of doctrine. It is also true that it is not necessary to believe in creation of the heavens and the Earth in six contiguous 24-hour days in order to be a Christian. But it is also true that the doctrine of creation is a key test case revealing the attitudes of theologians, pastors, elders, and church members toward the authority of Scripture and the proper approach to its interpretation.

The test is simple: Will you believe what God has written in its plainly-understood sense, or will you say, with the serpent in the Garden, "Has God really said?" To put it in the context of this chapter, will you believe the Word of God, and bring every thought captive to it, or must you first pass God's Word through perspectival filters – principally the perspectives of unbelievers whose theories about origins reflect, at their core, an unwillingness to acknowledge God as Creator and thus open the door to His claims upon them

39. The full *Report* is reproduced by the PCA Historical Center at www.pcanet.org/history/creation/report.html.

as His creatures? In *John* 5:40 Jesus said to the Jews what is also true of these unbelievers: "But you are not *willing* to come to Me that you may have life."

In that same passage, Jesus tells them: "If you believed Moses, you would believe Me; for he wrote about Me. But if you do not believe his writings, how will you believe My words?" The issue at that moment in the Gospel account was not the doctrine of creation, but the principle Jesus stated still applies. We are grossly inconsistent if we say that we believe the words of God the Son in the New Testament but do not believe the words of His inspired penmen in the Old. If we do not trust Moses' words given under the inspiration of the God the Holy Spirit, how can we say that we trust the words of God made flesh? Where do we draw such a dividing line, and who gives us the right to draw it? Perspectivalism and the hermeneutic of trust presume to grant us that right, but they cannot, because God does not.

For the pastor or teacher, the test posed by the doctrine of creation is even more pointed: Will you be consistent in your attitude toward the Word of God from beginning to end, or will you lead those under your care into the swamp of equivocation? Are you willing to take a stand that is contrary to the false wisdom of this world, and thus be identified with the One who said in the same passage, "I do not receive honor from men"? Are you willing to be such an example to the people of God, by exposing yourself to the criticism of the world?

Sadly, the OPC as a denomination has not passed this test.[40] And what is the result? The OPC, along with the PCA

40. Sadly, many post-Darwinian theologians of Old Princeton, including such godly men as Charles Hodge, Benjamin B. Warfield, and J. Gresham Machen, embraced perspectives on *Genesis* that com-

and many other churches, fails to bear a clear testimony to the authority of the Word of God, both to its own members and to the outside world.

This was vividly demonstrated in the following incident. *Answers in Genesis*,[41] an organization whose motto is "Upholding the authority of the Bible from the very first verse," applied to government authorities for re-zoning of land near Cincinnati, Ohio, for construction of a Creation Museum. The museum will teach the truth about *Genesis* and proclaim the Gospel for which the creation record is foundational. The project was approved, but only after a protracted legal fight led by national humanist organizations.

At one public hearing, a humanist spokesman said this: "We wouldn't mind so much if they wanted to build a church — but they want to build a creation museum to change our minds!"[42] Such a statement speaks volumes about the reputation of churches like the OPC and PCA, which have refused to take an unequivocal stand on the authority of Scripture and have instead compromised with the unbelieving world. Jesus Christ commissioned His church to seek to change the minds of men by preaching the Gospel of *repentance* (*Luke* 24:47). In the original language the word translated "repentance" is *metanoia*, a *change of mind*. The Bible's accounts of the creation of the universe and the fall of man are foundational to that Gospel. The church cannot credibly call unbelievers to *change their*

promised with evolutionary thinking. The steady advance of compromise on the historicity of the early chapters of *Genesis* in Reformed churches is a part of their legacy, along with so much that is good.

41. www.answersingenesis.org

42. *AIG Update* newsletter, January 29, 2005.

minds based on an infallible Word from God, if it cannot *make up its own mind* to accept the plain meaning of Scripture – whether it is the meaning of the word *day* in *Genesis,* or the meaning of other doctrinal words such as *regeneration, faith, justification,* and *sanctification.*

Needed: A Hermeneutic of Biblical Authority

God calls upon His church not to practice a hermeneutic of trust, but a hermeneutic of Biblical authority. It is the entrance of *God's* Word that gives light (*Psalm* 119:130). We are to judge everything and everyone in that light (*1 John* 4:1). We may trust the teachings of other Christians only to the extent that they conform to the Word of God (*1 Timothy* 6:3-5). We are not to be tossed about by every wind of doctrine, but to speak the truth in love (*Ephesians* 4:14-15). Man is constantly changeable and changing. Only God and His Word are unchangeable and unchanging (*James* 1:17, *Psalm* 119:89). The Berean believers did not trust the word even of an apostle of Jesus Christ, but searched the Scriptures daily to find out whether the things that the Apostle Paul taught them were true (*Acts* 17:11). They practiced a hermeneutic of Biblical authority.

The apostles themselves, under the inspiration of the Holy Spirit, also practiced such a hermeneutic. The New Testament writers quoted the Old Testament over 270 times. They demonstrated that the Old Covenant revelation is the foundation of the New. They explained how much of the Old Testament was fulfilled in the coming of Christ and the establishment of His Church, and that much remains to be fulfilled in the events leading up to and culminating in His second coming. In doing these things under the inspiration of God, the apostles practiced the principles of grammatical-historical hermeneutics themselves. They were exceedingly careful in their handling of the existing Scriptures as they were directed to write the remainder of the canon. In some cases (*e.g., Galatians* 3:16) the apostles demonstrated that correct interpretation of Scripture – in fact, major points of doctrine – can hinge on minute details, such as a word being in the singular or plural.

Friendship with the Enemies of Scripture

Westminster Theological Seminary in Philadelphia has demonstrated a strong bias against grammatical-historical hermeneutics. Dr. Peter Enns, a professor at Westminster and current editor of its *Theological Journal*, has been a spokesman for this bias. In an article we cited in an earlier chapter,[43] Enns writes:

> A problem arises, however, when we observe how the Apostles handled the OT. Despite protestations to the contrary, grammatical-historical hermeneutics does not account for the New Testament's use of the Old.... [I]t must be stated clearly that the Apostles did not seem overly concerned to put this principle into practice.... [A]postolic hermeneutics, apart from the expenditure of significant mental energy and denial of plain fact, cannot be categorized as being "essentially" grammatical-historical....
>
> ...[W]e see again and again that the Apostles approached the Old Testament in ways that are adverse

43. Peter Enns, "Apostolic Hermeneutics and an Evangelical Doctrine of Scripture: Moving beyond a Modernist Impasse," *WTJ*, Fall 2003. Enns repeats much of this essay in his book, *Inspiration and Incarnation*.

to grammatical-historical exegesis but are firmly at home in the Second Temple world.

...What can be said about the interpretive *methods* of the NT authors can also be said of the interpretive *traditions* that find their way into their writings. Not only did the Apostles handle the OT in ways consistent with other Second Temple interpreters, but they also *transmit existing* interpretive traditions...[emphases in the original].

What were those "existing interpretive traditions" and who were the "other Second Temple interpreters"? Enns makes it clear that he is speaking of the extra-Biblical rabbinical writings of the time of the apostles (the "Second Temple" period).

This phenomenon, reflected in the NT as well as throughout much of Second Temple literature, is often referred to as the "retold" or "rewritten" Bible....

As examples, Enns cites a number of apocryphal books and other writings of the rabbis. But Jesus condemned such writings as not only non-authoritative but also antagonistic to the authentic Word of God:

Well did Isaiah prophesy of you hypocrites, as it is written: "This people honors Me with their lips, but their heart is far from Me. And in vain they worship Me, teaching as doctrines the commandments of men." All too well you reject the commandment of God, that you may keep your tradition...making the Word of God of no effect through your tradition which you have handed down [*Mark* 7:6-7, 9, 13].

Enns, however, claims that the apostles employed such rabbinical writings in the writing of the New Testament, and incorporated such traditions into the Scriptures.

> The "retold Bible" is not merely an ancient phenomenon. Rather, it is a phenomenon that has accompanied biblical interpretation throughout its history, including our own day....
>
> New Testament authors also bear witness to their participation in the phenomenon of the "retold Bible"....
>
> These interpretive traditions did not derive from a grammatical-historical reading of the OT. Moreover, it is certain that they did not even originate with the New Testament authors....
>
> It will not do to argue, as has been done, apparently in an effort to safeguard the hermeneutical integrity of the Apostles, that the Apostles were not really "interpreting" the Old Testament but "applying" it. It would need to be demonstrated that such a distinction would have been recognizable to Second Temple authors. But such a position seems motivated more by a desire to protect a particular doctrine of Scripture than it is by a direct assessment of the evidence. The same can be said for the related, and well-known, distinction between meaning and significance, that is, that the Apostles did not assign new meaning to the OT but only explained its significance for the church. Such a distinction, it is thought, safeguards a high view of Scripture.

Enns continues:

> Grammatical-historical hermeneutics insists that the interpretation of texts must begin with the words in front of us understood in the context in which these words were written.

This is only partly true. What he has just stated is one of the principles of sound hermeneutics we described earlier in this chapter. But it is not where we *begin*. Our beginning point must be that Scripture alone is the inspired Word of God, every word having been authored by the Holy Spirit. In the nearly 15,000 words of his essay, Enns makes only two passing references to inspiration, but never states it as the starting point for interpretation. Lip service to the doctrine of inspiration notwithstanding, it is clear that human wisdom is his actual starting point. And as we have already seen with Gaffin and Poythress, this is typical of the Westminster faculty.

The hermeneutic of trust not only breeds the wrong kind of trust within the church – a misplaced trust in human wisdom – but also the wrong kind of trust between men of the church and men of the unbelieving world. The attitudes and practices of men at Westminster Seminary and in the OPC demonstrate this as well.

As we noted in an earlier chapter, the *Westminster Theological Journal* has published several articles by WTS graduate and Biblical skeptic Paul H. Seely. In those essays Seely denies inerrancy, consistently placing the perspectives of unregenerate men above the authority of Scripture.

Seely denies the Biblical account of the nature and extent of the flood, saying that it is "falsified by archaeology."[44] He denies the historicity of the *Genesis* record of the division of human language at the time of the building of the Tower of Babel.[45] He claims that the use of the word *raqiya'* ("firma-

44. Paul H. Seely, "Noah's Flood: Its Date, Extent, and Divine Accommodation" in *Westminster Theological Journal*, Volume 66, Fall 2004, 301.

45. Paul H. Seely, "The Date of the Tower of Babel and Some

ment") in *Genesis* 1:7 and elsewhere was an accommodation to man's false understanding that the sky was a solid dome; in other words, Seely says that God the Holy Spirit incorporated scientific error into Scripture.[46] Seely claims that God in *Genesis* also accommodated fallacious human understandings by teaching that the Earth was a flat disc consisting of a single continent floating on a circular sea.[47]

Seely frequently echoes the redemptive-historical thinking of Gaffin and others, seeing Biblical revelation as events rather than as a system of doctrine, and most of Scripture as merely a series of interpretations of those events. When it is viewed in this way – as principally the words of men – it is only natural for Seely to conclude that the Biblical record need not be infallible when touching upon matters of science.[48] In a May 2005 debate regarding the *Genesis* flood on the Yahoo® Presbyterians-OPC Internet discussion group, Seely stated:

Theological Implications" in *Westminster Theological Journal*, Volume 63, No. 1, Spring 2001, 15-38.

46. Paul H. Seely, "The Firmament and the Water Above," in *Westminster Theological Journal*, Volume 53, No. 2, Fall 1991, 227-240 and Volume 54, No. 1, Spring 1992, 31-46. For a refutation of Seely's error see James Patrick Holding, "Is the *raqiya'* ('Firmament') a Solid Dome?" in *Creation Technical Journal*, Vol. 13, No. 2, November 1999, 44-51, also available online at www.answersingenesis.org/tj/v13/i2/firmament.asp.

47. Paul H. Seely, "The Geographical Meaning of 'Earth' and 'Seas' in *Genesis* 1:10," *Westminster Theological Journal*, Volume 59, 213-255. For a refutation of Seely's error see James Patrick Holding, "Is the *'erets'* ('Earth') Flat?" in *Creation Technical Journal*, Vol. 14, No. 3, December 2000, 51-54, also available online at www.answersingenesis.org/tj/v14/i3/flat_earth.asp.

48. Paul H. Seely, essay in the *Journal of the American Scientific Affiliation*, as quoted in Harold Lindsell, *The Battle for the Bible*, 130-131.

2 *Timothy* 3:16 contextually limits the authority of
Scripture to matters of faith and morals. When it says
that Scripture is authoritative for "correction," it contextually is referring to matters of faith and morals, not
the correction of geology, astronomy, or any other
science.... The absolute inerrancy of Scripture (inerrant
in science as well as in faith and morals) is not a necessary doctrine of Scripture. It cannot be proven from
Scripture.[49]

The *American Heritage Dictionary of the English Language*
defines science as "the observation, identification, description, experimental investigation, and theoretical explanation
of phenomena." If the Bible is not "inerrant in science" –
things empirically observed and investigated – then on
what basis are we to trust the accounts of the plagues in
Egypt, the parting of the Red Sea and the Jordan River, the
presence of God's *shekinah* glory above the mercy seat,
God's provision of manna for Israel in the wilderness, the
miracles performed by Jesus and the apostles, the Trans-
figuration, or the Resurrection? Where does one draw lines
in the pages of Scripture between the errant and the
inerrant, and by whose authority? If we say that it is permissible to draw such lines, on what basis can anyone say
that the signers of the *Auburn Affirmation*, who denied the
miracles and the virgin birth of Christ, were wrong three
generations ago?

It is not only in the scientific realm that WTS and the
OPC condone friendship with the enemies of Scripture. In
1991, Dr. Moisés Silva, former WTS professor of hermeneu-

49. Paul H. Seely, "Re: Noah's Flood," groups.yahoo.com/group/
presbyterians-opc/message/28105.

tics and former licentiate in the OPC Presbytery of Philadelphia, wrote a review of James Dunn's book, *Jesus, Paul
and the Law* for the *Westminster Theological Journal*. Dunn is
one of the principal theorists of the New Perspective on
Paul and its denial of the doctrine of justification by faith
alone. Silva said that he considers Dunn's theology to have
"serious weaknesses," but:

> I do not consider Dunn to have set a particularly
> egregious example of poor Pauline exegesis. On the
> contrary, there is much in this book that I have found
> fascinating, provocative, and worthy of careful study.
> The very length of this review article is an indication of
> my admiration for his work.... At any rate, my quarrel
> is less with Dunn's distinctive thesis [the New Per-
> spective on Paul's claim that justification is *not* by faith
> alone] than with an approach that characterizes im-
> portant segments of NT scholarship. Traditional Re-
> formed theology can learn and appropriate a great deal
> from recent Pauline research,[50] but it need not fear the
> dissolution of one of its central tenets, *sola fide*.[51]

In a subsequent review of Dunn's *The Epistle to the Galatians*, Silva speaks glowingly of "Dunn's contribution to our
understanding of Paul's message." He says this, despite
acknowledging "Dunn's almost systematic ignoring of
Philippians 3:9 in his attempt to understand Paul's view of

50. Here, in a footnote, Silva cites the work of Don B. Garlington, a
student of Dunn and a New Perspectivist himself, saying that "he has
on the whole succeeded quite admirably in integrating contemporary
Pauline exegesis and sensitive theological reflection."

51. Moisés Silva, "The Law and Christianity" in *Westminster Theological Journal*, Volume 53, No. 2, Fall 1991, 353.

justification," and despite the fact that Dunn "suggests that the Christian is 'still hanging' on the cross with Christ." Silva then concludes: "But one would have to be perverse not to recognize that, all things considered, this is a work of exceptionally fine quality."[52]

One wonders how Dunn's Gospel-rejecting exegesis could be "not...particularly egregious." One wonders how a book that denies the sufficiency of Christ and the secure position of the redeemed, and ignores the Bible's teaching that justification is by faith apart from law-keeping, can be "a work of exceptionally fine quality." One wonders how Silva can say that the Reformed church need not fear the dissolution of the doctrine of justification by faith alone when his favorable review lends undeserved credibility to the work of a theologian who repudiates it. But the dimensions of the inclusivism promoted by the hermeneutic of trust transcend the boundaries of truth and error.

Westminster has also been increasingly favorable toward the teachings of New Perspective spokesman N. T. Wright. The Spring 1994 issue of *WTJ* included a flattering review of Wright's *The Climax of the Covenant: Christ and the Law in Pauline Theology*, in which Wright radically deconstructs and redefines the Biblical covenants to eliminate justification by faith alone. The reviewer (a Gordon-Conwell Seminary professor) said that he "was delighted beyond expression to find in print a *covenantal* analysis of Paul's thought."[53] He said that Wright's "assault on aspects of the scholarly

52. Moisés Silva, Review of Dunn's *The Epistle to the Galatians* in *Westminster Theological Journal*, Volume 57, No. 2, Fall 1995, 487.

53. T. David Gordon, Review of N. T. Wright's *The Climax of the Covenant: Christ and the Law in Pauline Theology* in *Westminster Theological Journal*, Volume 56, No. 1, Spring 1994, 198. Emphasis in the original.

consensus that have never been adequately argued is courageous." As an example he cited "Wright's denial of the popular 'two-covenant' theory" (the concept of old and new covenants under the Covenant of Grace) which Wright mistakenly says makes the church "an exclusively Gentile possession," a notion he labels "anti-Semitic." Yet the reviewer later states: "Lest I lose whatever academic reputation I might have had heretofore, I had better find a fault or two with this work. First, Wright could have been more precise in defining covenant."[54] Such is the confusion at Westminster (and at Gordon-Conwell) that a reviewer can be "delighted beyond expression" to find a book that supposedly gives a *"covenantal* analysis of Paul's thought" – but without precisely defining *covenant.*

Dr. Douglas J. Green, Associate Professor of Old Testament at Westminster, is another New Perspective enthusiast. In January 2004 Green revealed that he is not the only one on the WTS faculty, though some of his colleagues are still somewhat "in the closet."

> Recently, frustration has been expressed at the failure of certain professors at Westminster Theological Seminary (PA) to express publicly their sympathy for the New Perspective in general and Tom Wright in particular. While I cannot speak for any of my colleagues, I will speak for myself.
>
> ...When respected Reformed theologians describe Wright's views as "dangerous" and "an attack on the very heart of the gospel" and more extreme voices denounce "Wright's anti-Christian theology," it is hardly an environment that encourages seminary professors –

---

54. Gordon, 200.

let alone those who teach at Westminster – to stand up and say, "Hold on, maybe Wright's on to something here. Let's be a little less suspicious and see what we can learn."

...I react positively to the basic outlines of Wright's reading of Paul.

So for those who may be interested, I have appended below an expanded version of comments that I made last year in the context of internal faculty discussions about the New Perspective....

...These comments should not be particularly controversial, especially for those who embrace a redemptive-historical approach to Scripture.... [T]hese remarks will make most sense when read in the context of the hermeneutical and theological distinctives of Westminster Theological Seminary (PA)....

I fundamentally agree with the analysis that sees *Wright's approach to Paul as compatible with Calvin's emphasis on union with Christ.* At Westminster Seminary, union with Christ – rather than justification by faith – is viewed as the organizing center of Pauline soteriology. This emphasis – along with the tradition of redemptive-historical hermeneutics and the consequent subordination of *ordo salutis* [the Biblical order of salvation described in passages such as *Romans* 8:29-30] to *historia salutis* in theology [the Biblical Theology movement's false notion that revelation consists of stories or events and not systematic doctrine] – *should* encourage a sympathetic reading of Wright....[55]

---

55. Douglas J. Green, "N. T. Wright – A Westminster Seminary Perspective," first posted as message number 2866 on the Yahoo® Groups

In footnotes to the preceding paragraph, Green makes it clear that when he speaks of the doctrine of "union with Christ" he means not Calvin's orthodox teaching, but the heterodox version of that doctrine set forth in Richard B. Gaffin's *Resurrection and Redemption*, which we discussed at length in chapter six. In other words, Green himself sees compatibility between the teachings of Wright and Gaffin, and makes it clear that *Gaffin's false teaching is the teaching of Westminster Seminary as an institution.*

As we stated earlier, one wonders if the two-thirds of OPC ministers (and others in the PCA and elsewhere) who are Westminster Theological Seminary graduates ever read their *alma mater's* theological journal,[56] or realize what has been taught to the men who come before their presbyteries for licensure and ordination to the ministry. Thirty years ago, some OPC presbyteries at least recognized that young men were spouting heresy when they came before them repeating the teachings of Norman Shepherd. But such discernment has virtually disappeared today, displaced by the hermeneutic of trust: If you've come to us from Westminster, you must be alright, even if you don't sound like it. One can reasonably conclude that Westminster has been so effective "in inducting Orthodox Presbyterian ministerial candidates into a culture of interpretation" that it has become difficult if not impossible for many of these men to see that their *alma mater* – and consequently their denomi-

Wrightsaid List, January 5, 2004; reproduced with his permission at www.ntwrightpage.com/Green_Westminster_Seminary_Perspective.pdf. Emphases in the original.

56. We could cite many more examples along the same lines from past volumes of the *WTJ*.

nation – are both in the deepest and most fundamental trouble. Sadly, many of these men are in the thick of the trouble themselves.

An Unsafe House

As we said at the beginning of this chapter, the principles and methodology of hermeneutics are like the unseen supports of a house – the foundation under the basement, the wood inside the walls. The house – the part that we see – is the interpretation of the Scriptures, and the system of doctrine we derive from that interpretation.

If we employ sound interpretive principles, and we employ them carefully and consistently, our system of doctrine will be correctly derived from the words of Scripture. We will believe the right things, because we will believe what God says. Spiritually speaking, our doctrine will be a house that is safe for us to live in.

But if sound interpretive principles and methodology have been gradually undermined, our system of doctrine will be increasingly unsound. Our system of doctrine will not be correctly derived from the words of Scripture, and will often rely instead on the words of men. We will believe the wrong things, because we are being deceived. Spiritually speaking, we will be living in a house that is increasingly in danger of collapse. If we go on living in that house, we will do so at the peril of our souls.

Use of the hermeneutic of trust in the OPC has gradually undermined sound interpretive principles and methods. Human authority has displaced Biblical authority. This is the hallmark of the Biblical Theology movement, perspectivalism, and redemptive-historical approach to Scripture.

When such false principles are applied to the Gospel, as is being done in the OPC and elsewhere, the result is just the kind of confusion that the enemy of men's souls desires.

Many men in the OPC have adopted a perspective that redefines justification by faith as Norman Shepherd and others do: a final declaration of righteousness at the Last Judgment, based on personal righteousness achieved through covenant faithfulness. Others define justification by faith as Scripture does: God's once-for-all legal declaration that a sinner is righteous at his conversion, based on the imputed righteousness of Christ alone, and received by faith alone. Yet the logic of the hermeneutic of trust says that those who have the Gospel right are to embrace those who have the Gospel wrong as brothers in Christ, and live together in harmony within the same church. The results are deadly: The preaching of the authentic Gospel is displaced by the preaching of a "faith" that does not save. Many people in the pews are resting in the false comfort of a false gospel that is carrying them contentedly on their way to Hell.

Under such conditions it is not surprising that Norman Shepherd's heresies, which were allowed to take root over thirty years ago, have spread like a cancer in the years since. It is not surprising that Shepherd and his followers continue to be welcome in many parts of the OPC. It is not surprising that Richard Gaffin's teachings have become the dominant position at Westminster Seminary in Philadelphia, and have flowed from there into the churches of the OPC and other denominations. It is not surprising that John Kinnaird's heresy conviction was overturned, that a perspectivalist view of a key passage (*Romans* 2:13) was used to support that decision, or that those who had found him guilty were said to be the ones in error.

It is not surprising that the OPC General Assembly should endorse the false principle, in the creation committee *Report*, that inclusivist interpretations of confessional standards trump the faithful interpretation of Scripture. It is not surprising that articles in the *Westminster Theological Journal* that deny or radically redefine the doctrine of Biblical inerrancy have produced no outcry of alarm.

It is not surprising that Douglas Green, along with other members of the Westminster faculty and administration,[57] attended the 2005 Auburn Avenue Pastors Conference to listen to three days of false teaching from both featured speakers. It is not surprising that Richard Gaffin amicably shared the platform with N. T. Wright at AAPC 2005. Nor is it surprising that Gaffin's lectures at that conference set forth his own "new perspective on Paul" which is just as much another gospel as Wright's.

And it is not surprising that the OPC should feel the need to assemble a study committee with representatives of various *perspectives* on the doctrine of justification (including Richard Gaffin), to give its judgment regarding teachings that were forever settled as heresy in the pages of the New Testament.

The Orthodox Presbyterian Church has become, doctrinally and spiritually speaking, an unsafe house. Over a period of decades, the sound principles and methodology of grammatical-historical hermeneutics have been displaced

57. In addition to Green and Gaffin, the other WTS professors attending Auburn 2005 were Peter Enns; J. Alan Groves, head of the Old Testament Department; Dan G. McCartney, head of the New Testament Department; and Stephen S. Taylor, Associate Professor of New Testament, all from the Philadelphia campus; also Steven Vanderhill, WTS Vice President and dean of the Dallas campus.

by redemptive-historical interpretations. Commitment to a Bible-derived system of doctrine has been displaced by an artificial, inclusivist confessionalism where doctrine is no longer even derived directly from the words of God in Scripture but from interpretations of the words of fallible men in the *Confession* and *Catechisms*.

What is worse, thousands of people in the pews are being deceived. Spiritually speaking, they are living in a house that is in imminent danger of collapse, though most do not realize it. Most of them continue living contentedly in that house, week after week, assuming that their denomination is still a bastion of doctrinal conservatism and that liberalism is something on the outside. Those who go on living in such a house, and under such misconceptions, do so at the peril of their souls.

Chapter 9

How Did It Happen?

*And Elijah came to all the people, and said,
"How long will you falter between two opinions?
If the LORD is God, follow Him; but if Baal, follow him."
But the people answered him not a word.*
1 Kings 18:21

A t the beginning of this book, we said that the cancer of neo-liberalism has grown and spread, slowly and subtly, for at least three decades in the Orthodox Presbyterian Church and beyond. We asked readers to examine the evidence, which we said is ample and growing.

In the first eight chapters we have presented some of that evidence, but by no means all; the whole would fill several volumes this size. We have seen how the cancer of neo-liberalism spread from Westminster Theological Seminary into the Orthodox Presbyterian Church, and how it has spread beyond it into other denominations and institutions.

The evidence substantiates the definition of neo-liberalism we gave at the outset: *It is the denial of fundamentals of authentic Biblical Christianity by reputedly conservative churchmen, who simultaneously claim that they remain completely faithful to Scripture and to the doctrinal standards of their churches.* Neo-liberals pretend to be what they are not, and profess to believe what they do not.

As we have shown, neo-liberalism principally manifests itself in the denial of the inerrancy, infallibility, and author-

287

ity of Scripture and the denial of the Gospel doctrine of justification by faith (mere belief) in Christ alone. But from
those two fundamental errors, as we have seen, the cancer
spreads to corrupt sound teaching on other foundational
truths including creation, the covenants, baptism, the
church, sanctification, adoption, glorification, the Last Judgment, even the doctrine of Christ himself.

We have shown that neo-liberalism bears many of the
marks of the old liberalism that came to dominate the
PCUSA three generations ago. We have demonstrated the
unmistakable parallels between developments in the PCUSA
that led to the formation of the OPC in 1936 and developments in the OPC itself today. We have seen that neo-
liberalism gives new life to centuries-old heresies; the errors
of church history are being repeated. We have shown that it
is neo-liberals who are the schismatics, not those who oppose them; it is the neo-liberals who have departed from
Scripture and have thus sown discord. We have also seen
that neo-liberals employ strategies and tactics that can only
be described as ungodly.

As we said at the outset, to call the situation a crisis is no
overstatement.

Some of you, perhaps many, began reading this book
with skepticism. Some doubted that such a thing as neo-
liberalism existed. Some were bound by the no-liberals-in-
our-church paradigm we described in chapter two. Some
doubted that neo-liberalism had spread, like a cancer, from
Westminster Theological Seminary in Philadelphia into the
pulpits and agencies of the Orthodox Presbyterian Church
and beyond. Some doubted the claims that deep and lasting
spiritual damage had been done.

If you have gotten this far in this book, and you are
convinced that there is a spiritual crisis in the OPC and

beyond, we thank God the Holy Spirit for His gracious work. We take no credit for persuading anyone; if you have been convinced, it may well be despite our lack of skill in presenting the evidence. If you are not yet convinced, we pray for the sake of your soul that in time you will be, because nothing less than the welfare of your soul, and the souls of your family members, is at stake.

There remain, however, two questions yet to be fully addressed: *How did it happen? How should Christians respond?* In this chapter we shall address the first question, and in our final chapter we shall turn to the second.

How, then, did it happen? How did a seminary and a denomination that began well come to this? How did the cancer begin, and how did it spread? We have touched on the answer along the way, but now we shall focus on it: *There has been a profound loss of spiritual discernment in Christian academia and in the church. This loss of discernment is the result of the influences of secular thinking – what Scripture calls "the wisdom of this world" or "the wisdom of this age"* (1 Corinthians 1:20, 2:6). This loss of discernment made the growth and spread of neo-liberalism possible.

In what specific ways does the loss of discernment manifest itself in Christian academia and in the church? How does it bear upon the present crisis? We can name at least ten ways, and we shall discuss them in this chapter.

Loss of Discernment Regarding Scripture

There has been a catastrophic loss of discernment in Christian academia and the church regarding the authority and interpretation of Scripture. This is foundational. Much of Reformed academia has abandoned (or holds increasing contempt for) grammatical-historical principles and methods for the interpretation of Scripture. As men trained in this mindset have made their way into the churches, the problem has spread. Christian academia and the church seem to have forgotten that grammatical-historical princeples and methods, as we saw in chapter eight, are derived from Scripture and therefore carry Biblical authority. This loss of discernment has facilitated the rise of the Biblical Theology movement and redemptive-historical methods, with their man-centered approaches to Scripture. It has also facilitated the rise of perspectivalism, where all perspectives are valid in principle for the interpretation of Scripture, and the Bible is no longer acknowledged to be its own interpreter. Human wisdom has become the measure of all things, and the wisdom of this present age says that there is no singular truth, only the viewpoints of various communities of interpreters.

Because academia and the church have increasingly abandoned the sure foundation of Scripture as its own interpreter, seminary professors, many ministers, and even people in the pews have become like the philosophers of Mars Hill, who "spent their time in nothing else but either to tell or to hear some new thing" (*Acts* 17:21). When we are open to anything and everything, and blindly trust our spiritual well-being to the learned specialist, we are vulnerable to the snare of equating "fresh interpretation" with superior insight. The neo-liberals have long ago fallen into this trap themselves, and lead others into it by the thousands.

This is not to deprecate theological education if it is of the right kind – self-consciously committed to Scripture alone as the Word of God. Christians whose formal theological training is limited, or who have none at all, are better off than the most learned theologian if they are fully committed to the authority of Scripture and its proper interpretation, when the learned theologian is not. The "lay" Christian who employs sound principles of interpretation and does the work of a Berean will soon understand just how wrong and how spiritually deadly the "fresh interpretations" of the neo-liberals actually are.

We need to remember the warning of Peter concerning those who twist the Scriptures:

> Therefore, beloved, looking forward to these things, be diligent to be found by Him in peace, without spot and blameless; and consider that the longsuffering of our Lord is salvation — as also our beloved brother Paul, according to the wisdom given to him, has written to you, as also in all his epistles, speaking in them of these things, in which are some things hard to understand, which untaught and unstable people twist to their own destruction, as they do also the rest of the Scriptures.
>
> You therefore, beloved, since you know this beforehand, beware lest you also fall from your own steadfastness, being led away with the error of the wicked; but grow in the grace and knowledge of our Lord and Savior Jesus Christ [2 *Peter* 3:14-18].

Loss of Discernment Regarding Systematics

The loss of discernment regarding the interpretation of Scripture has facilitated the neglect of (and often a barely-concealed contempt for) systematic theology in Christian academia. The fact that Scripture contains a God-breathed system of doctrine, consistent from *Genesis* to *Revelation*, must be one of the Bible believer's key guiding principles. When we devalue or abandon this principle, as the modern

Biblical Theology movement does, the result is a growing ignorance of the system of doctrine contained in Scripture. Under such conditions it is all too easy to abandon systematic presentation of Bible doctrine through chapter-by-chapter, verse-by-verse preaching of the Word, and to focus instead on pet doctrinal theories allegedly supported by pet passages. Isolated and narrow treatment of doctrinal subjects can easily lead to un-Biblical treatment of them. And that, history shows us, is also how cults are born. Some schools of thought in neo-liberalism, such as the Federal Vision, evince cultish traits.

While Christian academia and the church need to regain lost discernment about the systematic nature of Bible doctrine, they also need to be carefully constrained in the use of confessions and catechisms. In the context of the classroom or the church these can be helpful tools for understanding the systematic nature of Bible doctrine and studying that system. But they are no substitute for the immersion of all Christians – professors and students, ordained men and church members – in the Word of God itself, and in an ever more intimate knowledge of the Living Word, Jesus Christ. That is the way the people of God will come to think God's thoughts after Him.

Practically speaking, a way of thinking that puts confessions and catechisms above Scripture is inculcated into the minds of many Reformed ministers from the beginning. Men who come before presbyteries for licensure and ordination to the ministry are often coached to simply recite passages from the *Confession* and *Catechisms* in response to questions during their theological examinations, rather than to cite Scripture itself and expound the system of doctrine directly from it. This practice plays into the hands of neo-liberals by helping to conceal men's true positions as well as their lack of grounding in systematics, permitting error to cloak itself in the language of orthodoxy. In this regard, it is also telling that all the OPC offered the church in the *71ˢᵗ General Assembly Statement on Justification* was a rote recitation of passages from the *Confession* and *Catechisms*.[1] Neo-liberals profess loyalty to those words, while preaching another gospel that is contrary to the system of doctrine revealed in Scripture. They get away with it because of widespread ignorance of that system of doctrine.

It is no wonder, then, that such problems among men of the pulpits also affect people in the pews. Many members of Reformed churches who have memorized long portions of the *Catechisms* cannot quote from memory more than a bare handful of Scripture passages such as *John* 3:16 and the Lord's Prayer. Many who have spent untold hours being instructed from the *Confession of Faith* could not find God's covenant with Abraham in the Bible on their own, or explain what it means from Scripture itself; many do not know where to find the New Testament's frequent warnings concerning false teachers; many do not know enough Scripture to lead someone to Christ; in fact, many know relatively little about Christ. Many people in Reformed churches simply do not know how to use their Bibles to understand its system of doctrine. They have not been equipped to search the Scriptures to see if the things they are hearing in the church and in the classroom are true. That is a sad commentary on the state of the Reformed church.

The remedy for this is direct, continual, intimate contact with the Word of God. Academia and the church must not place confessions and catechisms between the people of

1. The *Statement* appears at www.opc.org/GA/justification2004.pdf.

God and His Word, which is what Rome does with its traditions. Confessions and catechisms, rightly used, are tools for teaching the Word itself, and for teaching submission to it. It is the Word of God that is the sword of the Spirit, not the words of men. It is the Word of God that is forever settled in Heaven. It is the Word of God that is alive and powerful. It is the Word of God that is the discerner of the thoughts and intents of the heart. It is the Word of God that we are instructed to commit to memory so that we might not sin, and so that we can discern truth from error. It is the entrance of the Word that gives light and understanding. It is the Word of faith preached, heard, and believed, that saves sinners by bringing them to the knowledge of Christ.

Christian academia and the church must continually remind the people of God that the best thing men can do is to understand and believe the system of doctrine revealed in Scripture, and submit to its authority in every area of life. They must also remind God's people that the best confession men have devised is a moon having no glory of its own, which merely reflects the blazing sunlight of Scripture.

Christian academia and the church must always practice two key principles concerning God's Word: It is complete, and it is univocal. These principles underpin systematic theology. Employing these principles means that Scripture must be approached and understood as a whole, not as a collection of disjointed parts. The believer's interest can never be merely in what Moses, Isaiah, Paul, James, or Peter has to say about a given matter of doctrine in a particular book or passage, because not a single word of Scripture is the mere word of man. In and of themselves, each of the human writers had nothing authoritative to say; but the Spirit of God spoke through every one of them, and therefore they wrote with one voice, without contradiction or paradox, from *Genesis* to *Revelation*. God the Holy Spirit gave one, and only one, system of doctrine to His people.

> Now the Spirit expressly says that in latter times some will depart from the faith, giving heed to deceiving spirits and doctrines of demons, speaking lies in hypocrisy, having their own conscience seared with a hot iron [1 *Timothy* 4:1-2].

> For a bishop [overseer] must be...holding fast the faithful word as he has been taught, that he may be able, by sound doctrine, both to exhort and convict those who contradict [*Titus* 1:7-9].

> [The Bereans] received the word with all readiness, and searched the Scriptures daily to find out whether these things were so [*Acts* 17:11].

> Be mindful of the words which were spoken before by the holy prophets, and of the commandment of us, the apostles of the Lord and Savior [2 *Peter* 3:2].

> All Scripture is given by inspiration of God, and is profitable for doctrine, for reproof, for correction, for instruction in righteousness, that the man of God may be complete, thoroughly equipped for every good work. I charge you therefore before God and the Lord Jesus Christ, who will judge the living and the dead at His appearing and His kingdom: Preach the word! Be ready in season and out of season. Convince, rebuke, exhort, with all longsuffering and teaching. For the time will come when they will not endure sound doctrine, but according to their own desires, because they have itching ears, they will heap up for themselves teachers;

and they will turn their ears away from the truth, and be turned aside to fables. But you be watchful in all things, endure afflictions, do the work of an evangelist, fulfill your ministry [2 *Timothy* 3:16-4:5].

Loss of Discernment Regarding Doctrinal Consistency

There has been a loss of discernment in Christian academia and the church regarding the necessity of doctrinal consistency. Some false teachers have gained a popular following based largely on the fact that they take conservative positions on certain issues. But their outward conservatism is a spiritual Trojan horse. Once these false teachers have gained entry among the undiscerning, the way is open for them to spread heresy on much more vital matters. The loss of discernment regarding the imperative of doctrinal consistency often goes hand in hand with the loss of discernment regarding the systematic nature of Bible doctrine.

N. T. Wright has articulately defended certain doctrines where he is closer to Biblical truth – for example, the historicity of Christ's resurrection.[2] But at the same time Wright, through his extensive speaking and voluminous writing, teaches heresy regarding justification by faith and other essential doctrines. Douglas Wilson has gained a following as a leader in the classical Christian school movement.[3] But

2. Dr. D. James Kennedy featured Wright in a Coral Ridge Ministries television program, *Who Is This Jesus: Is He Risen?* broadcast on March 20, 2005, and also sold on DVD.

3. Wilson is the author of *The Case for Classical Christian Education* (Wheaton, Illinois: Crossway Books, 2002) and a frequent speaker at Christian school conferences.

at the same time he teaches grievous error on a wide spectrum of doctrines.[4] Dr. Peter Lillback has attracted a growing audience in his roles as a conservative activist on social issues and as a leader in educating Americans about the nation's Christian heritage.[5] But at the same time he defends and promulgates the heresies of Norman Shepherd.

Because Wright, Wilson, Lillback and others take positions that are popular with conservatives on certain doctrines or social issues, many who are not discerning about doctrinal consistency make the mistake of assuming that these men teach authentic Biblical Christianity across the board. Thus the undiscerning have opened the door for such men to exert broad theological influence, and to poison the church. The Pharisees were the social conservatives and leaders in religious education of their day. They made much of their heritage as well. But they too had abandoned the authority of Scripture and preached salvation by faith-plus-works. Jesus repeatedly condemned their hypocrisy, and made it clear that their heritage and conservatism meant nothing apart from personal faith in Him alone (*e.g.*, *Matthew* 23; *John* 3:10, 8:36-59).

Loss of Discernment Regarding the Gospel

Today, false teachers add many things to the authentic Gospel. Some of them are Biblical in their proper context: doctrines such as baptism, sanctification, adoption, and

4. For a detailed critique of Wilson's theology see John W. Robbins and Sean Gerety, *Not Reformed at All: Medievalism in "Reformed" Churches* (Unicoi, Tennessee: The Trinity Foundation, 2004).

5. Lillback is, in addition to his other positions, president of The Providence Forum.

participation in the visible church. These stem from the Gospel or are related to it, but they are not the Gospel itself. Other additions to the Gospel, such as a "final justification" at the Last Judgment, are not Biblical at all. All of these additions to the authentic Gospel take us back to the Dark Ages before the Reformation. The Reformers recovered the Biblical distinctions that had long been shrouded in darkness by Rome. Christians today must regain discernment concerning the nature of the Gospel. We must remember that it is not something to be done, or experienced, or participated in, but simply *believed*:

> Moreover, brethren, I declare to you the Gospel which I preached to you, which also you received and in which you stand, by which also you are saved, if you hold fast that word which I preached to you – unless you believed in vain. For I delivered to you first of all that which I also received: that Christ died for our sins according to the Scriptures, and that He was buried, and that He rose again the third day according to the Scriptures [1 *Corinthians* 15:1-4].

We need also to remember the later warning of Paul to these same Corinthians about their subsequent lack of discernment regarding the true nature of the Gospel:

> I am jealous for you with godly jealousy. For I have betrothed you to one husband, that I may present you as a chaste virgin to Christ. But I fear, lest somehow, as the serpent deceived Eve by his craftiness, so your minds may be corrupted from the simplicity that is in Christ. For if he who comes preaches another Jesus whom we have not preached, or if you receive a different spirit which you have not received, or a different

gospel which you have not accepted – you may well put up with it! [2 *Corinthians* 11:2-4].

Loss of Discernment Regarding Evangelism and the Church

There can be no evangelism – for that matter, there is no *basis* for evangelism – without a Biblical view of sin. Sin is what makes evangelism necessary in the first place. But neo-liberal false teachings about salvation all involve a diminished view of sin. Neo-liberals say that one becomes part of the covenant community through baptism and remains in the covenant community through law-keeping and partaking of the Lord's Supper.[6] Neo-liberals say that one develops a personal righteousness and is justified at the Last Judgment on that basis. What is diminished – and often entirely missing – is the Bible's teaching regarding the utter sinfulness of sin, and the thoroughness of the pollution of sin in every part of our being. Justification is not, according to neo-liberal theology, as much about the restoration of man's relationship with a holy creator God that has been broken because of sin as it is about establishing human relationships with others within the visible church.

The neo-liberal false gospels do not require the church member to face the issue of personal sin squarely and see himself as God sees him – already declared guilty, already condemned, already on the brink of Hell, and utterly helpless and hopeless apart from believing in the propitiation of the wrath of God by the blood of Jesus Christ. It is only when a member of the visible church (or someone who is not, for that

6. Under this influence, a growing number of churches refer to the Supper as the "service of covenant renewal."

matter) is moved by the preaching of the Word and the work of the Holy Spirit to face the issue of his sin, and to believe in Christ's propitiation, that he becomes a member of the *invisible* church – the true Church of Christ for all eternity.

The false gospels provide a psychological escape for those who seek a "salvation" that does not require them to fully face up to the desperation of their sin problem. As Jesus said to Nicodemus:

> [T]his is the condemnation, that the light has come into the world, and men loved darkness rather than light, because their deeds were evil. For everyone practicing evil hates the light and does not come to the light, lest his deeds should be exposed [*John* 3:19-20].

Thus also the covenant successionists deceive many into thinking there is no need to evangelize baptized children. But the sin problem is inescapable for young and old, baptized or unbaptized, and evangelism is essential.

We need to look to Scripture, not the sinful human mind, for our authority regarding evangelism and the nature of the church. The loss of discernment concerning the true nature of evangelism and the distinction between the visible and the invisible church has facilitated the proclamation of false comfort to sinners. Christ's words throughout the *Gospels*, and *Romans* 1 through 3, plainly teach the centrality of the depth of man's sin and his inability to save himself. One can choose to deny or to obscure that truth, but only at one's eternal peril. It remains the truth by which God will judge all men.

The fourth and fifth chapters of *Romans*, the book of *Galatians*, and the end of *2 Corinthians* 5, all plainly teach that justification is God's act in declaring sinners righteous, thus restoring a right "vertical" relationship with Him. Scripture is clear: Justification is not about our "horizontal" relationships with one another in the visible church. We must maintain a Biblical view of the evangelistic message:

> Blessed is he whose transgression is forgiven, whose sin is covered. Blessed is the man to whom the Lord does not impute iniquity, and in whose spirit there is no deceit.... I acknowledged my sin to You, and my iniquity I have not hidden. I said, "I will confess my transgresssions to the Lord," and You forgave the iniquity of my sin [*Psalm* 32:1, 2, 5].

Loss of Discernment Regarding the World

There has been a loss of discernment concerning secular acceptance and approval. This is most noticeable in Christian academia, but the problem also affects the church as a result. Dr. James White observes:

> Large numbers of Christian scholars, with few and precious exceptions, have chosen to walk the path of scholarship in general, choosing acceptance by the world as their highest priority.
>
> This may seem a sweeping generalization, but the assertion is all too easily proven...even Christian scholars have adopted the methodologies of secularism. Most importantly, even conservative Christian scholars have adopted a view of the foundation of the Christian faith (Scripture) that is not derived from a Christian worldview but from a secular paradigm.
>
> ...this fact accounts for the diminishment of the emphasis upon justification as a divine truth that is elemen-

tal to the church's proclamation within the context of the Christian ministry.[7]

Dr. Ligon Duncan notes that N. T. Wright's promotion of the New Perspective on Paul from his position of prominence as a bishop in the Anglican Church has helped gain acceptance for "evangelicals trying to work in a mainstream academic setting.... This is very impressive to a New Testament scholar who is scared of being viewed as a 'fundamentalist' by his/her colleagues, but who wants to stay an evangelical and still be respectable."[8] The same mentality grips those who are willing to deny the doctrine of creation in six literal days because they fear secular ridicule, and therefore embrace one of the popular compromise views of the *Genesis* account so they can still be called "evangelical." So it was also in Jesus' day:

> Nevertheless even among the rulers many believed in Him, but because of the Pharisees they did not confess Him, lest they should be put out of the synagogue; for they loved the praise of men more than the praise of God [*John* 12:42-43].

As we saw in chapter three, neo-liberals' doctrines are often nothing more than old heresies warmed over. But they often add new ingredients to the recipe, usually scavenged from the work of unbelieving scholars. The intellectual lineage of the New Perspective on Paul includes the works of Emil Schürer (1844-1910), a German liberal theologian;

7. James R. White, *The God Who Justifies* (Bloomington, Minnesota: Bethany House Publishers, 2001), 36.

8. J. Ligon Duncan, "Attractions of the New Perspective(s) on Paul," reproduced at www.christianity.com/partner/Article_Display_Page/0,, PTID307086 I CHID559376 I CIID1660662,00.html.

Claude Montefiore (1858-1938), a founder of Liberal Judaism; George Foot Moore (1851-1931), a liberal American Presbyterian; Max Weber (1864-1920), the German sociologist who advocated "value-free" social science; Rudolf Bultmann (1884-1976), a noted spokesman for liberal/skeptical methods of Biblical interpretation who advocated replacement of "traditional" theology with existential philosophy; and Krister Stendahl (born 1921), liberal Lutheran Bishop of Stockholm and former dean of Harvard Divinity School.

The loss of discernment about secular acceptance and approval can naturally lead to seeking the unbelieving world's counsel on spiritual matters as well. A number of Reformed seminaries are contributing members and users of the services of In Trust, a consortium of seminaries and divinity schools, whose mission is

> to educate and inform those responsible for the governance of the graduate theological schools of North America. In Trust provides the members of its audience with the insights they need to function more effectively as leaders, illuminates the issues likely to engage their governing boards, and offers forums in which they can share with each other what they have learned.[9]

Over one hundred schools are In Trust members and associates. The vast majority of them are Roman Catholic, Jewish, and mainline liberal Protestant institutions; but also among them are the PCA's Covenant Theological Seminary, Gordon-Conwell Theological Seminary, Reformed Theological Seminary, Westminster Theological Seminary in Philadelphia, and Westminster Seminary in California.

9. From the mission statement at www.intrust.org.

The president of In Trust is Dr. Christa R. Klein, an associate professor of church history at St. Mary's Seminary (Roman Catholic) in Baltimore.[10] Over the years the members of the In Trust board of governors and staff have come primarily from unbelieving institutions – religious in name, pagan in reality. The In Trust web site states:

> Our board of governors is drawn widely from the world of theological education and governance. The members' extensive experience guides us as we chart our future, broaden our approach, and model good governance for those we would teach.

In Trust publishes a quarterly magazine of the same name which offers advice to its member institutions. In an article titled "Presidential Vision: Anticipating Where the Church is Heading," Vincent DePaul Cushing, a Franciscan priest, former In Trust board member, and consultant to In Trust member seminaries, writes:

> Today, some respected churches and confessions choose to flee into a romantic, cherished past, a past impossible to regain.

10. Klein's husband Leonard was a prominent long-time pastor in the liberal Evangelical Lutheran Church in America (ELCA). They both converted to Roman Catholicism in 2003. In June 2005 Leonard Klein was ordained to the ministry of Transitional Deacon in the Roman Catholic Church. Since Vatican Council II the papacy has placed greater emphasis on this office (and that of Permanent Deacon) as a "way home to Rome" for Protestant ministers. By being ordained as deacons, Protestant ministers converting to Romanism can perform most of the functions of a priest – assisting in the celebration of the Mass, preaching at Mass, and performing baptisms, marriages, and funerals. The only major differences between a deacon and a priest in the Romanist system are that the deacon cannot officiate at the Mass or (supposedly) offer absolution of sins.

We must develop a vibrant, energy-laden, compelling vision of where the church should be going.

Note what it is we need to envision. It is not the vision of where the school is going, but rather where the church should be going. Then in the light of that, one asks, "What is the best education for ministry to ensure that that church will come to be?" Moreover, envisioning the church's future and enabling its realization are noble tasks and constitute a vibrant intellectual challenge for the thoughtful [seminary] president.

The president's task, thus, is to engage in social analysis, then use the findings to envision the school's future as an education for the ministry. This means being steeped in the Christian tradition as the foundation for exploring the key questions of catechesis and hermeneutics.

I believe the president and [seminary] board are, by position and vocation, futurists who believe in the possibility of the institution making a difference in the future that will carry forth the gospel as a treasure of meaning and a statement of hope.[11]

Just what "gospel" this is, just which confessions belong to "a romantic, cherished past, a past impossible to regain," how questions of catechesis and hermeneutics are to be "explored" through social analysis, and where the In Trust consortium thinks "the church should be going," we can only imagine. But In Trust does give us clues. *In Trust* magazine editor Jay Blossom writes:

11. Vincent DePaul Cushing, "A Presidential Vision: Anticipating Where the Church Is Headed," *In Trust* magazine, Summer 2000, reproduced at www.intrust.org/magazine/pastarticle.cfm?&id=220.

North American theological education is a riotous garden, filled with bees, bugs and blooms of all kinds. At In Trust, we share some of that bounty, try to make sense of it, and offer tips for the gardeners of such a great gift.[12]

Here is a sampling of *In Trust* articles providing "tips" for those who tend this garden of apostasy and syncretism:

- A transcript of a speech on the education of ministers by Josef Ratzinger, now Pope Benedict XVI.

- "A Sacred Heart: Meditations on Vulnerability, Leadership, and a Life Fully Lived," in which "the authors, both Jewish, obliquely explore two Christian images, the Crucifixion and the Catholic devotion of the Sacred Heart of Jesus,[13] to plumb the spiritual depths of inspired leadership."

- "Go Out into All the World: How Schools Attract Those Who Would Be Doers of the Word."

- "Capitalizing on Our Differences."

- "Bridging the Divide: Conversations Lead to Collaboration and Cooperation."

- "Let Not Theology Put Asunder."

The last three articles explored ways to bring varying theological "perspectives" together in seminaries and minimize doctrinal differences.

---

12. www.intrust.org/who/staff.cfm.

13. This idolatrous veneration of the "wounded heart of Jesus," includes prayers to it using special beads, offerings, a feast day, and other acts of devotion. Devotees "cling firmly to it as one of their strongest hopes of ennoblement and salvation." See "Devotion to the Sacred Heart of Jesus," *Catholic Encyclopedia*, www.newadvent.org/cathen/07163a.htm.

In 2001, the In Trust magazine included an article which lamented the fact that a female Master of Divinity student at Westminster Theological Seminary was "rebuffed" when she sought, along with her husband, to come under care of a PCA presbytery (the first step toward licensure and ordination to the ministry).[14]

The In Trust web site includes an area where the member schools in this theological Babel are asked to pray for one another, and member institutions can post specific prayer requests. Machen well described such a thing as "prayer in the house of Rimmon."[15]

The spirit of Antichrist is in all of this. Yet a number of the Reformed seminaries mentioned above not only helped found such an endeavor, but according to the In Trust web site they continue to lend their support and use its services year by year. As we noted in chapter one, nearly half the members of the current Westminster Philadelphia faculty have degrees from apostate seminaries and graduate schools; most of those schools are also members of In Trust.

In sharp contrast to all of these examples, Scripture commands believers not to seek the acceptance, approval, or counsel of the secular world (which includes false religions) in spiritual matters. We must recognize that if anyone is not regenerated by the Holy Spirit, and if any individual or organization is not in submission to the Word of God, then they have absolutely nothing to say to the true Church of the Lord Jesus Christ about what its theology is or should be, or how it should train men for the ministry.

14. Bob Bettson, "How Congregations Can Promote Vocations," *In Trust* magazine, first quarter 2001, reproduced at www.intrust.org/magazine/article.cfm?id=178.

15. *J. Gresham Machen: Selected Shorter Writings*, 147.

Adulterers and adulteresses! Do you not know that friendship with the world is enmity with God? Whoever therefore wants to be a friend of the world makes himself an enemy of God. Or do you think that the Scripture says in vain, "The Spirit who dwells in us yearns jealously"? [*James* 4:4-5].

They are of the world. Therefore they speak as of the world, and the world hears them. We are of God. He who knows God hears us; he who is not of God does not hear us. By this we know the spirit of truth and the spirit of error [*1 John* 4:5-6].

Let no one deceive himself. If anyone among you seems to be wise in this age, let him become a fool that he may become wise. For the wisdom of this world is foolishness with God. For it is written, "He catches the wise in their own craftiness," and again, "The Lord knows the thoughts of the wise, that they are futile." Therefore let no one boast in men. For all things are yours...and you are Christ's, and Christ is God's [*1 Corinthians* 3:18-23].

For you see your calling, brethren, that not many wise according to the flesh, not many mighty, not many noble, are called. But God has chosen the foolish things of the world to put to shame the wise, and God has chosen the weak things of the world to put to shame the things which are mighty; and the base [lowly] things of the world and the things which are despised God has chosen, and the things which are not, to bring to nothing the things that are, that no flesh should glory in His presence. But of Him you are in Christ Jesus, who became for us wisdom from God – and righteousness and sanctification and redemption – that, as it is written, "He who glories, let him glory in the Lord" [*1 Corinthians* 1:26-31].

Loss of Discernment Regarding Human Wisdom

Many of the neo-liberal spokesmen are clever, articulate, and even witty speakers and writers. They definitely have a way with words. Many of them are personally charming and engaging. Some of them have taken on a celebrity status among their followers. The undiscerning, focusing on these outward appearances, let down their guard and open their minds to heresy with hardly a second thought. One wonders how they would have reacted to the Apostle Paul:

> But as for myself, having come to you, brethren, I came, not having my message dominated by a transcend-dent rhetorical display or by philosophical subtlety when I was announcing to you the testimony of God, for, after weighing the issues, I decided not to know anything among you except Jesus Christ and this very One as crucified. And as for myself, when I faced you, I fell into a state of weakness and fear and much trembling. And my message and my preaching were not couched in specious words of philosophy but were dependent for their efficacy upon a demonstration of the Spirit and of power, in order that your faith should not be resting in human philosophy but in God's power [1 Corinthians 2:1-5].[16]

> Now I urge you, brethren, note those who cause divisions and offenses, contrary to the doctrine which you learned, and avoid them. For those who are such do not serve our Lord Jesus Christ, but their own belly, and by smooth words and flattering speech deceive the hearts of the simple [Romans 16:17-18].

16. Kenneth S. Wuest, *The New Testament: An Expanded Translation* (Grand Rapids, Michigan: William B. Eerdmans Company, 1961).

But evil men and impostors will grow worse and worse, deceiving and being deceived [2 *Timothy* 3:13].

For such are false apostles, deceitful workers, transforming themselves into apostles of Christ. And no wonder! For Satan himself transforms himself into an angel of light. Therefore it is no great thing if his ministers also transform themselves into ministers of righteousness, whose end will be according to their works [2 *Corinthians* 11:13-15].

The Apostle urges believers to stand firm in Christ and in the Scriptures,

that we should no longer be children, tossed to and fro and carried about with every wind of doctrine, by the trickery of men, in the cunning craftiness of deceitful plotting, but, speaking the truth in love, may grow up in all things into Him who is the head – Christ [*Ephesians* 4:14-15].

Loss of Discernment Regarding Church History

Neo-liberals frequently take advantage of their hearers' lack of familiarity with church history to distort that history in support of their false teachings. They often get away with it because average churchgoers, as well as many ordained men, don't know any better.

Admittedly, not everyone has the time or desire to become a student of church history, much less an expert. But Christians must recognize the fact that just because neo-liberals quote the Reformers, that does not make them careful students (or honest reporters) of church history. On the contrary, they are all too willing to play fast and loose with the facts of church history and the words of the Reformers to advance their agendas. Advocates of the Federal Vision and New Perspective on Paul frequently erect "straw man" versions of the teachings of Augustine, Luther, and others on which to launch their attacks. Neo-liberals frequently distort the words of Calvin and the Scottish Reformers to portray them as legalists, baptismal regenerationists, and covenant successionists. As Ligon Duncan observes, "If you don't know what the Reformers said, then you are vulnerable to having someone else tell you what they said, and tell you wrong, and you'll have no way of telling the difference."[17]

Neo-liberals also take advantage of the general loss of discernment regarding more recent church history. They engage in a good deal of revisionism to distance themselves from the false principles of the *Auburn Affirmation*, when in fact they readily embrace those principles (as we saw in chapter four). And if anyone expresses alarm about conditions in the OPC and calls attention to the strong parallels with developments in the PCUSA three generations ago, the neo-liberals and their enablers insist that "this isn't 1936," when, in fact, spiritually speaking, it is.

A chilling it-can't-happen-here sense of spiritual pride often accompanies this ignorance of church history. "After all," as one long-time presbyter told me more than once, and in all seriousness, "this is the *Orthodox* Presbyterian Church."

Christians need to understand that neo-liberalism, and the churches' ineffectual response to it, repeats the errors of church history. They need to understand that Scripture-submissive vigilance is the price of the preservation of sound doctrine. That is the reason we included two chapters of historical background in this book. Those who refuse to

17. Duncan, "The Attractions of the New Perspective(s) on Paul."

understand and learn from the errors of the past are bound not only to repeat them, but to suffer the resulting spiritual damage. Those who remain committed to authentic Biblical Christianity need to expose and refute neo-liberals' twisting of church history as well as their twisting of Scripture.

Loss of Discernment Regarding Doctrinal Indifference

Neo-liberals rely on the cooperation or inaction of the doctrinally indifferent to carry out their agenda. This is yet another important parallel between the crisis in the PCUSA three generations ago and the crisis in the OPC today.

The core liberals who signed the *Auburn Affirmation* comprised only fifteen percent of the ordained ministers and elders in the PCUSA, but they effectively controlled the denomination. It is quite probable that today the core neo-liberals – those who self-consciously embrace another gospel and openly reject the exclusive authority of Scripture – form roughly the same percentage in the OPC.

Machen and others estimated that perhaps another ten to fifteen percent of the PCUSA's ordained ministers and elders agreed with the signers of the *Auburn Affirmation*, but were unwilling to state their position as publicly. My research for this book indicates that today a similar percentage of the OPC's ordained men agree with the views of the core neo-liberals, but do not say so publicly.

This means that when the OPC was formed in 1936, probably only twenty-five to thirty percent of the ministers and ruling elders in the PCUSA could be identified as liberals. Likewise, it means that probably thirty percent or fewer can be identified as neo-liberals in the OPC today. Some would say this estimate is too high or too low. But in any event it appears that *self-conscious, open neo-liberalism* is a minority view in the OPC today, just as *self-conscious, open liberalism* was a minority view in the PCUSA three generations ago.

How, then, did a liberal minority come to dominate the PCUSA in the 1920s and 1930s, to the point where the formation of the OPC became necessary? And how does a neo-liberal minority dominate the OPC today?

The answer is this: *Now, as then, liberals rely on the cooperation, or at least inaction, of the doctrinally indifferent.* Three generations ago many referred to this group as the "moderates," but Machen more accurately described them by their mindset: "doctrinal indifferentism." The doctrinally indifferent were ministers, elders, and church members alike. They formed the plurality in the PCUSA's general assemblies and presbyteries. They also occupied most of the church pews. As we shall see, the doctrinally indifferent made up more than two-thirds of the membership of the PCUSA three generations ago.

Who are the doctrinally indifferent? It would be inaccurate to say that these people are merely *generally* indifferent, that is, apathetic. The doctrinally indifferent do care about other things. Their watchword is tolerance. They see controversy as one of the greatest evils, and they see tolerance of varying views under one big confessional tent as the way to avoid controversy, the way to put aside seemingly petty strife and focus on the greater good. We must all trust one another and work together, they say, even though we differ on basic doctrine (or, as they like to say, "we express the same doctrine differently"). Doctrinal disputes are an airing of dirty laundry that must be avoided. The pluralism and relativism of the secular mind dominate their thinking, and this produces spiritual indifference in matters of doctrine. Intolerance of error becomes the only intolerable thing. Machen's description of the doctrinally indifferent in the PCUSA applies equally to their counterparts in the OPC (and the Reformed church at large) today:

> ...[I]t is undoubtedly true that in many quarters there is a most lamentable ignorance regarding the greatest issue of the day [Christianity versus liberalism]. Such ignorance, with the indifference to which it gives rise, is sometimes very disheartening to those who are contending for the faith....
>
> Far more serious, however...is the injury to the souls of the indifferent people themselves. In very many cases, people who decry controversy have already lost, or are in process of losing, their own hold upon the great verities of the faith. They may not be conscious of relinquishing a single doctrine or a single fact that the Bible records. But the trouble is that what is not con-sciously given up in their minds has been removed from their hearts; they live only on the periphery of the Christian religion, and the really great things are lost from view. By such persons, whether in the pulpit or in the pew, the gospel is not indeed denied. But what is almost a worse thing than that is done – the gospel is not denied, but is simply ignored.[18]

Three generations ago, the doctrinally indifferent simply wanted peace at any price. When the controversy over the *Auburn Affirmation* was beginning to rage in 1924, Dr. Charles Erdman was elected moderator of the PCUSA General Assembly on this platform: "We need a moderator who stands for presenting a united front rather than the

18. J. Gresham Machen, "What Is the Gospel?" in *J. Gresham Machen: Selected Shorter Writings*, 124-125.

encouragement of controversy." Erdman himself said this: "I want the constructive work of the Presbyterian Church to go on without interruption on account of any doctrinal controversy." Machen responded:

> It would be impossible to put in any clearer way than is here done by Dr. Erdman the position of doctrinal indifferentism. And it would be impossible to imagine a position to which I am more conscientiously and more profoundly opposed. How can the constructive work of the Presbyterian church go on without interruption on account of any doctrinal controversy? The thing for which the Presbyterian church exists, I hold, is the propagation of a certain doctrine that we call the gospel of the Lord Jesus Christ. Only in that doctrine is Christ offered to men as their Savior. The church might do many other things—it might tinker with social conditions, it might use all sorts of palliative measures with men who have not been born again – but only by persuading men to accept the blessed "doctrine" or gospel can it save human souls. The church, I hold, is in the world to propagate a message; and if its propagation of the message is not clear, then, whatever else it does, it cannot possibly he said to be engaged in its "constructive work." [19]

The doctrinally indifferent also said that if there were problems in the church, Presbyterian polity must simply be allowed to do its work through the courts of the church. Erdman had said of the liberals in the PCUSA, "I believe the question about Dr. Fosdick and those who agree with him[20]

19. J. Gresham Machen, "Statement to the Committee to Investigate Princeton," in *J. Gresham Machen: Selected Shorter Writings*, 306-307.

20. See discussion of Fosdick and the *Auburn Affirmation* in chapter four.

should be settled according to the constitutional law of the Church. If these men are not loyal, let the law act."

Machen responded, "But what is meant by letting 'the law act'? A law never acts of itself; it does not act unless there is someone to enforce it."[21] Machen and other conservatives understood, as the doctrinally indifferent did not or would not, that church law can only be effective if administered by godly, Spirit-filled men committed to the one true Gospel and the authority of Scripture. Properly used, it is an orderly method for holding churches and individuals accountable to the authority of the Word of God. But in the PCUSA, as in the OPC three generations later, church law was badly abused. Not one of the nearly 1,300 signers of the *Auburn Affirmation* was ever disciplined in a court of the PCUSA; not a single case was ever brought to trial. All such efforts were blocked by liberals with the aid of the doctrinally indifferent. Machen described their attitude:

> With regard to that issue [authentic Christianity versus liberalism], three positions are possible and are actually being taken today. In the first place, one may stand unreservedly for the old faith and unreservedly against the indifferentist tendency in the modern church; in the second place, one may stand unreservedly for [liberalism] and against the old faith; and in the third place, one may ignore the seriousness of the issue and seek, without bringing it to a head, to preserve the undisturbed control of the present organization in the church.... Dr. Robert E. Speer [head of the PCUSA mission board at the time] certainly presents himself not as a [liberal] but as an adherent of the historic Christian faith;

21. Machen, "Statement to the Committee to Investigate Princeton."

yet he takes no clear stand in the great issue of the day, but rather adopts an attitude of reassurance and pallia- tion, according high praise and apparently far-reaching agreement to men of very destructive views.

It is this palliative or reassuring attitude which, we are almost inclined to think, constitutes the most serious menace to the life of the church today; it is in some ways doing more harm than clear-sighted [liberalism] can do. The representatives of it are often much further from the faith than they themselves know, and they are leading others much further away than they have been led themselves.[22]

Today the doctrinally indifferent in the OPC occupy the same position as their counterparts of three generations ago. Because they shun controversy over doctrine, and prize a false peace and counterfeit unity at all costs, they are often willingly ignorant of the facts of the present crisis. There are none so blind as those who will not see. In many cases they themselves have lost their grasp of the message of the Gospel. Therefore they cannot understand that this Gospel has for decades been under the most serious attack in the OPC, how damaging those attacks have been, and what is at stake as a result.

They do not understand that defending the faith is more than a formula of words. Today, when aroused from slumber and confronted with the facts, the doctrinally indifferent echo men like Erdman three generations ago. They protest that *if* the neo-liberals are not loyal – as though that were an

22. J. Gresham Machen, "Review of Robert Speer's *Some Living Issues*," in *J. Gresham Machen: Selected Shorter Writings*, 444-445. We have placed the terms "liberalism" and "liberal" in brackets in this passage where Machen used the equivalent terms "modernism" and "modernist."

open question – the courts of the church must be allowed to do their work. What they do not understand – or often do understand but refuse to admit – is that the courts of the OPC *have* done their work for thirty years. But the church courts have not prevented the crisis, they have caused it – and it is the doctrinally indifferent who have made that possible.

The doctrinally indifferent have facilitated the agenda of the neo-liberals for three decades. Without their cooperation, neo-liberals could not have concealed the teaching of another gospel at Westminster Seminary in the 1970s. Without their support, neo-liberals could not have prevented action against Norman Shepherd by the courts of the church in the 1970s and 1980s. Without their compliance and love of false peace, neo-liberals could not have sought to punish the godly men who exposed the evil taking place at Westminster Seminary and in the Presbytery of Philadelphia, and neo-liberals could not have succeeded in sullying those men's reputations. Without the aid of the doctrinally indifferent, neo-liberals could not have put a defender of the faith like Dr. Clinton Foraker out of his pulpit without judicial process. Without the compliance of the doctrinally indifferent, neo-liberals could not have succeeded in overturning John Kinnaird's heresy conviction. Without the cooperation of the doctrinally indifferent, neo-liberals would not have succeeded in stopping numerous efforts to right the wrongs of the Shepherd and Kinnaird cases. Without the support of the doctrinally indifferent, neo-liberals could not have come to dominate the faculty of Westminster Theological Seminary, where for decades they have promoted false gospels, and now ever more openly deny the inerrancy and unique authority of Scripture. Without the doctrinally indifferent vocally promoting it, there could be no deadly hermeneutic of trust at work in Reformed seminaries and churches.

Like Pontius Pilate and the careless Gallio of Achaia (*Acts* 18:12-17), the doctrinally indifferent have long sought to avoid taking clear positions on the most vital issues. They refuse to stand for authentic Christianity and against the counterfeit of neo-liberalism. Yet by "taking no position" they *do* take one. By consistently refusing to take the side of those who defend authentic Biblical Christianity, they have consistently given aid and comfort to the enemies of Christ.

Loss of Discernment Regarding Protestantism

There has been a loss of discernment concerning the nature of Roman Catholicism, what it means to be a Protestant, and the need to be vigorously Protestant. Today too few evangelicals, even in the Reformed church, really understand why the Reformation took place and what is at stake if it is reversed. Because of this, they do not understand that the spread of neo-liberalism means the reversal of the Reformation and the return to a spiritual Dark Age. Few neo-liberals publicly admit it, but the logical end of their doctrinal agenda will wipe out all that was recovered by the Reformers in the sixteenth century. Neo-liberals increasingly shun the name Protestant; today their preferred formulation for their movement in the direction of Rome is "Reformed catholicity."

Most nominal Protestants do not realize that Rome's centuries-old position, which is diametrically opposed to authentic Biblical Christianity on the central issues of Scripture and salvation, remains unchanged – as these passages from contemporary Catholic writings demonstrate:

> Protestants claim the following three qualities for justification: certainty, equality, the impossibility of ever losing it. Diametrically opposed to these qualities are those defended by the Council of Trent:

319

- uncertainty [no one can be sure he is justified]
- inequality [some are more justified than others]
- amissibility [justification can be lost].

Since these qualities of justification are also qualities of sanctifying grace, see [the entry on] Grace.[23]

[And so, from the entry on Grace] Every adult soul stained...with original sin...must, in order to arrive at the state of justification, pass through a short or long process of justification, which may be likened to the gradual development of the child in its mother's womb....

The Catholic idea maintains that the formal cause of justification does not consist in an exterior imputation of the justice of Christ but in a real, interior sanctification.... Although the sinner is justified by the justice of Christ, inasmuch as the Redeemer has merited for him the grace of justification, nevertheless he is formally justified and made holy by his own personal justice and holiness.[24]

The reason for the uncertainty of the state of grace lies in this, that without a special revelation nobody can with certainty of faith know whether or not he has fulfilled all the conditions that are necessary for achieving justification.[25]

23. "Justification" in *The Catholic Encyclopedia*, Vol. 8, www.new advent.org/cathen/08573a.htm. See also Dr. Ludwig Ott, *Fundamentals of Catholic Dogma*, (Rockford, Illinois: Tan Books, 1974), 261-263. The cover describes this book as "A one-volume encyclopedia of the doctrines of the Catholic Church, showing their sources in Scripture and Tradition and their definition by Popes and Councils." The book bears the *imprimatur* (mark of official approval) of Rome.

24. "Sanctifying Grace" in *The Catholic Encyclopedia*, reproduced at www.newadvent.org/cathen/06701a.htm. See also Ott, 250-252.

25. Ott, 262.

...[O]ver and above faith other acts are necessary for justification, such as fear, and hope, charity, penance with contrition, almsgiving.... Faith alone does not justify.

The "justification by faith alone" theory was by Luther styled the article of the standing and falling [of the] church (*articulus stantis et cadentis ecclesiae*), and by his followers was regarded as the material principle of Protestantism, just as the sufficiency of the Bible without tradition was considered its formal principle. Both of these principles are un-Biblical....[26]

Neo-liberal teachings on Scripture and salvation are essentially those of Rome above. Men like Norman Shepherd and N. T. Wright readily admit that they seek to reunite evangelicals and Roman Catholics. Since justification by faith alone and the authority of Scripture over church tradition were the basis of the sixteenth century break, it is their view that evangelicals and Catholics must reach an understanding on these points that will facilitate re-union.

But Antichristian Rome is patiently intransigent while neo-liberals are increasingly eager suitors; the ever more one-sided "compromises" in the *Evangelicals and Catholics Together* documents demonstrate this clearly. Reaching an "understanding" with Rome by definition means the surrender of authentic Biblical Christianity recovered at the Reformation, and Rome will not be satisfied until the surrender is complete. Thus neo-liberalism's displacement of Protestantism in Reformed churches such as the OPC and PCA is a most welcome development to the Papists. The conditions that Martyn Lloyd-Jones observed in the United

26. *Catholic Encyclopedia*, entry on "Sanctifying Grace." See also Ott, 5-6, 253-254, 272-291.

Kingdom forty-five years ago are the conditions in much of the Reformed church around the world today:

> What of the state of the church?...We are going back to the pre-Reformation position.
>
> What about the state of doctrine in the church? Before the Reformation, there was confusion. Is there anything more characteristic of the church today than doctrinal confusion, doctrinal indifference – a lack of concern and a lack of interest? And then perhaps the most alarming of all, the increase in the power, influence, and numbers of the Church of Rome, and the Romanizing tendencies that are coming into and being extolled in the Protestant church! There is no question about this. This is a mere matter of fact and observation. There is an obvious tendency to return to the pre-Reformation position; ceremonies and ritual are increasing and the Word of God is being preached less and less, sermons are becoming shorter and shorter. There is an indifference to true doctrine, a loss of authority, and a consequent declension....
>
> I wonder, Christian people, whether I am exaggerating when I suggest that at the present time we are really engaged in a great struggle for the very life of the Christian church, for the essence of the Christian faith? As I see the situation, it is nothing less alarming than that.[27]

Five watchwords – the five *solas* – summarized the great truths reclaimed at the Protestant Reformation. If these are lost, all that was recovered at the Reformation is lost:

27. D. Martyn Lloyd-Jones, "Remembering the Reformation," in *Knowing the Times*, 94.

- *Sola Scriptura*: Our doctrine is from Scripture alone.

- *Solus Christus*: We are saved by Christ's work alone.

- *Sola Gratia*: Salvation is by grace alone.

- *Sola Fide*: Justification is by faith alone.

- *Soli Deo Gloria*: The glory belongs to God alone.

Today, neo-liberalism denies them all.

Neo-liberalism exchanges *Sola Scriptura* for man's fallible perspectives on Scripture; neo-liberals place their elastic interpretations of confessional standards above Scripture.

Neo-liberalism exchanges *Solus Christus* for Christ-plus-works; the sufficiency of the imputation of His righteousness to sinners is denied.

Neo-liberalism exchanges *Sola Gratia* for a view of "grace" which denies that God's favor will, in the end, be unmerited except through the merits of Christ.

Neo-liberalism exchanges *Sola Fide* for justification by man's faithfulness.

Thus neo-liberalism in practice denies *Soli Deo Gloria*: It removes Christ from His throne; it removes Scripture from the place of sole authority; human works and human wisdom are in the ascendant. Neo-liberalism suppresses the truth in unrighteousness, exchanging the truth of God for the lie (*Romans* 1:18, 25).

True Christians must oppose this with all their being. They must learn once again what it means to be truly and vigorously Protestant. James R. White declares:

> It is my firm conviction that "Protestant" means absolutely, positively *nothing* unless the one wearing the term believes, breathes, lives, and loves the un-

compromised, offensive-to-the-natural-man message
of justification by God's free grace by faith in Jesus
Christ *alone*. As the term has become institutionalized,
it has lost its meaning. In the vast majority of instances
today a Protestant has no idea what the word itself
denotes, what the historical background behind it was,
nor why he should really care. And a label that has
been divorced from its significance no longer functions
in a meaningful fashion. We need a Reformation in our
day that will again draw the line clearly between those
who embrace the gospel of God's grace in Christ and
those who do not. And how one answers the question
"How is a man made right with God?" determines
whether one embraces that gospel or not.[28]

The Holy Spirit calls us to be Protestants. Scripture commands us in the most unequivocal terms to be true to the
unalloyed Gospel and the unique authority of Scripture,
both long veiled in darkness by Rome but brought back into
the light at great cost by the Reformers.

For you were once darkness, but now you are light
in the Lord. Walk as children of light (for the fruit of
the Spirit is in all goodness, righteousness, and truth),
finding out what is acceptable to the Lord. And have
no fellowship with the unfruitful works of darkness,
but rather expose them. For it is shameful even to
speak of those things which are done by them in secret.
But all things that are exposed are made manifest by
the light, for whatever makes manifest is light.

28. White, 26. Emphasis in the original.

Therefore He says: "Awake, you who sleep, arise from the dead, and Christ will give you light." See then that you walk circumspectly, not as fools but as wise, redeeming the time, because the days are evil [*Ephesians* 5:8-16].

Chapter 10

The Biblical Imperative

Therefore "Come out from among them
and be separate," says the Lord.
2 *Corinthians* 6:17

W e turn, now, to our final question: *What is the Biblical response to the present spiritual crisis in the OPC?* We must put the question in those terms, and we must seek the answer in those terms. Unless believers' response has clear Scriptural warrant, we are sure to go wrong.

We find that the Biblical response is a Biblical imperative. It is the same today as it has been in all such spiritual crises in the history of God's people: separation from unrepentant false teachers and their errors, and separation from a church body that is under their control. *Those who remain true to Christ and His Word must leave the Orthodox Presbyterian Church, and realign on the basis of Biblical principles, because the Bible tells us to do so.*

The Holy Spirit gives us this imperative repeatedly in the pages of Scripture. The Reformers understood the imperative of separation from apostasy in their day, Spurgeon understood it in his, and Machen understood it three generations ago. None of these stalwarts wanted to separate from their churches; they hoped for repentance. When it was not in evidence, they took the only course that Scripture would allow. Believers must do the same today. It is not the easy

326

course, but the Lord declares that He will bless no other. Indecision and half measures will only lend support to the present evil, and imperil souls.

In this chapter we shall examine the Scriptures that define the imperative of separation, as well as Scriptures that give us the discernment necessary to know when to separate from a church body and how to realign on a basis that will please Christ. God the Holy Spirit has been gracious to spell these things out for us; if we search the Scriptures we shall find that He has not left us in doubt, nor has He left us to our own fluctuating opinions. Scripture tells us the marks of a true church of Jesus Christ. It also tells us how to identify false teaching and false teachers, and what our attitude toward them must be. And, Scripture gives us the Biblical imperative – what we must do when a denomination has come to be controlled by false teachers. The Word is also clear in telling us that any other response is sinful.

The OPC and the Marks of a True Church

Scripture teaches that a true church of Jesus Christ bears these three marks: the faithful proclamation of the authentic Gospel;[1] the faithful administration of the sacraments of baptism and the Lord's Supper;[2] and the faithful exercise of Biblical discipline.[3] The Orthodox Presbyterian Church long

1. *Matthew* 24:14; *Mark* 16:15; *Romans* 1:16-17; *Galatians* 1:6-9.

2. *Matthew* 28:18-19; *Acts* 2:38-39; *Romans* 6:3-4; *Ephesians* 4:4-6; *Luke* 22:19-20; 1 *Corinthians* 11:23-26.

3. *Matthew* 18:15-18; *Romans* 16:17; 1 *Corinthians* 5:11-13; 2 *Corinthians* 2:6-8, 6:14-15, 13:1; *Galatians* 6:1; 1 *Thessalonians* 5:14; 2 *Thessalonians* 3:6, 14-15; 1 *Timothy* 5:20, 6:3-5; *Titus* 2:15, 3:10-11; 2 *John* 10-11; *Jude* 22-23. "Biblical discipline" means not merely the bringing of charges and the prosecution of judicial cases. That is what must happen in the last

ago ceased to bear these marks, and year by year departs ever further from them.

The OPC long ago ceased to proclaim the one true Gospel to the exclusion of all false gospels. The evidence we have examined could not be more clear. False gospels proclaiming a saving union with Christ through water baptism, and justification by faith-plus-works, have over the course of decades moved from quiet protection to open endorsement in the denomination. These false doctrines are firmly entrenched, and the OPC has demonstrated repeatedly that it is unwilling to rid itself of them.

The OPC long ago ceased to require the teaching of the truth regarding the sacraments to the exclusion of all error. The neo-liberal teachings that water baptism marks the point of conversion, and that baptized children need not be evangelized, are an accepted part of the theological landscape in the OPC. Acceptance of the doctrine of justification through covenant faithfulness has led to the false doctrine of the Lord's Supper as a meal of covenant renewal. In reality the Supper is the commemoration of the blessed fact that those who are by nature covenant breakers have been brought into a right relationship with God by believing on Jesus Christ, the seed of Abraham, who fulfilled all the requirements of the covenant on our behalf, once for all.

---

resort. Church discipline begins with careful attention to sound doctrine and manner of life among God's people, brought about through training in the inspired Word which "is profitable for doctrine, for reproof, for correction, for instruction in righteousness" (2 *Timothy* 3:16). We are not the family of God because we exercise discipline; we exercise discipline because we are the family of God. It is becoming to the faith to guard the spiritual well-being of the family, and it is a testimony that adorns the Gospel of Christ before the world.

False teaching on the sacraments has naturally led to a departure from the faithful administration of those sacraments. Men who hold false doctrines concerning the sacraments are permitted to go on administering them in their churches, spreading their heretical views on the significance of baptism and the Lord's Supper. In the OPC's presbyteries and general assemblies, ordained men serve the Supper without a second thought to other ordained men who are in long-standing, public, and unrepented sin concerning the Gospel – men who are under the anathema of God. If that were not enough of an offense to the Savior, these men who are in such long-standing and unrepented sin are also permitted to serve the Supper in presbyteries and general assemblies themselves.

The OPC has for three decades failed to exercise godly discipline in matters of essential doctrine. We have seen that the Presbytery of Philadelphia and the General Assembly were given half-a-dozen opportunities to deal with the error of Norman Shepherd and his supporters, and failed in every one, just as the men of the PCUSA failed to discipline a single one of the Auburn Affirmationists three generations ago. Churches of the OPC continue to welcome Norman Shepherd, Richard Gaffin, and others who preach another gospel to their pulpits without an eyebrow being raised. The OPC has for many years permitted men who openly embrace another gospel to hold positions of authority in its governing bodies, committees, and agencies. Likewise, the denomination has failed to support preachers of the true Gospel in their stand against opponents of the truth. When godly men have sounded the alarm against error, it has been the habit of the OPC to "shoot the messengers," or at least silence them, rather than heed their message.

Recognizing False Teachers

The Holy Spirit has not only told us the marks of a true church of Jesus Christ and how to recognize departure from them; He has also told us how to recognize false teachers.

We must have the proper starting point. We can only identify false teachers using the objective measuring rod of Scripture; mere opinions are irrelevant. The Bible tells us that false teachers creep into the church unnoticed (*Jude* 4). They secretly bring in destructive heresies and cause sound doctrine to be ridiculed (*2 Peter* 2:1-3). They are false apostles, deceitful workers, masquerading as apostles of Christ while they are in reality Satan's ministers, sowing the seeds of spiritual destruction (*2 Corinthians* 11:13-15). They are evil men and imposters, who grow worse and worse, deceiving and being deceived (*2 Timothy* 3:13). They are men who have become corrupted in their minds, resisting the truth, and are disapproved – that is, they do not meet the test of authenticity concerning the true faith (*2 Timothy* 3:8). They do not abide in the true doctrine of Christ (*2 John* 9), and in fact deny the true Christ Himself (*Jude* 4). They cause divisions and offenses by teaching things contrary to sound doctrine (*Romans* 16:17-18). They deceive through smooth words and flattering speech (*Romans* 16:18).

False teachers have crept into Westminster and other seminaries largely unnoticed. The men they have instructed in their false teachings have likewise come into the church for the most part without being recognized. They have secretly brought in destructive heresies. They cause sound doctrine to be ridiculed. They claim that their teachings are superior to what has been taught in past generations. They say they represent progress in theology. They allege that misconceptions regarding the covenants, the person and work of Christ, baptism, justification, sanctification, the church, and the Last Judgment have become embedded in Reformed doctrine over the centuries. Neo-liberals claim that their teachings serve to correct these supposedly long-held misconceptions. But what they are really saying, at the end of the day, is that our forebears in the faith – from the apostles themselves onward – have been wrong on the most basic elements of Christian doctrine. What the neo-liberals are really doing is denying authentic Biblical Christianity.

These reputedly conservative churchmen do this while simultaneously claiming that they remain completely faithful to Scripture and to the confessional standards of the church. Pretending to be what they are not, and professing to believe what they do not, they are "deceiving and being deceived" (2 *Timothy* 3:13).

What they are teaching is dangerously wrong. The souls of men, women, and children are at stake. These teachers are proclaiming "another gospel, which is not another" and their source of authority is the wisdom of this world rather than Scripture. The Word of God reserves its strongest condemnation for those who persist in such teaching. They are under God's curse (*Galatians* 1:6-9). They are to be marked and avoided (*Romans* 16:17-19). Let Christians who wish to stand for the truth make no mistake about this.

No one could dare say these things without clear authority. Scripture has that authority, and it says these things. They are matters of fact and not opinion. And, as we shall see, God has placed the responsibility of discernment in the hands of every believer, not rulers of the church only. God has not left these matters to question; the marks of the false teachers described in the pages of the New Testament are clearly the marks of neo-liberal teachers today. To deny this would be to deny the true faith.

Biblical Conduct Toward False Teachers

The Holy Spirit has not only instructed us clearly on the marks of a true church and how to recognize false teachers; the Lord also requires believers to adopt a Biblical attitude toward false teachers and conduct ourselves accordingly.

The New Testament states that once we have identified false teachers by the standard of Scripture, they are first of all to be commanded to desist. They are to be shunned, so that they might become ashamed and repent; but in the beginning they are still to be treated as brethren and not as enemies (*Matthew* 18:15, 2 *Thessalonians* 3:14-15, 1 *Timothy* 1:3). But if men persist in false doctrine, after the first and second admonition (not the tenth or twentieth) they are to be rejected (*Matthew* 18:15-17, *Titus* 3:10). The people of God are commanded to note them and avoid them (*Romans* 16:17). They are to withdraw themselves from them, certainly not make them leaders of the church (2 *Thessalonians* 3:6, 1 *Timothy* 5:5). They are not to offer them even a single word of encouragement or support, and not even meet with them privately, because doing even those seemingly harmless things is to share in their evil deeds (2 *John* 10-11). Those who persist in error and do not submit to correction are to be treated as lost sinners who are in need of the Gospel themselves, no matter what titles they may hold in the church or in academia (*Matthew* 18:17).

For over thirty years, the OPC has collectively refused to command those who preach another gospel to desist. It has not shunned them, so that they might become ashamed and repent. It has not rejected them. It has not noted and avoided them. It has not pointed them out to the people of God and told them to beware. The OPC has not withdrawn itself from such men. It has not refused to meet with them publicly or privately. It has not treated these unrepentant, habitual sinners concerning the Gospel as men who are in need of evangelization themselves, regardless of what titles or positions they may hold.

On the contrary, the Orthodox Presbyterian Church has given these men and those who openly support them places of honor and authority in the church. It has given neo-liberals the responsibility for educating and training its ministers. It has placed neo-liberals, and the men they have trained, in most of its pulpits. It has elected neo-liberals and their supporters to serve as moderators, clerks, and committeemen of its General Assemblies and presbyteries for many years. It has placed neo-liberals in positions of authority on its committees for home and foreign missions, Christian education, revisions to the proof texts of its doctrinal standards, revisions to its directory for worship, committees that examine men for licensure and ordination to the ministry, as well as its study committees on various issues. These false teachers, with the cooperation and support of the doctrinally indifferent, have used these positions of power and authority to control the denomination.

Adopting a Biblical attitude toward false teachers and dealing with them accordingly is never the easy or convenient thing to do. But in the OPC it has become the thing that is almost never done. Scripture is clear and unequivocal. The Holy Spirit leaves no room for doubt as to the Biblical course. Following that course will have a cost. Those who stand for the truth will suffer the loss of friends. Truth and error may even divide families, much less congregations, presbyteries, or general assemblies, but Jesus told us this would be the case:

> Therefore whoever confesses Me before men, him I will also confess before My Father who is in Heaven. But whoever denies Me before men, him I will also deny before My Father who is in Heaven.
>
> Do not think that I came to bring peace on Earth. I did not come to bring peace but a sword. For I have come to "set a man against his father, a daughter against her mother, and a daughter-in-law against her mother-in-law"; and "a man's enemies will be those of his own household." He who loves father or mother more than Me is not worthy of Me. And he who loves son or daughter more than Me is not worthy of Me. And he who does not take his cross and follow after Me is not worthy of Me. He who finds his life will lose it, and he who loses his life for My sake will find it [*Matthew* 10:32-39].

We may submit to God's commandments or not, but they are still the truth, and obedience is the only acceptable course, even if it is a difficult one.

What to Do When False Teachers Control the Church

The Orthodox Presbyterian Church long ago ceased to bear the marks of a true church of Jesus Christ. Neo-liberals – false teachers concerning the Gospel and much more – are in control of the denomination, with the aid of the doctrinally indifferent. This did not happen yesterday; it has been building to a crisis point for thirty years.

Under such conditions, there can be but one possible Biblical response from those who continue to stand for the truth. *Scripture commands true believers to separate from apostasy. Scripture also commands true believers, once separated, to realign on sound principles. Separation involves a Biblical attitude toward a church that has failed to recognize false teachers for what they are, has failed to deal with them in accordance with the commandment of God, and instead has actually placed them in charge.*

Just as Israel was commanded to make no covenant with the pagan nations of Canaan (*Deuteronomy* 7:2), Christians are commanded not to be unequally yoked together with unbelievers. 2 *Corinthians* 6:14-7:1 instructs believers in the imperative of separation:

> Do not be unequally yoked together with unbelievers. For what fellowship has righteousness with lawlessness? And what communion has light with darkness? And what accord has Christ with Belial [literally, Satan, or a pagan god]? Or what part has a believer with an unbeliever? And what agreement has the temple of God with idols? For you are the temple of the living God. As God has said: "I will dwell in them, and walk among them. I will be their God, and they shall be My people."
>
> Therefore, "Come out from among them and be separate," says the Lord. "Do not touch what is unclean, and I will receive you." "I will be a Father to you, and you shall be My sons and daughters," says the Lord Almighty.
>
> Therefore, having these promises, beloved, let us cleanse ourselves from all filthiness of the flesh and spirit, perfecting holiness in the fear of God.

We are commanded to recognize that fellowship with unrepentant false teachers and their adherents cannot possibly be true Christian fellowship. We are commanded to separate from a church that has not dealt with the evil in its midst; it is, in fact, no longer a true church of Christ. We are commanded to recognize what is at stake: light versus darkness, truth versus error, belief versus unbelief, worship of the true Christ versus worship of an Antichristian counterfeit. It is a matter of spiritual life versus spiritual death. Those who remain in the truth can have no part with false teachers – no communion, no harmony, no accord with them. We are commanded to come out from among them, to be separate, to stop even touching that which is spiritually unclean. Only then, says the Lord, can true believers themselves be in proper fellowship with Him.

Truly these are hard sayings. This is not the easy path. But these are the commandments of God. We must rely on God to tell us the truth about the present crisis, and to enable us to do what must be done. Man looks on the outward appearance. We tend to rely on our own variable opinions and emotions, and the opinions and emotions of others. But God looks on the heart (1 *Samuel* 16:7). He has told us what is really in the hearts of false teachers – even when they themselves are blind to their own heart-condition. We tend to make judgments based on human standards. But the Lord has been gracious to give us an infallible standard by which to clearly identify false teaching and false teachers. The question is: Will we read it and heed it? God has warned us to separate ourselves from them, just as the children of Israel were commanded to get away from the tents of Korah, Dathan, and Abiram when they rebelled against God, lest they be destroyed with them (*Numbers* 16). Ministers of Satan are masquerading as apostles of Christ in many places in the Orthodox Presbyterian Church. Separation from apostasy is the imperative of the hour.

Separating from the OPC

It is also important to consider the practical aspects of separation from the Orthodox Presbyterian Church. The OPC *Form of Government* specifies a procedure for the withdrawal of a congregation from the denomination:

> A congregation may withdraw from the Orthodox Presbyterian Church only according to the following procedure:
>
> a. Before calling a congregational meeting for the purpose of taking any action contemplating withdrawal from the Orthodox Presbyterian Church, the session shall inform the presbytery, ordinarily at a stated meeting, of its intention to call such a meeting, and shall provide grounds for its intention. The presbytery, through representatives appointed for the purpose, shall seek, within a period not to exceed three weeks after the presbytery meeting, in writing and in person, to dissuade the session from its intention. If the session is not dissuaded, it may issue a written call for the first meeting of the congregation. The call shall contain the session's recommendation, with its written grounds, together with the presbytery's written argument.
>
> b. If the vote of the congregation favors withdrawal, the session shall call for a second meeting to be held not less than three weeks, nor more than one year, thereafter. If the congregation, at the second meeting, reaffirms a previous action to withdraw, it shall be the duty of the presbytery to prepare a roll of members who desire to continue as members of the Orthodox Presbyterian Church and to provide for the oversight of these continuing members.

c. The presbytery shall be given the opportunity, at any congregational meeting at which withdrawal is being considered, to dissuade the congregation from withdrawing.[4]

Sessions and congregations that recognize the imperative to separate from the OPC may be inclined to follow this process, but that would be not only wrong but also spiritually dangerous. Submitting to the stated procedure is to submit to the spiritual authority of a body that has, by abandoning the marks of a true church, lost the right to exercise such authority and the ability to exercise it in a godly manner. Submitting to the stated procedure also gives neo-liberals and their supporters – men "who deceive through smooth words and flattering speech" (*Romans* 16:18) – three separate opportunities to dissuade a session and congregation through further deception. Through the first eight chapters of this book we saw that neo-liberals and their adherents are quite willing to employ ungodly tactics to advance their position and hold onto territory already gained. No minister or session should expose themselves or their congregation to that danger.

Some will object that if ministers and sessions do not follow the stated procedure for withdrawal, they are violating their ordination vows. This argument is specious. It is the neo-liberals, their adherents, and many of the doctrinally indifferent who long ago forsook *their* ordination vows to uphold the truth of the Gospel and the unique authority of Scripture. It is they who led the Orthodox Presbyterian Church to abandon the marks of a true church of Christ.

4. *Form of Government of the Orthodox Presbyterian Church*, Chapter 16, section 7.

Conservative ministers and ruling elders did not take vows to remain in submission to an apostate church. They did not make vows of unconditional fidelity to a church body; they made vows of unconditional fidelity to the Lord of the Church and to His Word. The Lord and the Word command faithful ministers and ruling elders to lead by example in separating from apostasy, not remaining in submission to it or having fellowship with it in any way.

Instead, ministers and sessions need to prepare their congregations to separate. How can that be done? The case of the writer's home congregation may be instructive.

Our session had become aware of the nature and extent of the spiritual crisis in the OPC and was contemplating recommending separation to the congregation. But before taking such a step, the session believed that the congregation had a right to a full explanation of the present crisis, and that the session as shepherds of the flock of God had an obligation to provide one.

So before deciding to recommend separation from the OPC, the session authorized a Sunday evening study series on the doctrinal issues at stake.[5] The study consisted of three phases. The first phase laid a firm foundation from Scripture regarding the authority and inerrancy of the Word, the doctrine of the covenants, justification by faith alone, sanctification, the Last Judgment, and related matters. This may seem unnecessary in a sound church where these doctrines have been carefully taught, but it helped to ensure that everyone was on the same footing for the second phase of the study.

5. The study materials are available in print and electronic form under the title *Justification by Faith Alone: Timeless Truths and Contemporary Errors*. Contact the author by e-mail at pelliott@teachingtheword.org.

The study then shifted its focus to the errors commonly being taught – Shepherdism, Federal Vision theology, and the New Perspective on Paul. The approach to this phase of the study was to: 1. quote from the purveyors of these heresies; 2. point out the errors in their teachings from Scripture; and 3. state positively the correct doctrine from Scripture, reinforcing the first phase of the study, so that the people of God would be ready to give an answer for the hope that is within them (1 Peter 3:15).

The final phase of the study examined what it means to "contend earnestly for the faith which was once for all delivered to the saints" (Jude 3).

The congregation subsequently separated from the OPC by voting on a resolution of separation prepared by the session and addressed to the presbytery. This resolution stated the church's reasons for leaving the OPC. It also made it clear that the congregation was *separating from the authority* of a body that has abandoned the marks of a true church of Jesus Christ, rather than *withdrawing under the authority* of that body as if it still possessed the Biblical qualifications to exercise spiritual authority.

Realignment on Sound Principles

This brings us to the second element of the Biblical response to the present crisis. True believers, once separated from apostasy, must realign into a new denomination or denominations on the basis of sound principles, or join with other existing churches and denominations that are still sound. Scripture commands this as well. Isolation is not an option.

In 1962, Dr. Martyn Lloyd-Jones gave two addresses to a British ministerial fellowship on the Biblical basis of Christian unity. In them he enumerated nine principles which I commend to those who answer the call to separate from the OPC as a sound basis for realignment. I quote him at length because the entire statement is vitally pertinent to the present situation:

1. *Unity must never be isolated or regarded as something in and of itself.*

2. *It is equally clear that the question of unity must never be put first.* We must never start with it, but always remember the order stated so clearly in *Acts* 2:42, where fellowship follows doctrine: "They continued steadfastly in the apostles' doctrine and fellowship, and in breaking of bread, and in prayers." That, as we have seen, is precisely the order in which they are placed in both *John* 17 and *Ephesians*. The present tendency to discount and to depreciate doctrine in the interests of unity is simply a denial and a violation of plain New Testament teaching.

3. *We must never start with the visible church or with an institution, but rather with the truth which alone creates unity.* Failure to realize this point was surely the main trouble with the Jews at the time when our Lord was in this world. It is dealt with in the preaching of John the Baptist, who said, "Bring forth therefore fruits worthy of repentance, and begin not to say within yourselves, We have Abraham to our father: for I say unto you, that God is able of these stones to raise up children unto Abraham" (*Luke* 3:8). Our Lord teaches the same thing in *John* 8:32-34. The Jews had objected to His saying "the truth shall make you free," their argument being that they were Abraham's seed, and were never in bondage to any man. He draws attention to their rejection of His Word and their attempts to kill Him, and concludes: "If ye

341

were Abraham's children, ye would do the works of Abraham.... Ye do the deeds of your father.... Ye are of your father the devil" (*John* 8:39, 41, 44). Their fatal assumption was that the fact that they were Jews guaranteed of necessity their salvation, that membership of the nation meant that they were truly children of God. As John the Baptist indicated, the notion was entirely mechanical; God could produce such people out of stones.

The apostle Paul also deals with this confusion when he says in writing to the Romans: "For he is not a Jew, which is one outwardly; neither is that circumcision, which is outward in the flesh: but he is a Jew, which is one inwardly; and circumcision is that of the heart, in the spirit, and not in the letter; whose praise is not of men, but of God" (*Romans* 2:28, 29). He repeats this in the words, "For they are not all Israel, which are of Israel" (*Romans* 9:6). This is further enforced by the statement, "Know ye therefore that they which are of faith, the same are the children of Abraham" (*Galatians* 3:7). And also, "And if ye be Christ's, then are ye Abraham's seed, and heirs according to the promise" (*Galatians* 3:29).

The same mistake of starting with the visible institution rather than with truth was also made at the time of the Reformation. What Luther was enabled to see, and what accounted for his courageous stand, was this self-same point. He refused to be bound by that mighty institution, the Roman Catholic Church, with her long centuries of history. Having been liberated by the truth of justification by faith he saw clearly that truth must always come first. It must come before institution and traditions, and everything – every institution, even the church – must be judged by the Word of truth. The invisible church is more important than the visible church, and loyalty to the former may involve either expulsion or separation from the latter, and the formation of a new visible church.

4. *The starting point in considering the question of unity must always be regeneration and belief of the truth.* Nothing else produces unity, and, as we have seen clearly, it is impossible apart from this.

5. *An appearance or a façade of unity based on anything else, and at the expense of these two criteria, or which ignores them, is clearly a fraud and a lie.* People are not one, nor in a state of unity, who disagree about fundamental questions such as (a) whether we submit ourselves utterly to revealed truth or rely ultimately upon our reason and human thinking; (b) the historic fall, and man's present state and condition in sin, under the wrath of God, and in complete helplessness and hopelessness as regards salvation; and (c) the person of our Lord Jesus Christ and the utter, absolute necessity, and sole sufficiency, of His substitutionary atoning work for sinners. To give the impression that they are one simply because of a common outward organization is not only to mislead the world which is outside the church [and those within as well – pme] but to be guilty of a lie.

6. *To do anything which supports or encourages such an impression or appearance of unity is surely dishonest and sinful.* Truth and untruth cannot be reconciled, and the difference between them cannot be patched over. Error is always to be exposed and denounced for truth's sake, and also, as we have seen, for the sake of babes in Christ. This is also important from the standpoint of the statement in *John* 17:21, "that the world may believe that thou hast sent Me." Nothing so surely drives the world

away from the truth as uncertainty or confusion in the church with respect to the content of her message.

That is undoubtedly the main cause of the present declension in religion. The world will not be impressed by a mere coming together in externals while there is central disagreement about the fundamentals of the faith. It will interpret it as an attempt on the part of church authorities to save their institution in much the same way as it sees business men forming combines and amalgamations with the same object and intention. The question the world is still asking is, What is Christianity? What is your teaching? Have you anything authoritative and powerful to offer us? It is interested in this rather than in organizational matters, and rightly so. It is also ready to respond to it.

7. *To regard a church, or a council of churches, as a forum in which fundamental matters can be debated and discussed, or as an opportunity for witness-bearing, is sheer confusion and muddled thinking.* There is to be no discussion about "the foundation," as we have seen. If men do not accept that, they are not brethren and we can have no dialogue with them. We are to preach to such and to evangelize them. Discussion takes place only among brethren who share the same life and subscribe to the same essential truth. It is right and good that brethren should discuss together matters which are not essential to salvation and about which there is, and always has been, and probably always will be, legitimate difference of opinion. We can do no better at that point than quote the old adage, "In things essential unity, in things indifferent liberty, in all things charity."

Before there can be any real discussion and dialogue and exchange there must be agreement concerning

344

primary and fundamental matters. Without the acceptance of certain axioms and propositions in geometry, for
example, it is idle to attempt to solve any problem. If
certain people refuse to accept the axioms, and are constantly querying and disputing them, clearly there is no
point of contact between them and those who do accept
them. It is precisely the same in the realm of the church.
Those who question and query, let alone deny, the great
cardinal truths that have been accepted throughout the
centuries do not belong to the church, and to regard
them as brethren is to betray the truth. As we have
already reminded ourselves, the apostle Paul tells us
clearly what our attitude to them should be: "A man that
is an heretick after the first and second admonition
reject" (*Titus* 3:10). They are to be regarded as unbelievers who need to be called to repentance and acceptance
of the truth as it is in Christ Jesus. To give the impression
that they are Christians with whom other Christians
disagree about certain matters is to confuse the genuine
seeker and enquirer who is outside [and also to confuse
those within the church – pme]. But such is the position
prevailing today. It is based upon a failure to understand
the nature of the New Testament church which is "the
pillar and ground of the truth" (*I Timothy* 3:15). In the
same way it is a sheer waste of time to discuss or debate
the implications of Christianity with people who are not
agreed as to what Christianity is. Failure to realize this
constitutes the very essence of the modern confusion.

8. *Unity must obviously never be thought of primarily in
numerical terms, but always in terms of life.* Nothing is so
opposed to the biblical teaching as the modern idea that
numbers and powerful organization alone count. It is the
very opposite of the great biblical doctrine of "the

remnant," stated, for instance, so perfectly by Jonathan to his armour-bearer as they faced alone the hosts of the Philistines, in the words: "Come, and let us go over unto the garrison of these uncircumcised: it may be that the Lord will work for us: for there is no restraint to the Lord to save by many or by few" (*I Samuel*. 14:6). Still more strikingly, perhaps, is it taught in the incident of Gideon and the Midianites, where we read of God reducing the army of Israel from 3,000 to 300 as a preliminary to victory (*Judges* 7).

God has done His greatest work throughout the centuries through remnants, often even through individuals. Why is it that we forget Micaiah the son of Imlah, and Jeremiah, and Amos, John the Baptist, the mere twelve disciples; and Martin Luther standing alone defying some twelve centuries of tradition and all the power of a mighty church? This is not to advocate small-ness or exclusiveness as if they had some inherent merit; but it is to suggest that the modern slavish attitude to bigness and organization cuts right across a central bib-lical emphasis. Indeed it suggests ignorance of, and lack of faith in, the power of the Holy Spirit.

9. *The greatest need of the hour is a new baptism and outpouring of the Holy Spirit in renewal and revival.* Nothing else throughout the centuries has ever given the church true authority and made her, and her message, mighty. But what right have we to pray for this, or to expect that He will honour or bless anything but the truth that He Himself enabled the authors of the Old Testament and the New Testament to write? To ask Him to do so is not only near blasphemy but also the height of folly. Reformation and revival go together and cannot be separated. He is the Spirit of truth, and He will honour

346

nothing but the truth. The ultimate question facing us these days is whether our faith is in men and their power to organize, or in the truth of God in Christ Jesus and the power of the Holy Spirit. Let me put it another way: Are we primarily concerned about the size of the church or the purity of the church, both in doctrine and in life? Indeed, finally it comes to this: Is our view of the church Roman Catholic (inclusivist, organizational, institutional, and hierarchical) or Reformed, emphasizing the universal priesthood of all believers and the need for keeping the church herself constantly under the judgment of the Word?[6]

Un-Biblical Solutions

Scripture is clear on the solution to the present crisis, and it is just as clear in telling us what are *not* proper solutions. All other options are, in one way or another, ungodly ones. In this section we shall address four that are frequently proposed.

1. *The Camping solution.* Harold Camping, owner and president of Family Radio, uses that worldwide network as a bully pulpit to teach that the church age has ended, we are now in the Great Tribulation, and the church of Jesus Christ in terms of local organized congregations no longer exists. The organized church, he says, has become the synagogue of Satan, who is now on its throne. God is no longer saving people through the ministry of organized churches. Therefore, says Camping, Christians must leave organized churches and meet in "fellowships" in which there are no

6. D. Martyn Lloyd-Jones, "The Basis of Christian Unity," in *Knowing the Times*, 159-163. Quoted by permission.

pastors, deacons, or elders, and there is no practice of baptism or observance of the Lord's Supper. And, true believers are to no longer financially support organized churches but are to support Family Radio.[7]

Harold Camping has shown himself to be a false prophet before, having predicted in the early 1990s that Christ would return in September 1994.[8] Camping recently announced a new date, 2011, on his daily radio program. Scripture instructs us that

> when a prophet speaks in the name of the Lord, if the thing does not happen or come to pass, that is the thing which the Lord has not spoken; the prophet has spoken it presumptuously; you shall not be afraid of him [*Deuteronomy* 18:22].

It also warns us:

> For I testify to everyone who hears the words of the prophecy of this book: If anyone adds to these things, God will add to him the plagues that are written in this book; and if anyone takes away from the words of the book of this prophecy, God shall take away his part from the Book of Life, from the holy city, and from the things which are written in this book [*Revelation* 22:18-19].

Camping's teachings on the church could simply be dismissed as absurd if they had not gained a loyal and cultish following, including some people who have left the OPC. His doctrines *are* absurd; he bases them on highly symbolic,

7. These teachings are found in Camping's booklets, *Has the Church Age Come to an End?* (Oakland, California: Family Stations, Inc., 2000) and *The End of the Church Age...and After* (2004).

8. Harold Camping, *1994?* (Ashland, Ohio: Vantage Press, 1992).

allegorical, and inconsistent interpretations of isolated Scripture passages, and his interpretations have no foundation in grammatical-historical principles. Space does not permit a full discussion here, but the church needs to be warned that Harold Camping teaches deep error not only regarding the church but on many other things, including salvation itself.[9] Camping denies that faith is the instrument of salvation; he claims that if God used faith as an instrument this would somehow add a work to salvation.[10] Yet at the same time Camping often says on his Open Forum radio program that people must "beg and plead" with God to save them.

Many people who disagree with Camping listen to Family Radio for the good Christian music, extensive Bible reading, and other things that are in themselves worthy. But along the way, around the clock, listeners are periodically indoctrinated by Camping and his approved teachers who repeat and reinforce his false doctrines. Christians should beware of Harold Camping on the most basic matters of doctrine, much less consider Camping's teachings on the church to be a solution to the present crisis. He has proven himself a false teacher who is to be noted and avoided. Christians do not need to flee from the organized church; they need to flee from Harold Camping.

Scripture is clearly opposed to Camping's basic propositions. Space permits us to address but three. First, Christ has not, as Camping alleges, forsaken His church, nor is Satan on its throne:

9. For a detailed critique of Camping's heresy, see James R. White, *Dangerous Airwaves: Harold Camping Refuted and Christ's Church Defended* (Amityville, New York: Calvary Press, 2002).

10. White, 142.

> I will build My church, and the gates of Hades shall not prevail against it [*Matthew* 16:18].

> For this reason I bow my knees to the Father of our Lord Jesus Christ, from whom the whole family in Heaven and Earth is named.... To Him be glory in the church by Christ Jesus to all generations, forever and ever [*Ephesians* 3:14, 21].

Second, Christ has not, as Camping teaches, suspended the sacraments:

> For as often as you eat this bread and drink this cup, you proclaim the Lord's death till He comes [*1 Corinthians* 11:26].

> All authority has been given to Me in Heaven and on Earth. Go therefore and make disciples of all the nations, baptizing them in the name of the Father and of the Son and of the Holy Spirit, teaching them to observe all things that I have commanded you; and lo, I am with you always, even to the end of the age [*Matthew* 28:18-19].

Third, Camping-style isolation is simply not an option for believers:

> Let us hold fast the confession of our hope without wavering, for He who promised is faithful. And let us consider one another in order to stir up love and good works, not forsaking the assembling of ourselves together, as is the manner of some, but exhorting one another, and so much the more as you see the Day approaching [*Hebrews* 10:23-25].

Camping cites many problems in the contemporary church as supposed proof of his "end of the church" doctrine. But there have been such problems in the church from the beginning: legalism (*Acts* 15; *Galatians*); compromise and corruption (*Revelation* 2); problems in worship (1 *Corinthians* 11); lukewarmness (*Revelation* 3); injustice (*Acts* 6); immorality (1 *Corinthians* 5); ungodly contentions (*James* 4). Such problems certainly abounded in the sixteenth century, but the Reformers knew better than to declare that the end of the church age had come. On the contrary, they championed separation from apostasy and realignment of the organized true church on sound principles. Because the church is in the world, the world is in the church, and believers are not perfected in this life, the church can never exist in the absence of many such problems until Jesus returns. To say that the church has come to an end because these things exist in it today is to deny the Biblical doctrine of the church and the lordship of Christ over His church. On the contrary, one of the marks of a true church of Jesus Christ is that it deals with such matters by exercising godly discipline according to Scripture.

2. "*Wait and see what the Justification Study Committee does.*" This is one of several suggested responses to the crisis that rest on the false assumption that separation from the OPC is premature. On the contrary, the formation of the study committee is *prima facie* evidence that the time has come for separation – in fact it is past time. The study committee is made up of men from across the spectrum of the groups within the OPC. It has been appointed to study teachings that were clearly earmarked as heresy even before the canon of Scripture was completed. Overshadowing the proceedings of this committee is the OPC's inclusivist, perspectivalist hermeneutic of trust. Behind the erection of such a committee is the history of thirty years of failure to condemn another gospel and to reject those who teach it.

The appointment of a study committee is but one more

chapter in that record of failure. The General Assembly has appointed Richard Gaffin, one of the chief purveyors and defenders of the heresy, to that committee. The OPC studied these doctrines twenty-five years ago during the Shepherd controversy and failed to condemn them; in the ensuing years it has facilitated the spreading of them far and wide. No man who is true to the Gospel and knows the history of the last three decades in the OPC should even be participating in such a committee. The entire proceeding is a commentary on just how deeply in trouble the OPC really is.

I have asked some who hold this wait-and-see position, "Just what is it that you are waiting for?" The answers are vague, and usually reflect a hope for some sign of "movement in the right direction." But this is not a situation where mere movement in the right direction is by any means sufficient. Souls are at stake, and have been for decades. There must be a clean and uncompromising break with error, and a clear and unequivocal condemnation of heresy and the heretics. The OPC has shown repeatedly that it lacks the stomach for this. With the neo-liberals in control of the OPC's presbyteries and general assemblies through the aid of the doctrinally indifferent, and the no-rules-just-right hermeneutic of trust as its operating principle, no such break with error is possible within the context of the existing denomination.

3. *The "exit strategy" response.* This is another proposed solution to the crisis that rests on the false notion that separation is premature. When churches and groups began leaving the OPC after the Kinnaird verdict, some other ministers and elders who chose to stay told us, "We sympathize with what you are doing and we would like to leave as well. But there is no place to go, no denomination for us to join, and we will not opt for independent status, not even

temporarily." Now that new denominations are beginning to form – partly in response to that lament – many of these same men have shifted their ground. Now they are saying, "Well, if and when things get bad enough in the OPC, one of the new denominations will be part of our exit strategy."

This raises the question, What is "bad enough"? We challenge these men once again: If you take an honest look at the evidence in this book and in other sources, and take an honest look around you in the denomination, what more is there to wait for? Will you wait until people in your own congregation have been infected with the neo-liberal cancer? Will you wait until it happens to you yourself? Do you, as a minister or ruling elder, not understand that you are no less susceptible to the influences of the neo-liberals and their errors than the general membership of your church? Can you in good conscience lend your congregation's financial support to a body that long ago ceased to proclaim the one true Gospel to the exclusion of all false gospels? Can you continue to give your people the impression, by remaining in the denomination, that it is sound and worthy of their support? Do you not understand that Scripture commands you to set the example, as the apostles did, in leading your people to "come out from among them and be separate"?

4. *The "stay and fight" response.* Some believe that they must stay in the OPC and fight the battle from within. Some believe the battle can still be won from within, while others believe that it is simply not permissible to leave the denomination, win or lose, because to leave would constitute schism. Both contentions are specious. What many do not realize or will not recognize is that the battle *has* been fought for over thirty years, and the neo-liberals have won every time. But the neo-liberals and their enablers have largely suppressed the knowledge that such a conflict has even existed. There is

no mention of these controversies over essential doctrine in official histories of the OPC. There has been no frank discussion of them in the denominational magazines, *New Horizons* and *The Ordained Servant*. Instead, as in the PCUSA three generations ago, denominational publications have been used to give the false impression that the denomination remains as faithful as ever to the Scriptures and its confessional standards. Neo-liberals and their allies, with the cooperation of the doctrinally indifferent, control the OPC; they have controlled it for many years. When liberals are in control of a denomination, conservatives must leave. Machen wrote:

> If the liberal party really obtains full control of the councils of the Church, then no evangelical Christian can continue to support the Church's work. If a man believes that salvation from sin comes only through the atoning death of Jesus then he cannot support by his gifts and by his presence a propaganda which is intended to produce an exactly opposite impression. To do so would mean the most terrible bloodguiltiness which it is possible to conceive. If the liberal party, therefore, really obtains control of the Church, evangelical Christians must be prepared to withdraw no matter what it costs. Our Lord has died for us, and surely we must not deny Him for favor of men.[11]

The stay-and-fight mindset assumes that to leave would be to stop fighting or to admit defeat. This is not the case at all. But what this mindset also assumes is that those who remain true to authentic Biblical Christianity must attempt to conduct whatever "fight" they can, under the corrupt authority of a denomination where men who are the enemies

11. Machen, *Christianity and Liberalism*, 166.

of the Gospel hold sway. That approach has been tried – and blocked at every turn – for thirty years.

Some who hold the stay-and-fight position contend that leaving the OPC under any circumstances would constitute schism. Machen in his time strongly opposed such thinking. He believed, wrote Ned B. Stonehouse, that

> [s]eparation from a Church could be countenanced only if it was demonstrated that that organization had abandoned the authority of the Word of God for another authority, only, that is, if it proved thereby that it was not really a Church of Jesus Christ. Under such circumstances, however, *it would virtually be an act of schism to remain,* for then one would be separating oneself from the true Church of Jesus Christ.[12]

Machen understood that separation from apostasy is not schism, but that remaining in a church that has departed from the faith is itself an act of schism, and aids and abets the lie that such a body is still a true church of Christ.

Answering Further Objections

We now move on to answer a few other objections that have been raised against the Biblical imperative of separation from the OPC and realignment on sound principles.

1. *Some say that only a church court has the right to declare anything to be heresy.* Those who make this claim say that since the OPC has not declared the doctrines of Norman Shepherd, Richard Gaffin, and their followers to be heresy, no one else has the right to do so. It will be objected that we

12. Ned B. Stonehouse, *J. Gresham Machen: A Biographical Memoir* (Grand Rapids, Michigan: Wm. B. Eerdmans, 1954), 494. Emphasis added.

do not have the right to make such statements in this book, nor do other denominations have the right to make such statements in official pronouncements of their assemblies.

But these claims and conclusions are false. We encountered and refuted this objection while considering the neo-liberals' embrace of the principles of the *Auburn Affirmation* in chapter four, and again earlier in this chapter. Christ and the apostles expected both ordained men and regular church-goers to recognize false teaching and false teachers. Ordained men have a particular responsibility, both individually and collectively, to warn the flock of God and to deal with the error. Church discipline of heretics begins with such individual judgments based on the Word of God.

Furthermore, we are not dealing with matters where contemporary individuals would be the first to label the teachings of neo-liberalism as heresy. Far from it. The apostles and the first Council of Jerusalem did so in the pages of Scripture. Not to label neo-liberal teachings on Scripture and salvation as heresy is to reject the judgment of Scripture itself.

2. *Some protest that the OPC has not officially endorsed heresy.* This is the flip side of the preceding argument. A church, so this objection goes, does not become a heretical body until it officially endorses heresy. Besides, they say, those whom conservatives have judged to be heretics still say that they believe the Scriptures and hold to the confessional standards of the church. We must take their word for it. The OPC has not officially accepted false teachings, and there really are no false teachers; therefore there is no reason to separate from the denomination.

The fact is that there *are* false teachers in the OPC, and their false teachings are readily accepted and have done enormous damage, as we have amply demonstrated. Some simply will not face these facts. But does that mean that we should look for official statements from presbyteries or the General Assembly titled, "Why We Endorse Justification by Faith Plus Works" or "Covenant Baptism Is the Instrument of Salvation"? Of course not. Likewise it is misleading for the leadership of the OPC to say that they have made no official pronouncement endorsing these things; that they have not changed the OPC's doctrinal standards; and, therefore those who say the OPC has accepted false teaching are wrong.

This attitude ignores the fact that Scripture tells us (and church history abundantly demonstrates) that this is not how error begins and spreads. The Biblical image is that of a *little* leaven leavening the whole lump. And as Paul told the young Timothy, "their message will spread like cancer" (2 *Timothy* 2:17).

Machen dealt with this no-official-endorsement canard in his time:

> When shall we cease benumbing ourselves with a baseless optimism; when shall we cease saying that the Presbyterian church is "essentially sound"; when shall we be willing to face the facts before God?
>
> The facts, alas, are perfectly clear to the man who is not afraid to see. Two mighty forces have been contending for control of the Presbyterian Church in the U. S. A. One is the religion of supernatural redemption that is presented in the Bible and in the *Confession of Faith*; the other is the naturalistic or indifferentist Modernism that finds expression in the *Auburn Affirmation*. Between these two forces, there are many attempts at compromise. We do not presume to look into the hearts of men; we do not presume to say just who in the church is a Christian and who is not; we do not presume to say how far a man can mistakenly serve the cause of unbelief

and yet be united to Christ by faith. But whatever may be said about individual *men*, it is perfectly clear that the two *forces* are diametrically opposed; it is perfectly clear that between the Bible and the *Auburn Affirmation* there can be no peace but only a deadly war.

It is perfectly clear, moreover, that in this warfare the anti-evangelical contention has so far won the victory. Of what avail is it to point to general professions of adherence to the faith of the church by this ecclesiastical official or that? The simple fact is that the *policy* of the church organization as a whole is exactly that which so effectively serves the purposes of unbelief in all the churches of the world – discouragement of controversy, tolerance of anti-Christian propaganda, bitter intolerance of any effort to make the true condition of the church known, emphasis on organization at the expense of doctrine, neglect of the deep things of the Word of God. Let us not deceive ourselves, my friends. The Presbyterian Church in the U. S. A. includes, indeed, many true Christian men and women; but in its corporate capacity, through its central organization, it has ceased to witness, in any clear and true sense, to the Lord Jesus Christ.[13]

Open official endorsement of false teaching is not among the first things to happen. It usually happens – as it did in the PCUSA – long *after* a body has ceased to bear the marks of a true church of Christ. The PCUSA never *officially* endorsed the *Auburn Affirmation*. The PCUSA has never to this day *officially* denied the *Westminster Confession of Faith*. It was not until three decades after conservatives left to form

---

13. J. Gresham Machen, "The Nature and Mission of the Church," in *Selected Shorter Writings*, 264-265. Emphases in the original.

the OPC that the liberal PCUSA approved the heretical *Confession of 1967*. Even then, the liberals were careful to erect this new confession *alongside* the PCUSA's other doctrinal standards, not officially in place of them.[14] But the liberals had long ago created an environment in which doctrinal standards didn't matter anyway. The *Confession of 1967* merely formalized the apostasy that had long existed. If formal, open, official endorsement of false teaching were the measure of things, then conservatives should not have left the PCUSA to form the OPC for at least another thirty years.

Furthermore, there *has* been official (albeit quiet) endorsement of error in the OPC. We saw this in the Presbytery of Philadelphia's votes on Shepherd's *Thirty-Four Theses* in the late 1970s. We saw it again in the General Assembly Advisory Committee *Report* in the Kinnaird case. We saw it once more in the OPC's promotion of the hermeneutic of trust.

3. *Still others argue that you can't leave a church, you have to be thrown out.* They point to the example of the proceedings against Machen and others in the mid-1930s, and say that conservatives must continue the fight from within until they are excommunicated. By definition that means that conservatives must wait until the neo-liberals and their enablers have corrupted enough souls to bring expulsion of the faithful about. It means that conservatives must stay and submit to the ungodly strategies of the apostates. It means they must be accessories to the proclamation of another gospel. It means they must expose their congregations to such spiritual danger for who knows how long. That cannot possibly be the godly thing to do.

14. In fact, the PCUSA has adopted a *Book of Confessions* representing a multiplicity of theological perspectives, to which new and increasingly liberal documents are being added over time.

4. *Still others protest that it is wrong to create more "micro-denominations."* This is a specious argument on several levels. First, it raises the question: What is "micro" and who defined it? Second, it assumes that size is the measure of right and wrong. As Martyn Lloyd-Jones said, this is not a valid starting point. Unity in the truth is the proper starting point, and the numbers, large or small, are God's doing.

The pattern that we see through all of Scripture is a remnant, a strait gate, a narrow way, and few finding it. It is significant that the Lord Jesus during His earthly ministry discussed this very thing in connection with false teachers:

> Enter by the narrow gate; for wide is the gate and broad is the way that leads to destruction, and there are many who go in by it. Because narrow is the gate and difficult is the way which leads to life, and there are few who find it.
>
> Beware of false prophets, who come to you in sheep's clothing, but inwardly they are ravenous wolves. You will know them by their fruits. Do men gather grapes from thorn bushes or figs from thistles? Even so, every good tree bears good fruit, but a bad tree bears bad fruit. A good tree cannot bear bad fruit, nor can a bad tree bear good fruit. Every tree that does not bear good fruit is cut down and thrown into the fire. Therefore by their fruits you will know them.
>
> Not everyone who says to Me, "Lord, Lord," shall enter the kingdom of Heaven, but he who does the will of My Father in Heaven. Many will say to Me in that day, "Lord, Lord, have we not prophesied in Your name, cast out demons in Your name, and done many wonders in Your name?" And then I will declare to

them, "I never knew you; depart from Me, you who practice lawlessness!" [*Matthew* 7:13-23].

Furthermore, the OPC itself is and has always been a "micro-denomination" by any human measure. The OPC has just over 300 congregations, fewer than 400 ministers, and about 28,000 members. The PCUSA today has over 11,000 congregations, 14,000 ministers, and 2.4 million members. Size is not a measure of loyalty to the truth in either case (nor are rates of growth or decline).

Fellowship in the authoritative Word and in the true Gospel, mutual accountability before God in doctrine and in life – these are the things that matter to the Lord of the Church, who says that where even two or three are gathered in His name, and on that basis (*Matthew* 18:15-20), He is in their midst.

In 1936, conservatives who left the PCUSA to form the OPC numbered less than *one half of one percent* of the PCUSA's ordained men. Seven decades later, the OPC is still less than one percent of the size of the PCUSA.

The liberal minority, plus the doctrinally indifferent who cooperated with them, made up a majority sufficient to carry out the liberal agenda in the PCUSA. That was the dynamic that necessitated the formation of the OPC out of the theological ruins of the PCUSA. The same dynamic is at work today in the OPC. Neo-liberals and the doctrinally indifferent together make up a substantial majority, thus enabling the neo-liberals to exercise control and promote their theological agenda.

This should neither surprise nor discourage those in the OPC who remain true to the Gospel and the authority of Scripture. In his day, Elijah thought he was alone in remaining true to God, but the Lord assured him that He had reserved seven thousand in Israel – out of millions – who had not bowed the knee to Baal (*1 Kings* 19:13-18). On the day of Pentecost, when Peter preached powerfully, "Be saved from this perverse generation," just three thousand souls – out of a million or more from all corners of the world who were in Jerusalem for the feast – responded to the call (*Acts* 2:40-41). The pattern throughout Scripture is that of God accomplishing His work through remnants that are numerically insignificant to the worldly mind.

On the night of April 14, 1912, the *Titanic*, the largest ship afloat – of which it was said, "Even God could not sink this ship" – struck an iceberg in the North Atlantic. Within a few hours she sank in 12,000 feet of water, taking 1,507 people to their deaths. There were not enough lifeboats to carry all the people on board, but most of the boats that were provided pulled away from the sinking ship only partially loaded. Many of the people who perished believed it was safer to remain on the large but mortally wounded ship than to trust their lives to the safety of a small but sound boat.

It is not overly dramatic to say that the people of the Orthodox Presbyterian Church – and of other purportedly conservative denominations that have let the truth slip from their grasp – face a similar decision in the spiritual realm. The Holy Spirit plainly tells us that the issue is spiritual life and death. It is the worst kind of folly to assume that a denomination is "spiritually unsinkable" or that there is safety in size or numbers. There is safety only in the truth, and that truth is found in Jesus Christ and His Word alone.

At the beginning of this book, we observed that various groups of people inside and outside the OPC will respond in differing ways to the present spiritual crisis. This book has been a call to action for each of them.

A Call to Action for Those Who Were Unaware

Some have, until now, been truly unaware of the rise of neo-liberalism in their denomination. There are, among you, a few pastors, many ruling elders, and perhaps most of the members of OPC congregations. The denominational leadership of the OPC bears much of the responsibility for keeping many of its elders and members in the dark. There has been practically no public discussion – especially no *official* discussion – of the deepest controversies that have occurred along the path to the present crisis.

In the local church setting, many pastors and sessions have simply wished to avoid controversy. Some of those pastors have known the facts of the crisis but have hesitated to discuss them with their sessions. In other cases, pastors have informed their elders, but the sessions have chosen not to make the facts known to their congregations. Some pastors and sessions have remained silent because they actually fear that their people will awaken to action. Some say they are motivated by a desire to maintain peace and unity in the church, to prevent disturbance. But keeping God's people in ignorance actually undermines the doctrinal purity without which true peace and unity cannot exist, without which the church cannot fulfill its mission, and without which the people of God are in danger.

Some other pastors and sessions have remained silent because of a misconception about Presbyterian polity – that "good churchmanship" requires them to keep silent in the face of evil, not only in their local churches but even in their presbyteries and general assemblies. But that only plays into the hands of neo-liberals who, as we have seen, stand ready to manipulate church law and the rules of parliamentary procedure to further their ends.

Many church members who are now understanding the spiritual crisis for the first time are no doubt deeply disappointed. Many of you came to the OPC after troublesome experiences in other churches which had their own difficulties. Perhaps you came to faith in Christ in the OPC. You saw the OPC as a safe haven, a place of soundness and sweet fellowship. But even if your local church is still sound, please understand that the denomination as a whole is not, and that the Biblical imperative of separation from apostasy applies no less to you and your congregation than it does to your fellow believers who find themselves in the minority in congregations that are largely unsound.

Others who are learning of the crisis for the first time perhaps grew up in the OPC and have been in it for many years. Perhaps you have raised children in it, and they have raised children in it. Perhaps you still think of the OPC as the church of Machen. Please understand, as difficult as it may be to accept the fact: The OPC long ago ceased to be the church that Machen and other stalwarts of the faith founded three generations ago. It has forsaken the marks of a true church of Christ, just as the PCUSA did in Machen's day.

For those who have until now been uninformed or misinformed, whatever the reason, this book has been a call to become fully acquainted with the spiritual crisis in the OPC, and to understand the Biblical course of action. We encourage you to examine the evidence, both in this book and elsewhere, carefully. We urge you to carefully consider what the Scriptures have to say about the imperative of separation from apostasy, no matter what the cost. We urge you to be Bereans, to search the Scriptures to see if these things are so. And for those who have hesitated to sound the alarm as faithful watchmen should, this book has been a call to fulfill your God-given responsibility.

364

A Call to Action for Those Now Taking a Stand

Secondly, this book has been addressed to faithful pastors, elders, and church members who have recognized the growth of neo-liberalism in the OPC (though perhaps, until now, not by that name) and have actively opposed it.

In some cases congregations have stood firmly with their pastors and elders. Other ordained men have taken their stand without congregational or even sessional support. Within some congregations where neo-liberalism is rampant or doctrinal indifference holds sway, individuals and groups have arisen to oppose the growing error, and to alert others.

We praise the Lord that He has raised you up for such a time as this. For those of this faithful remnant, this book has been a call to recognize the dangers of remaining in the OPC, and to acknowledge that the time has come to separate from it. We urge you to be obedient to that Biblical imperative, no matter what the cost.

A Call to Believers Outside the OPC

There is also another group, outside the OPC, for whom we hope this book has been helpful and challenging. Some of the things that we have said about the Orthodox Presbyterian Church in these pages could also be said of other churches, denominations, and institutions where the cancer of neo-liberalism has spread. Faithful pastors, elders, deacons, and members of churches in other denominations may have recognized the crisis in the OPC as their own crisis as well. If so, we pray that you will recognize that the Biblical imperative applies to you as well.

An Appeal to the Doctrinally Indifferent

This book has also been addressed to the doctrinally indifferent – pastors, elders, and church members who have been aware of developments but have ignored, denied, or tolerated the growing apostasy. "Doctrinal indifference" is the term Machen used to describe the mindset of those who, by their cooperation or inaction, facilitated control of the PCUSA by the liberals in the 1920s and 1930s. Today, neo-liberals also rely on the cooperation or inaction of the doctrinally indifferent to exert control in the OPC.

We pray that the Lord will awaken those who have been doctrinally indifferent to recognize that neutrality regarding truth and error is impossible, that doctrinal inclusivism is a grave error, and that Christ calls on you to take an unambiguous stand for the truth no matter what the cost.

An Appeal to Neo-Liberals and Their Adherents

Lastly, this book has been addressed to neo-liberals in the OPC, and to those who have openly joined their cause.

You do not see yourselves as false teachers, or the followers of false teachers. Many of you believe that your teachings are superior to what has been taught in past generations. You believe they represent progress in theology, and that they correct supposedly long-held misconceptions about Christianity and about the Reformation. But what you are really doing is denying authentic Biblical Christianity. You do this while simultaneously saying that you remain completely faithful to Scripture and to the confessional standards of the church. You cannot have it both ways.

We pray that you will come to understand that you have been deceived. Your minds have been corrupted from the simplicity that is in Christ (2 *Corinthians* 11:3), and you are corrupting thousands of others. Jesus Christ himself warned against this:

> During that hour the disciples came to Jesus, saying, "Who then is the greatest in the kingdom of Heaven?" And having called to himself a little child, He stood it in their midst and said, "Assuredly, I am saying to you, unless you reverse your present trend of thought and become as the little children, in no case shall you enter the kingdom of Heaven. Therefore, he who is of such a nature as to humble himself like this little child, esteeming himself small inasmuch as he is so, thus thinking truly, and because truly, therefore humbly of himself, this person is the greatest in the kingdom of Heaven....
>
> "But whoever causes one of these little ones who believe in Me to stumble, it would be to his profit that a millstone were hung about his neck and that he be drowned in the depth of the sea. Woe to the world because of stumbling-blocks, for it is inevitable that stumbling-blocks come, but woe to the man through whom the stumbling-block comes" [*Matthew* 18:1-10].[15]

As we said at the outset, those who continue to stand for the truth fear for your souls. We fear that you, like Esau, having fallen short of the grace of God, will find "no place for repentance, though he sought it diligently with tears" (*Hebrews* 12:17). We continue to pray that the Holy Spirit will awaken you to understand that you have been deceived by the evil one, and we pray that godly sorrow will produce repentance. Indeed, we continue to pray that it may be said of you what Paul said to the church at Corinth:

15. Wuest, *The New Testament: An Expanded Translation.*

Now I rejoice, not that you were made sorry, but that your sorrow led to repentance.... For godly sorrow produces repentance leading to salvation, not to be regretted; but the sorrow of the world produces death. For observe this very thing, that you sorrowed in a godly manner: What diligence it produced in you, what clearing of yourselves, what indignation, what fear, what vehement desire, what zeal, what vindication! In all things you proved yourselves to be clear in this matter [2 Corinthians 7:9-11].

And finally, a word to all readers: Let all those who say they would stand for the truth now take that stand. In all questions where God and men are at odds, we must obey God rather than men. This is not a time for complacency, or indifference, or fear of men rather than fear of God. Some may think that heeding the Biblical imperative involves risks that are too great to take. But the position of true risk is the position that stands against the truth. Those who take their stand for the truth will find in the end that it was no risk at all, because God will bless it. "Watch, stand fast in the faith, be brave, be strong" (1 Corinthians 16:13).

Appendix A

The Auburn Affirmation

The Auburn Affirmation was first published in January 1924. The document was initially signed by 150 ministers of the Presbyterian Church in the U. S. A. (PCUSA). By the end of May 1924 there were 1,294 signers, including both ministers and ruling elders, and only one man had asked that his name be removed. The text reproduced below is from the May 5, 1924 printing issued by The Jacobs Press, Auburn, New York.

An Affirmation
designed to safeguard the unity and liberty of the Presbyterian Church in the United States of America submitted for the consideration of its ministers and people.

We, the undersigned, ministers of the Presbyterian Church in the United States of America, feel bound, in view of certain actions of the General Assembly of 1923 and of persistent attempts to divide the church and abridge its freedom, to express our convictions in matters pertaining thereto. At the outset we affirm and declare our acceptance of the Westminster Confession of Faith, as we did at our ordinations, "as containing the system of doctrine taught in the Holy Scriptures." We sincerely hold and earnestly preach the doctrines of evangelical Christianity, in agreement with the historic testimony of the Presbyterian Church in the United States of America, of which we are loyal ministers. For the maintenance of the faith of our church, the preservation of its unity, and the protection of the liberties of its ministers and people, we offer this Affirmation.

The church's guarantee of liberty (1) concerning the interpretation of the Confession of Faith, and (2) concerning the interpretation of the Scriptures

I. By its law and its history, the Presbyterian Church in the United States of America safeguards the liberty of thought and teaching of its ministers. At their ordinations they "receive and adopt the confession of Faith of this Church, as containing the system of doctrine taught in the Holy Scriptures." This the church has always esteemed a sufficient doctrinal subscription for its ministers. Manifestly it does not require their assent to the very words of the Confession, or to all of its teachings, or to interpretations of the Confessions by individuals or church courts. The Confession of Faith itself disclaims infallibility. Its authors would not allow this to church councils, their own included: "All synods or councils since the apostles' times, whether general or particular, may err, and many have erred; therefore they are not to be made the rule of faith or practice, but to be used as a help in both" (Conf. XXXI, iii). The confession also expressly asserts the liberty of Christian believers, and condemns the submission of the mind or conscience to any human authority: "God alone is lord of the conscience, and hath left it free from the doctrines and commandments of men which are in any thing contrary to his Word, or beside it, in matters of faith or worship. So that to believe such doctrines, or to obey such commandments out of conscience, is to betray true liberty of conscience; and the requiring of an implicit faith, and an absolute and blind obedience, is to destroy liberty of conscience, and reason also" (Conf. XX, ii).

The formal relation of American Presbyterianism to the Westminster Confession of Faith begins in the Adopting Act of 1729. This anticipated and provided for dissent by individuals from portions of the Confession. At the formation of the Presbyterian Church in the United States of America, in 1788, the Westminster Confession was adopted as the creed of the church; and at the same time the church publicly declared the significance of its organization in a document which contains these words: "There are truths and forms, with respect to which men of good characters and principles may differ. And in all these they think it the duty, both of private Christians and Societies, to exercise mutual forbearance towards each other" (Declaration of Principles, v).

Of the two parts into which our church was separated from 1837 to 1870, one held that only one interpretation of certain parts of the Confession of Faith was legitimate, while the other maintained its right to dissent from this interpretation. In the Reunion of 1870 they came together on equal terms, "each recognizing the other as a sound and orthodox body." The meaning of this, as understood then and ever since, is that office-bearers in the church who maintain their liberty in the interpretation of the confessions are exercising their rights guaranteed by the terms of the Reunion.

A more recent reunion also is significant, that of the Cumberland Presbyterian Church and the Presbyterian Church in the United States of America, in 1906. This reunion was opposed by certain members of the Presbyterian Church in the United States of America, on the ground that the two churches were not at one in doctrine; yet it was consummated. Thus did our church once more exemplify its historic policy of accepting theological differences within its bounds and subordinating them to recognized loyalty to Jesus Christ and united work for the kingdom of God.

With respect to the interpretation of the Scriptures the position of our church has been that common to Protestants. "The Supreme Judge," says the Confession of Faith, "by whom all controversies of religion are to be determined, and all decrees of councils, opinions of ancient writers, doctrines of men, and private spirits, are to be examined, and in whose sentence we are to rest, can be no other but the Holy Spirit speaking in the Scripture" (Conf. I, x). Accordingly our church has held that the supreme guide in the interpretation of the Scriptures is not, as it is with Roman Catholics, ecclesiastical authority, but the Spirit of God, speaking to the Christian believer. Thus our church lays it upon its ministers and others to read and teach the Scriptures as the Spirit of God through His manifold ministries instructs them, and to receive all truth which from time to time He causes to break forth from the Scriptures.

There is no assertion in the Scriptures that their writers were kept "from error." The Confession of Faith does not make this assertion; and it is significant that this assertion is not to be found in the Apostles' Creed or the Nicene Creed or in any of the great Reformation confessions. The doctrine of inerrancy, intended to enhance the authority of the Scriptures, in fact impairs their supreme authority for faith and life, and weakens the testimony of the church to the power of God unto salvation through Jesus Christ. We hold that the General Assembly of 1923, in asserting that "the Holy Spirit did so inspire, guide and move the writers of Holy Scripture as to keep them from error," spoke without warrant of the Scriptures or of the Confession of Faith. We hold rather to the words of the Confession of Faith, that the Scriptures "are given by inspiration of God, to be the rule of faith and life" (Conf. I, ii).

Authority under the constitution for the declaration of doctrine

II. While it is constitutional for any General Assembly "to bear testimony against error in doctrine" (Form of Govt. XII, v), yet such testimony is without binding authority, since the constitution of our church provides that its doctrine shall be declared only by concurrent action of the General Assembly and the presbyteries. Thus the church guards the statement of its doctrine against hasty or ill-considered action by either General Assemblies or presbyteries. From this provision of our constitution, it is evident that neither in one General Assembly nor in many, without concurrent action of the presbyteries, is there authority to declare what the Presbyterian Church in the United States of America believes and teaches; and that the assumption that any General Assembly has authoritatively declared what the church believes and teaches is groundless. A declaration by a General Assembly that any doctrine is "an essential doctrine" attempts to amend the constitution of the church in an unconstitutional manner.

Action of the General Assembly regarding the preaching in the First Presbyterian Church of New York City

III. The General Assembly of 1923, in asserting that "doctrines contrary to the standards of the Presbyterian Church" have been preached in the pulpit of the First Presbyterian Church of New York City, virtually pronounced a judgment against this church. The General Assembly did this with knowledge that the matter on which it so expressed itself was already under formal consideration in the Presbytery of New York, as is shown by the language of its action. The General Assembly acted in the case without giving hearing to the parties concerned. Thus the General Assembly did not conform to the procedure in such cases contemplated by our Book of Discipline, and, what is more serious, it in effect condemned a Christian minister without using the method of conference, patience and love enjoined on us by Jesus Christ. We object to the action of the General Assembly in this case, as being out of keeping with the law and the spirit of our church.

The doctrinal deliverance of the General Assembly

IV. The General Assembly of 1923 expressed the opinion concerning five doctrinal statements that each one "is an essential doctrine of the Word of God and our standards." On the constitutional grounds which we have before described, we are opposed to any attempt to elevate these five doctrinal statements, or any of them, to the position of test for ordination or for good standing in our church.

Furthermore, this opinion of the General Assembly attempts to commit our church to certain theories concerning the inspiration of the Bible, and the Incarnation, the Atonement, the Resurrection, and the Continuing Life and Supernatural Power of our Lord Jesus Christ. We all hold most earnestly to these great facts and doctrines; we all believe from our hearts that the writers of the Bible were inspired of God; that Jesus Christ was God manifest in the flesh; that God was in Christ, reconciling the world unto Himself, and through Him we have our redemption; that having died for our sins He rose from the dead and is our ever-living Saviour; that in His earthly ministry He wrought many mighty works, and by His vicarious death and unfailing presence He is able to save to the uttermost. Some of

374

us regard the particular theories contained in the deliverance of the General Assembly of 1923 as satisfactory explanations of these facts and doctrines. But we are united in believing that these are not the only theories allowed by the Scriptures and our standards as explanations of these facts and doctrines of our religion, and that all who hold to these facts and doctrines, whatever theories they may employ to explain them, are worthy of all confidence and fellowship.

Extent of the liberty claimed

V. We do not desire liberty to go beyond the teachings of evangelical Christianity. But we maintain that it is our constitutional right and our Christian duty within these limits to exercise liberty of thought and teaching, that we may more effectively preach the Gospel of Jesus Christ, the Saviour of the World.

The spirit and purpose of this affirmation

VI. Finally, we deplore the evidences of division in our beloved church, in the face of a world so desperately in need of a united testimony to the gospel of Christ. We earnestly desire fellowship with all who like us are disciples of Jesus Christ. We hope that those to whom this Affirmation comes will believe that it is not the declaration of a theological party, but rather a sincere appeal, based on the Scriptures and our standards, for the preservation of the unity and freedom of our church, for which most earnestly we plead and pray.

* * * * * * * * * * * * * * * * * *

Presenters' notes:

In issuing for the second time the Affirmation, first published in January 1924, the Conference Committee is fulfilling its promise to publish all signatures received up to April

15th. That the record may be complete, the Note Supplementary, issued in March, is also included. The committee urges on the attention of the ministers and people of the Presbyterian Church in the United States of America these considerations:

1. The number of signatures, 1,274, is far greater than the Committee had anticipated.[1] Furthermore, the Committee has certain knowledge, through many letters and conversations, that beside the signers there are in our church hundreds of ministers who agree with and approve of the Affirmation, though they have refrained from signing it.

2. No one can read this long list of signatures, containing honored names of men whose Christian character is known to all and whose ministries have been blessed with abundant fruits, without recognizing that these ministers cannot justly be charged with unfaithfulness to their ordination engagements, with revolt against rightful authority in the church, or with forsaking Christian belief. The support of such a company makes it evident that the principles restated in the Affirmation are in accord with the standards of our church.

3. The signers of the Affirmation are not a theological party. Among them are men who call themselves and are called conservatives, and men who call themselves and are called liberals. Differing as to certain theological interpretations, they are one in loyalty to our church, in devotion to the kingdom of God, and in faith in our Lord and Saviour Jesus Christ.

4. These signatures constitute an appeal to the church, both at large and as represented in its commissioners to the General Assembly, for a general adoption of this same spirit

---

1. The final total at the end of May 1924 was 1,294.

of mutual confidence and unity, for a recognition of the fact that our church is broad enough to include men honestly different in their interpretation of our common standards and yet loyal servants of Jesus Christ, and for a new consecration of the whole church to work for the world in obedience to our Lord.

Murray Shipley Howland
Robert Brewster Beattie
Philip Smead Bird
James E. Clarke
John J. Lawrence
Alexander MacColl
Malcolm L. MacPhail
William P. Merrill
William L. Sawtelle
Robert Hastings Nichols
George B. Stewart

Conference Committee

May 1924

Appendix B

Kinnaird Memorandum

Arlyn and Wanda Wilkening submitted a charge of heresy against ruling elder John O. Kinnaird to the session of Bethany OPC, Oxford, Pennsylvania, on March 18, 2002. Four days later, a member of the congregation discovered a memorandum written by Kinnaird that had been left behind on the church photocopier. The memo, from Kinnaird to the rest of the seven-man session majority, outlined a detailed strategy to engineer his acquittal. Kinnaird's plan stated two purposes: to have the session adopt his heretical theological statement as the official position of the church, and to dismiss the Wilkenings' charge without a trial. The memo, reproduced on the following pages, detailed two alternative versions of the scheme, labeled "Plan One – Safe" and "Plan Two – Risky."

Kinnaird's memo instructed his allies on the session to sequence the dockets of upcoming meetings to achieve his stated goals. They were to use specific parliamentary maneuvers to orchestrate proceedings to his benefit, such as moving from open session into executive (closed) session at one critical juncture, and moving into a committee of the whole to permit off-the-record discussions during open session at another point. He instructed his allies to make motions on his behalf at critical moments in those meetings – motions he would not be permitted by the OPC Book of Discipline to make himself because he was a potential heresy defendant. And, John Kinnaird instructed his fellow elders to vote to dismiss the Wilkening charge against him.

These actions clearly violated the OPC Book of Discipline's provision that "the accused may not sit in judgment on his own case at any stage thereof, including the preliminary investigation"

(Book of Discipline *chapter 4, section 3.a*), *to say nothing of Scripture's condemnation of wicked conspiracies (e.g.,* Psalm 10:2, 64:2; Proverbs 6:16-19*).*

PLAN ONE - Safe

Brothers:

March 25 will have Stevenson[1] on the chair.

April 1 will be in Executive Session.

April 15 is a regular Session Meeting.

I would appreciate your help in finally bringing my Theological Statements[2] to a vote. We can not do this while there is a pending charge, or a related complaint, against me. We now have Foraker's pending complaint on the Schmidt charge[3] case. We have a pending charge from the Wilkenings.

I would propose the following procedure to get the complaint and the charge off the agenda and to avoid some new charge or complaint coming on the agenda long enough so that we can have the agenda empty of charges and complaints while considering my Theological Statements. The procedure I would propose is somewhat complicated.

---

1. David J. Stevenson, who was Associate Pastor of Bethany OPC and an ally of John O. Kinnaird.

2. *Kinnaird Declaration and Theological Statement*, reproduced at www.trinityfoundation.org/KinnairdDeclarationTheologicalStatement.php.

3. The Schmidt charge alleged misconduct by John Kinnaird in a separate matter, and was also dismissed by the Bethany session without a trial.

Also, I am prohibited from making motions pertaining to the Wilkening charges. Therefore some planning needs to be done. We will need to assign somebody to make motions that I can not make. Here's the plan as I would propose it:

March 25

Postpone Kinnaird Theology [4] until April 15.

Complete the docket in open session.

April 1

Docket the Wilkening charges and the Foraker complaint in 1rst [sic] and end spots.

Seat my counsel [5] with privileges of the floor.

Invite the Wilkenings to observe the handling of the Wilkening charges.

Go into a committee of the whole (I'll explain below).

Discuss the Wilkening charges and specifications as to admissibility.

Come out of the committee of the whole.

Move that specifications 1, 2, and 3 be found to not support the charge.

Move the previous question (and vote in favor).

Move to postpone the vote until April 15 (and vote in favor).

Finish consideration on the Foraker complaint.

Complete the docket for April 1 and adjourn.

4. *Kinnaird Declaration and Theological Statement.*

5. Thomas E. Tyson.

At this point there will only a pending charge, ready to be voted on without any further debate, on the agenda. There can be no complaint re the Wilkening charges as we will have not yet taken any action.

Sometime - Notify potential observers that there will be a period of executive session first thing on the 15th and that it is expected to end about whatever hour, depending on what's on the docket.

April 15

Docket Wilkening Charges in 1rst [*sic*] spot.

Docket any other confidential items to follow the Wilkening charges.

Docket Kinnaird Theology[6] next.

Go into executive session.

Vote seriatim on the specifications (hopefully vote that they do not support the charge).

Move that the Wilkening charge not be admitted.

Vote on the admissibility of the charge (hopefully vote that it is not admissible).

Handle any other confidential matters.

Come out of executive session.

Handle Kinnaird Theology next (before anybody submits a complaint).

---

6. *Kinnaird Declaration and Theological Statement.*

Notes:

While in executive Session

- There can be only invited visitors.
- Action can be taken on motions.

In a committee of the whole

- Action can not be taken.
- Only a motion to come out of committee can be made.
- Discussion can be held without a motion on the floor.
- Discussion can be broader than any anticipated motion.

PLAN TWO - Risky

Brothers:

March 25 will have Stevenson[7] on the chair.

April 1 will be in Executive Session.

April 15 is a regular Session Meeting

I would prefer a procedure to get the present complaint and charge off the agenda and that prevents some new charge or complaint coming on the agenda so that we can have an agenda empty of charges and complaints long enough to consider my Theological Statements.[8] However, that procedure is somewhat complicated. Therefore here is a simpler procedure but one that runs considerable risk that a new charge or complaint might be filed before we can get to vote on my Theological Statements.

I am prohibited from making motions pertaining to the Wilkening charges. Therefore some planning needs to be done. We will need to assign somebody to make motions that I can not make.

Here's the plan as I would propose it.

March 25

Postpone Kinnaird Theology until April 15.
Complete the docket in open session.

---

7. David J. Stevenson, who was Associate Pastor of Bethany OPC and an ally of John O. Kinnaird.

8. *Kinnaird Declaration and Theological Statement.*

April 1

Docket the Wilkening charges and the Foraker complaint in 1rst [*sic*] and 2nd spots.

Seat my counsel[9] with privileges on the floor.

Invite the Wilkenings to observe the handling of the Wilkening charges.

Go into a committee of the whole (I'll explain below).

Discuss the Wilkening charges and specifications as to admissibility.

Come out of the committee of the whole.

Move that specifications 1, 2, and 3 be found not to support the charge.

Move that the previous question (and vote in favor).

Move that the vote be taken seriatim (and vote in favor).

Vote on Specification 1, then on 2, and then on 3 (and hopefully vote that they not be found in order).

Move that the Wilkening charges not be admitted (and hopefully vote that they not be admitted).

Dismiss the Wilkenings.

Finish consideration on the Foraker complaint.

Complete the docket for April 1 and opadjourn.

April 15

Docket Kinnaird Theology [10] as early as possible.

9. Thomas E. Tyson.

10. *Kinnaird Declaration and Theological Statement*.

Notes:

While in executive session

- There can be only invited visitors.
- Action can be taken on motions.

In a committee of the whole

- Action can not be taken.
- Only a motion to come out of committee can be made.
- Discussion can be held without a motion on the floor.
- Discussion can be broader than any anticipated motion.

Appendix C

Proposed (Rejected) Overture to the 2004 General Assembly

In November 2003, a group of concerned men in the Presbytery of Philadelphia of the Orthodox Presbyterian Church submitted an overture seeking to clarify the church's damaged witness concerning the doctrine of justification by faith alone. This overture, reproduced below, faced strong opposition in the Presbytery of Philadelphia. It was rejected by being tabled after a year-long filibuster by neo-liberals and their supporters (see chapter seven, "Efforts to Right the Wrong Defeated").

A shorter overture drafted along similar lines was defeated in the Presbytery of New Jersey.

An overture virtually identical to the one reproduced below was proposed in a session in the Presbytery of the Mid-Atlantic, but when it became apparent that there was little likelihood of passage in the full Presbytery, it was withdrawn.

In the Presbytery of the Midwest, a concerned session submitted an overture virtually identical to the one below. It was rejected by Alan D. Strange, the moderator of the presbytery, as out of order because in his view it would reopen the Kinnaird case. The signers submitted a watered-down version, but it was also ruled out of order for the same reason. In its place, the Presbytery of the Midwest passed a much weaker overture, which was subsequently adopted as a resolution by the 71st General Assembly.

The following is the text of the original overture submitted to the Presbytery of Philadelphia. Footnotes are as they appear in the original document.

Overture to the 71st (2004) General Assembly Regarding the 70th (2003) General Assembly's Decision Concerning the Doctrine of Justification

To the Presbytery of Philadelphia of the
Orthodox Presbyterian Church

The undersigned respectfully petition the Presbytery
to overture the 71st General Assembly as follows:

I. PREAMBLE

The vows that officers of the Orthodox Presbyterian Church take for ordination and installation into office include the vow to maintain the truths of the gospel and the purity, peace, and unity of the church. Commitment to that vow lay behind the origins of the OPC and its founding in 1936. We trust that it will be recognized that we who support this overture seek to pursue that commitment not only to the doctrinal purity of the Church, but to its peace and unity as well. We also trust that it will be recognized that there can be no true peace and unity without doctrinal purity.

When there is a difference in essential doctrines, adversarial attitudes may develop which endanger the purity, peace, and unity of the Church. At such times we need to exercise brotherly love, even as we earnestly contend for the faith with respect to purity of doctrine. We need also to entreat our Lord to enable His people to do, with forthrightness and objectivity, that which is necessary to maintain the truths of the gospel and the purity, peace, and unity of the church.

Who is sufficient for these things? Only God. May He help us.

II. PURPOSE

The purpose of this Overture is to rectify the present confusion that has compromised the doctrinal witness of the Orthodox Presbyterian Church, resulting from the 70th (2003) General Assembly's decision in a judicial case involving the doctrine of justification. We believe that the actions outlined in this Overture are necessary to accomplish that end, and thus to restore the purity, peace, and unity of the Church.

III. REMEDIAL ACTION

We therefore petition the 71st (2004) General Assembly to adopt the following resolution:

BE IT THEREFORE NOW RESOLVED THAT

The 71st (2004) General Assembly of The Orthodox Presbyterian Church declares its continued commitment to the teaching of the Word of God, the Westminster Confession of Faith, the Larger and Shorter Catechisms with regard to the doctrine of justification,

AND,

Inasmuch as an action of the 70th (2003) General Assembly in a judicial case involving the doctrine of justification tolerates views contrary to the teaching of the Standards,

THIS GENERAL ASSEMBLY

1. Affirms:
    a. That the action of the 70th (2003) General Assembly does not and cannot change the constitutional commitment of the Church to the Word of God and the subordinate Westminster Standards;

b. That the action of the Assembly nevertheless led to confusion both within and without the Church, and compromise of its witness, by allowing certain doctrinal statements brought into evidence in the trial to stand without comment, clarification or correction, and therefore

c. This confusion needs to be corrected.

2. Declares unequivocally the following beliefs:

a. Justification is not by works of any kind on man's part, nor do our works provide any contribution to that justification. Rather, justification is the irreversible declarative judicial act of God's free grace at conversion, wherein he freely pardons all our sins and accepts us as righteous in His sight, only on account of the righteousness of Christ imputed to us, and received by faith alone. God's justification of the ungodly is by grace alone, through faith alone, in Christ alone.

b. No one will be justified at the Day of Judgment because of his own obedience to the law. The judgment according to works at the Day of Judgment is not a second or further justification. Rather, justification at conversion is perfect and final through the perfect righteousness of Christ imputed to us, so that all believers will be openly acknowledged and acquitted at that Day as righteous, because of Christ's perfect obedience and imputed righteousness alone.

c. Justification is distinct from sanctification. Sanctification by the Holy Spirit is a blessing that all believers enjoy, to renew us in holiness, and in sanctified obedience to the law of God, which is holy, just, and good. But this sanctified obedience does not attain perfection in this life and cannot justify us before God. It is, rather, the outward evidence that we have been justified by the Lord our Righteousness alone.

3. Declares that it is impermissible within the Constitution of the Church:

    a. To teach explicitly, or by way of implication, that entrance into Heaven is on any basis other than the work of Jesus Christ, and

    b. To teach anything that states or implies that sanctification contributes anything to God's judicial acceptance of the believer either in this life or at the final judgment and, thus confuses justification and sanctification.

4. And therefore:

    a. Calls upon all officers to examine their beliefs and teachings, especially with respect to the doctrines of justification, sanctification, and the Day of Judgment, to make certain that their beliefs and teachings are in accord with the Word of God and our subordinate standards.

    b. Urges any who may hold contrary doctrines to repent and retract them.

    c. Warns all officers to be aggressively on guard against the onslaught of the erroneous teachings of our day, which lead to confusion and compromise on these doctrines.

d. Urges all officers and members to pray diligently for one another to these ends.

e. Urges all officers to give careful attention to instructing their congregations on these matters of doctrine, in accord with the Word of God and our subordinate standards.

f. Directs the Clerk of the Assembly to send this Resolution, within two weeks of the adjournment of the Assembly, to all ministers and sessions of the Church, and to all churches with which the OPC is in ecclesiastical relationship, and to the two ecumenical bodies of which the Orthodox Presbyterian Church is a member, namely, the North American Presbyterian and Reformed Council (NAPARC) and the International Conference of Reformed Churches (ICRC).

g. Calls upon the Committees on Christian Education, Foreign Missions, and Home Missions and Church Extension to take action at their respective next regular meetings to explicitly assure the Church publicly that their representatives and their publications will teach, clearly and consistently, in accord with the declarations and affirmations in this Resolution.

h. Directs that this Resolution be displayed prominently on the OPC web site (www.opc.org) at the earliest possible time.

i. Directs that this Resolution be displayed prominently in New Horizons at the earliest possible time.

III. GROUNDS

A. The (2003) General Assembly's Decision and Its Effects

1. How the Decision Produced Confusion

Some, perhaps many, may believe that the vote in deciding the judicial case was not an endorsement of the specific language appearing in the record of the case, nor even an endorsement of its general course, but only a refusal to find these views worthy of the severity of the censure imposed by the trial judicatory. Yet to sustain the appeal in toto, as was done, is liable to give the impression that those teachings are acceptable in our Church; in harmony with the Bible and the Westminster Standards; and therefore, to be regarded as the de facto teachings of the OPC. However, these teachings are in conflict with the historic Protestant gospel doctrines of justification and sanctification.

It is not acceptable that a General Assembly of the OPC should bring about confusion as to the Church's position on the doctrines of justification and sanctification, which were the crux of the case, not only among members of our own denomination, but also elsewhere in the Reformed community and beyond. Such confusion on basic doctrines not only compromises the clarity of our Church's testimony to the gospel of Christ but also endangers the purity, peace and unity of the Church, and indeed endangers the souls of men.

2. Teachings presented as evidence in the case that have led to confusion about the witness of the Orthodox Presbyterian Church:

    a. "It is those who obey the law who will be declared righteous on that Day of Judgement."[1]

    b. "It is not possible that any could be a brother to Jesus Christ and enjoy with Christ, in the Kingdom of Heaven, the presence of God the Father except that one be fully conformed to the image of Christ in true and personal righteousness and holiness.... [T]he imputation of the righteousness of Christ, which all Christians receive at justification...can[not] suffice for that purpose. Christ does not have an imputed righteousness; His righteousness is real and personal. If we are to be conformed to his image, we too must have a real and personal righteousness." [2]

    c. "Whereas in justification we receive credit for the righteousness of Christ, here [in sanctification] we receive, through the work of the Holy Spirit, a righteousness that is really and personally our very own, not just that of another credited to us, but our very personal own." [3]

    d. "Thus we rightly conclude that those inside the city [of Revelation 22] are those who have kept

1. John O. Kinnaird, "A Proposal for the Session" [also known as the *Kinnaird Declaration and Theological Statement*], October 25, 2001.

2. John O. Kinnaird, "A Proposal for the Session" [also known as the *Kinnaird Declaration and Theological Statement*], October 25, 2001.

3. John O. Kinnaird, message number 7846 entitled "Justification," posted on the Presbyterians-OPC Yahoo® Internet forum December 24, 2001, 2; evidence received by the trial judicatory at its first meeting, and discussed in two papers supplied to the judicatory and read aloud at its second meeting, November 23, 2002. [This document is reproduced at http://www.trinityfoundation.org/OPCListPosting12-24-01.php.]

the law of God and those only. So, a pretty simple answer to our last two questions. Inside the city are those who do righteousness and outside are those who do evil." [4]

e. "*Romans* 2 puts it this way. 'God will give to each person according to what he has done. To those who by persistence in doing good seek glory, honor and immortality, He will give eternal life. But for those who are self seeking and who reject the truth and follow evil there will be wrath and anger.' Now by this we know the decision, the judgement as to who enters the city and who stays outside for eternity will be made on that great day of judgement in accordance with what you have done in this life."[5]

f. "God has provided not only justification from the guilt of sin, he has also, for all those begotten from above by the seed of God, provided that holiness without which no one will see the Lord. *Hebrews* 12:14. These good works are a required condition if we would stand in the Day of Judgement and they are supplied by God to all His people.

"Every description of the Judgement events speaks of these good works. Without them, no one will see God. Our God is not unjust. His judgements are always righteous and in accord-

4. John O. Kinnaird, "Though the Waters Roar and the Mountains Quake," sermon preached September 22, 2000.

5. John O. Kinnaird, "Though the Waters Roar and the Mountains Quake," sermon preached September 22, 2000.

ance with the facts of the case. On the past two Lord's Days I shared over 25 texts and passages of Scripture with my Sunday School class on just these two concepts. They were about evenly divided between the concept that our God's judgements are always righteous and in accord with the facts of the case and the concept that the final judgement will be in accord with what we have done in this life." [6]

g. "There will be glory, honor, and peace on the Day of Judgement for everyone who does good. [*Romans* 2] v.10. Who are these people who thus benefit – who stand on the Day of Judgement? They are those who obey the law who will be declared righteous. [*Romans* 2] v.13. When God declares them righteous that is a forensic declaration of righteousness.... This is a judicial scene, the Day of Judgement. It is an act of God sitting as Judge. It is justification – a forensic act of God whereby he declares a person righteous. God is able to make this declaration on That Day because it is a truth. Something has happened to change those who were once sinful. What is it?...Paul says, [*Romans* 2] v. 14 and 15, these are those who by nature, a new nature, do the things required by the law."[7]

6. John O. Kinnaird, message number 8014 titled "justification" (*sic*) posted on the Presbyterians-OPC Yahoo® Internet forum January 6, 2002. [This document is reproduced at http://www.trinityfoundation. org/OPCListPosting1.php.]

7. John O. Kinnaird, message number 8014 .

B. Errors may creep into the church when unguarded or erroneous teachings are allowed to circulate unchecked.

  1. The Nature of the Errors

    a. That the obedience of believers (which the Westminster Confession calls "evangelical obedience") is not only the fruit and evidence of justification, but also the instrument, ground or component of justification (or any other grace that may be imagined as necessary to the obtaining of acquittal at the Last Judgment.)

    b. That justification is not one act but two.

    c. That the righteousness of Christ imputed to us and received by faith alone is not sufficient to gain for the true believer acceptance with God or entrance into the eternal kingdom.

    d. That God's reward of evangelical obedience, of which the Bible and our Confession speak, is eternal life.

    e. That justification is progressive.

    f. That anything less than "personal, entire, exact, and perpetual obedience" (WCF XIX:1) can obtain God's favor.

  2. The truths that these errors ignore or confuse:

    a. The absolute obedience required by God's moral law

    b. The utter inadequacy of our own obedience for justification

    c. The sufficiency of the righteousness of Christ

    d. The essential principles of imputation and substitution

    e. Christ our righteousness, and Perfect Substitute

    f. Complete and perfect justification through the righteousness and obedience of Christ alone, received by faith alone, apart from works of any kind on our part

    g. Salvation by grace alone

    h. Sanctification and justification clearly distinguished from each other

    i. Sanctification as the believer's deliverance from the dominion of sin, but not yet in this life from the presence of indwelling sin.

C. Error in Essential Doctrine Must Be Corrected

It is important that the Church understand that under our Constitution judicial decisions are final with reference only to that particular judicial decision; they do not establish a binding precedent. However, when a General Assembly becomes convinced that a judicial action of a prior Assembly tolerates serious doctrinal error, even if such a result was unintended, the General Assembly must act to remedy that situation. In a case of confusion arising from error on basic doctrine, such action is the more imperative.

D. The Scriptures clearly teach, and our secondary Westminster Standards likewise affirm, the following truths:

    1. Nothing less than perfect obedience of the law of God can save.

2. No man can keep the requirements of the law perfectly.

3. Therefore, the keeping of the law by man is excluded from justification.

4. The sole basis of our justification, the only basis on which we can enter the Kingdom of Heaven, is the real and personal righteousness of Christ our perfect substitute, imputed to sinners by grace through faith, apart from the law.

5. God declares the sinner righteous at conversion, imputing the perfect righteousness of Christ to him. Our justification is complete and final at conversion.

6. On the Day of Judgment, God will openly acknowledge and acquit His elect, affirming the forensic declaration of their justification that took place once and for all at conversion. At the Judgment we shall stand at Christ's right hand on the basis of His righteousness alone.

7. Obedience is required of believers, and the grace of sanctification does work obedience in us. But that obedience cannot qualify us for any further justification at the Day of Judgment. In sanctification sin is subdued, but not perfectly in this life because the remnants of it abide in every part of us until we are glorified. Our good works, done in obedience to God's commandments, though imperfect in this life, are the fruits and evidences of saving faith.

E. The Scriptures and the Standards directly and explicitly address each of these points.

1. Nothing less than perfect obedience of the law of God can save.

    a. Thus the Scriptures[8] teach:

        i. "And He said to him, 'You have answered rightly; do this and you will live'" (*Luke* 10:28).

        ii. "For not the hearers of the law are just in the sight of God, but the doers of the law will be justified" (*Romans* 2:13).

        iii. "Whoever shall keep the whole law, and yet stumble in one point, he is guilty of all" (*James* 2:10).

        iv. "Cursed is the one who does not confirm all the words of this law. And all the people shall say, 'Amen!'" (*Deuteronomy* 27:26).

    b. Thus the Westminster Standards affirm:

        i. "God gave to Adam a law, as a covenant of works, by which He bound him and all his posterity, to personal, entire, exact, and perpetual obedience, promised life upon the fulfilling, and threatened death upon the breach of it, and endued him with power and ability to keep it" (WCF XIX:1).

        ii. "This law, after the fall, continued to be a perfect rule of righteousness; and, as such, was delivered by God upon Mount Sinai, in ten commandments, and written in two

8. All Scripture quotations are from the *New King James Bible* unless otherwise noted.

tables: the first four commandments containing our duty towards God; and the other six, our duty to man" (WCF XIX:2).

    iii. "The moral law doth forever bind all, as well justified persons as others, to the obedience thereof; and that, not only in regard of the matter contained in it, but also in respect of the authority of God the Creator, who gave it. Neither doth Christ, in the gospel, any way dissolve, but much strengthen this obligation" (WCF XIX:5).

2. No man can keep the requirements of the law perfectly.

    a. Thus the Scriptures teach:

        i. "For as many as are of the works of the law are under the curse; for it is written, 'Cursed is everyone who does not continue in all things which are written in the book of the law, to do them' " (*Galatians* 3:10).

        ii. "Among whom also we all once conducted ourselves in the lusts of our flesh, fulfilling the desires of the flesh and of the mind, and were by nature children of wrath, just as the others" (*Ephesians* 2:3). "Moreover the law entered that the offense might abound" (*Romans* 5:20).

        iii. "They have all turned aside; they have together become unprofitable; there is none who does good, no, not one" (*Romans* 3:12).

iv. "Now we know that whatever the law says, it says to those who are under the law, that every mouth may be stopped, and all the world may become guilty before God" (*Romans* 3:19).

v. "Therefore the law is holy, and the commandment holy and just and good. Has then what is good become death to me? Certainly not! But sin, that it might appear sin, was producing death in me through what is good, so that sin through the commandment might become exceedingly sinful. For we know that the law is spiritual, but I am carnal, sold under sin. For what I am doing, I do not understand. For what I will to do, that I do not practice; but what I hate, that I do. If, then, I do what I will not to do, I agree with the law that it is good. But now, it is no longer I who do it, but sin that dwells in me. For I know that in me (that is, in my flesh) nothing good dwells; for to will is present with me, but how to perform what is good I do not find. For the good that I will to do, I do not do; but the evil I will not to do, that I practice" (*Romans* 7:12-19).

b. Thus the Westminster Standards affirm:

i. "From this original corruption, whereby we are utterly indisposed, disabled, and made opposite to all good, and wholly inclined to all evil, do proceed all actual transgressions" (WCF VI:4).

    ii. "This corruption of nature, during this life, doth remain in those that are regenerated; and although it be, through Christ, pardoned, and mortified; yet both itself, and all the motions thereof, are truly and properly sin" (WCF VI:5).

    iii. "Every sin, both original and actual, being a transgression of the righteous law of God, and contrary thereunto, doth, in its own nature, bring guilt upon the sinner, whereby he is bound over to the wrath of God, and curse of the law, and so made subject to death, with all miseries spiritual, temporal, and eternal" (WCF VI:6).

3. Therefore, the keeping of the law by man is excluded from justification.

    a. Thus the Scriptures teach:

       i. "Therefore by the deeds of the law no flesh will be justified in His sight, for by the law is the knowledge of sin" (*Romans* 3:20).

       ii. "Where is boasting then? It is excluded. By what law? Of works? No, but by the law of faith. Therefore we conclude that a man is justified by faith apart from the deeds of the law" (*Romans* 3:27-28).

       iii. "What then shall we say that Abraham our father has found according to the flesh? For if Abraham was justified by works, he has something to boast about, but not before God. For what does the Scripture say? 'Abraham believed God, and it was accounted to him for righteousness.' Now to him who works, the wages are not counted as grace but as debt. But to him who does not work but believes on Him who justifies the ungodly, his faith is accounted for righteousness, just as David also describes the blessedness of the man to whom God imputes righteousness apart from works: 'Blessed are those whose lawless deeds are forgiven, and whose sins are covered; blessed is the man to whom the Lord shall not impute sin' " (*Romans* 4:1-8).

iv. "For the promise that he would be the heir of the world was not to Abraham or to his seed through the law, but through the righteousness of faith. For if those who are of the law are heirs, faith is made void and the promise made of no effect, because the law brings about wrath; for where there is no law there is no transgression. Therefore it is of faith that it might be according to grace, so that the promise might be sure to all the seed, not only to those who are of the law, but also to those who are of the faith of Abraham, who is the father of us all" (*Romans* 4:13-16).

v. "For they being ignorant of God's righteousness, and seeking to establish their own righteousness, have not submitted to the righteousness of God. For Christ is the end of the law for righteousness to everyone who believes. For Moses writes about the right-

CHRISTIANITY & NEO-LIBERALISM

eousness which is of the law, 'The man who does those things shall live by them.' But the righteousness of faith speaks in this way, 'Do not say in your heart, "Who will ascend into Heaven?"' (that is, to bring Christ down from above) or, ' "Who will descend into the abyss?"' (that is, to bring Christ up from the dead). But what does it say? 'The word is near you, in your mouth and in your heart' (that is, the word of faith which we preach): that if you confess with your mouth the Lord Jesus and believe in your heart that God has raised Him from the dead, you will be saved" (*Romans* 10:3-9).

vi. "Knowing that a man is not justified by the works of the law but by faith in Jesus Christ, even we have believed in Christ Jesus, that we might be justified by faith in Christ and not by the works of the law; for by the works of the law no flesh shall be justified" (*Galatians* 2:16).

vii. "Yet the law is not of faith, but 'the man who does them shall live by them'" (*Galatians* 3:11).

b. Thus the Westminster Standards affirm:

i. "Those whom God effectually calls, He also freely justifieth; not by infusing righteousness into them, but by pardoning their sins, and by accounting and accepting their persons as righteous; not for any thing wrought in them, or done by them, but for Christ's

404

sake alone; nor by imputing faith itself, the act of believing, or any other evangelical obedience to them, as their righteousness; but by imputing the obedience and satisfaction of Christ unto them, they receiving and resting on Him and His righteousness by faith; which faith they have not of themselves, it is the gift of God" (WCF XI:1).

ii. "...true believers be not under the law, as a covenant of works, to be thereby justified, or condemned..." (WCF XIX:6).

4. The sole basis of our justification, the only basis on which we can enter the Kingdom of Heaven, is the real and personal righteousness of Christ our perfect substitute, imputed to sinners by grace through faith, apart from the law.

a. Thus the Scriptures teach:

i. "He shall see the labor of His soul, and be satisfied. By His knowledge My righteous Servant shall justify many, for He shall bear their iniquities" (*Isaiah* 53:11).

ii. "In His days Judah will be saved, and Israel will dwell safely; now this is His name by which He will be called: THE LORD OUR RIGHTEOUSNESS" (*Jeremiah* 23:6).

iii. "For if by the one man's offense death reigned through the one, much more those who receive abundance of grace and of the gift of righteousness will reign in life through the One, Jesus Christ. Therefore, as through one man's offense judgment came to all men, resulting in condemnation, even so through one Man's righteous act the free gift came to all men, resulting in justification of life. For as by one man's disobedience many were made sinners, so also by one Man's obedience many will be made righteous" (*Romans* 5:17-19).

iv. "For by grace you have been saved through faith, and that not of yourselves; it is the gift of God, not of works, lest anyone should boast" (*Ephesians* 2:8-9).

v. "God was in Christ reconciling the world to Himself, not imputing their trespasses to them, and has committed to us the word of reconciliation. Now then, we are ambassadors for Christ, as though God were pleading through us: we implore you on Christ's behalf, be reconciled to God. For He made Him who knew no sin to be sin for us, that we might become the righteousness of God in Him" (*2 Corinthians* 5:19-21).

vi. "And be found in Him, not having my own righteousness, which is from the law, but that which is through faith in Christ, the righteousness which is from God by faith" (*Philippians* 3:9).

vii. "Not by works of righteousness which we have done, but according to His mercy He saved us, through the washing of regeneration and renewing of the Holy Spirit, whom He poured out on us abundantly through

Jesus Christ our Savior, that having been justified by His grace we should become heirs according to the hope of eternal life" (*Titus* 3:5-7).

b. Thus the Westminster Standards affirm:

   i. "Faith, thus receiving and resting on Christ and His righteousness, is the alone instrument of justification: yet is it not alone in the person justified, but is ever accompanied with all other saving graces, and is no dead faith, but worketh by love" (WCF XI:2).

   ii. "Christ by His obedience and death, did fully discharge the debt of all those that are thus justified, and did make a proper, real, and full satisfaction to His Father's justice in their behalf. Yet, in as much as He was given by the Father for them; and His obedience and satisfaction accepted in their stead; and both, freely, not for any thing in them; their justification is only of free grace; that both the exact justice, and rich grace of God might be glorified in the justification of sinners" (WCF XI:3).

   iii. "Q: What is Justification? A: Justification is an act of God's free grace, wherein He pardoneth all our sins, and accepteth us as righteous in his sight, only for the righteousness of Christ imputed to us, and received by faith alone" (WSC 33).

5. God declares the sinner righteous at conversion, imputing the perfect righteousness of Christ to him. Our justification is complete and final at conversion.

   a. Thus the Scriptures teach:

      i. "Therefore let it be known to you, brethren, that through this Man is preached to you the forgiveness of sins; and by Him everyone who believes is justified from all things from which you could not be justified by the law of Moses" (*Acts* 13:38-39).

      ii. "That is why his faith was 'counted to him as righteousness.' But the words 'it was counted to him' were not written for his sake alone, but for ours also. It will be counted to us who believe in him who raised from the dead Jesus our Lord, who was delivered up for our trespasses and raised for our justification. Therefore, since we have been justified by faith, we have peace with God through our Lord Jesus Christ. Through him we have also obtained access by faith into this grace in which we stand, and we rejoice in hope of the glory of God" (*Romans* 4:22-5:2, ESV).

      iii. "What then shall we say to these things? If God is for us, who can be against us? He who did not spare His own Son, but delivered Him up for us all, how shall He not with Him also freely give us all things? Who shall bring a charge against God's elect? It is God who justifies. Who is he who condemns? It is Christ who died, and furthermore is also risen, who is even at the right hand of God, who also makes intercession for us. Who shall separate us from the love of Christ?" (*Romans* 8:31-35).

iv. "That in the ages to come He might show the exceeding riches of His grace in His kindness toward us in Christ Jesus. For by grace you have been saved through faith, and that not of yourselves; it is the gift of God, not of works, lest anyone should boast" (*Ephesians* 2:7-9).

b. Thus the Westminster Standards affirm:

i. "God did, from all eternity, decree to justify all the elect, and Christ did, in the fullness of time, die for their sins, and rise again for their justification: nevertheless, they are not justified, until the Holy Spirit doth, in due time, actually apply Christ unto them" (WCF XI:4).

6. On the Day of Judgment, God will openly acknowledge and acquit His elect, affirming the forensic declaration of their justification that took place once and for all at conversion. At the Judgment we shall stand at Christ's right hand on the basis of His righteousness alone.

a. Thus the Scriptures teach:

i. "Therefore whoever confesses Me before men, him I will also confess before My Father who is in heaven" (*Matthew* 10:32).

    ii. "Most assuredly, I say to you, he who hears My word and believes in Him who sent Me has everlasting life, and shall not come into judgment, but has passed from death into life" (*John* 5:24).

    iii. "Being justified freely by His grace through the redemption that is in Christ Jesus, whom God set forth as a propitiation by His blood, through faith, to demonstrate His righteousness, because in His forbearance God had passed over the sins that were previously committed" (*Romans* 3:24-25).

    iv. "And He will set the sheep on His right hand, but the goats on the left. Then the King will say to those on His right hand, 'Come, you blessed of My Father, inherit the kingdom prepared for you from the foundation of the world.'...And these will go away into everlasting punishment, but the righteous into eternal life" (*Matthew* 25:33-34, 46).

  b. Thus the Westminster Standards affirm:

    i. "Q: What shall be done to the righteous at the Day of Judgment? A: At the day of judgment, the righteous, being caught up to Christ in the clouds, shall be set on his right hand, and there openly acknowledged and acquitted, shall join with him in the judging of reprobate angels and men, and shall be received into Heaven, where they shall be fully and for ever freed from all sin and misery; filled with inconceivable joys, made perfectly holy and happy both in body and soul, in the company of innumerable saints and holy angels, but especially in the immediate vision and fruition of God the Father, of our Lord Jesus Christ, and of the Holy Spirit, to all eternity. And this is the perfect and full communion, which the members of the invisible church shall enjoy with Christ in glory, at the resurrection and day of judgment" (WLC 90).

7. Obedience is required of believers, and the grace of sanctification does work obedience in us. But that obedience cannot, and need not, qualify us for any further justification at the Day of Judgment. In sanctification sin is subdued, but not perfectly in this life because the remnants of it abide in every part of us until we are glorified. Our good works, done in obedience to God's commandments, though imperfect in this life, are the fruits and evidences of saving faith.

a. Thus the Scriptures teach:

i. "Knowing this, that our old man was crucified with Him, that the body of sin might be done away with, that we should no longer be slaves of sin" (*Romans* 6:6).

ii. "For sin shall not have dominion over you, for you are not under law but under grace" (*Romans* 6:14).

iii. "The Spirit Himself bears witness with our spirit that we are children of God, and if children, then heirs – heirs of God and joint heirs with Christ, if indeed we suffer with

411

Him, that we may also be glorified to-gether" (*Romans* 8:16-17).

iv. "Not that I have already attained, or am al-ready perfected; but I press on, that I may lay hold of that for which Christ Jesus has also laid hold of me. Brethren, I do not count myself to have apprehended; but one thing I do, forgetting those things which are behind and reaching forward to those things which are ahead, I press toward the goal for the prize of the upward call of God in Christ Jesus" (*Philippians* 3:12-14).

v. "For I know whom I have believed and am persuaded that He is able to keep what I have committed to Him until that Day" (*2 Timothy* 1:12).

vi. "Therefore we also, since we are surrounded by so great a cloud of witnesses, let us lay aside every weight, and the sin which so easily ensnares us, and let us run with en-durance the race that is set before us, looking unto Jesus, the author and finisher of our faith, who for the joy that was set before Him endured the cross, despising the shame, and has sat down at the right hand of the throne of God" (*Hebrews* 12:1-2).

vii. "To the general assembly and church of the firstborn, which are written in Heaven, and to God the Judge of all, and to the spirits of just men made perfect" (*Hebrews* 12:23).

viii. "But someone will say, 'You have faith, and I have works.' Show me your faith without your works, and I will show you my faith by my works.... Do you see that faith was working together with his works, and by works faith was made perfect? And the Scripture was fulfilled which says, 'Abraham believed God, and it was accounted to him for righteousness'" (*James* 2:18, 22-23).

ix. "If we say that we have no sin, we deceive ourselves, and the truth is not in us. If we confess our sins, He is faithful and just to forgive us our sins and to cleanse us from all unrighteousness. If we say that we have not sinned, we make Him a liar, and His word is not in us. My little children, these things I write to you, so that you may not sin. And if anyone sins, we have an Advocate with the Father, Jesus Christ the righteous. And He Himself is the propitiation for our sins, and not for ours only but also for the whole world" (*I John* 1:8-2:2).

b. Thus the Westminster Standards affirm:

i. "Q: Wherein do justification and sanctification differ? A: Although sanctification be inseparably joined with justification, yet they differ, in that God in justification imputeth the righteousness of Christ; in sanctification his Spirit infuseth grace, and enableth to the exercise thereof; in the former, sin is pardoned; in the other, it is subdued: the one doth equally free all believers from the revenging wrath of God, and that perfectly

in this life, that they never fall into condemnation; the other is neither equal in all,
nor in this life perfect in any, but growing up
to perfection" (WLC 77).

ii. "Q: Whence ariseth the imperfection of
sanctification in believers? A: The imperfection of sanctification in believers ariseth
from the remnants of sin abiding in every
part of them, and the perpetual lustings of
the flesh against the spirit; whereby they are
often foiled with temptations, and fall into
many sins, are hindered in all their spiritual
services, and their best works are imperfect
and defiled in the sight of God" (WLC 78).

iii. "These good works, done in obedience to
God's commandments, are the fruits and evidences of a true and lively faith" (WCF XVI:2).

iv. "The bodies of men, after death, return to
dust, and see corruption: but their souls,
which neither die nor sleep, having an immortal subsistence, immediately return to
God who gave them: the souls of the righteous, being then made perfect in holiness,
are received into the highest heavens, where
they behold the face of God, in light and
glory, waiting for the full redemption of their
bodies" (WCF XXXII:1).

F. The Dangers of an "Unclear Call"

The Advisory Committee which considered the case
in question admitted, in every one of their four "Concluding Observations," that the teaching embodied in

414

the documents before them had been deficient. They stated that the "words are not as clear and helpful as they should be"[9] and the "teaching has not been as clear as should be expected."[10]

The Advisory Committee also noted the confusing use of the word justification, which our standards use only for God's act "when a sinner first believes," and the phrase "openly acknowledged and acquitted" to refer to the result of the judgment of the last day for the righteous. The teachings before them, the Committee pointed out, occasionally use "the word justified to refer to what happens to the righteous at the last judgment."[11] They mildly observed also that "it is highly desirable ordinarily to use the words of our standards in speaking of these matters. Clarity in the defense of the essential Protestant doctrine of justification by faith alone requires (emphasis ours) that we use different words for different things."[12] The Committee further stated that the "teaching taken as a whole (emphasis ours) is less clear in this respect than is desirable for effective instruction."[13] Whatever may be the reasons for the failure to observe this necessity, the result is utter confusion concerning the place of works in one's entrance into the Kingdom of Heaven.

These admissions by the Advisory Committee, and the later implicit acceptance of them by the General

---

9.   Advisory Committee, "Concluding Observations," item 1.

10. Advisory Committee, "Concluding Observations," item 2.

11. Advisory Committee, "Concluding Observations," item 3.

12. Advisory Committee, "Concluding Observations," item 3.

13. Advisory Committee, "Concluding Observations," item 4.

Assembly in its decision, fly in the face of God's own stern warning to those who speak in any language: "If the trumpet does not sound a clear call, who will get ready for battle? So it is with you. Unless you speak intelligible words with your tongue, how will anyone know what you are saying?" (*1 Corinthians* 14:8-9, NIV;) the ESV has "give an indistinct sound"; the KJV has "makes an uncertain sound").

By sustaining the appeal without any exceptions whatsoever, the 70th General Assembly gave implicit approval to the entire position of the appeal. It should be noted that even the Advisory Committee's mild reservations noted above were not actions of the Assembly.

The overall position of the appeal having been fully cleared, other persons may assume, at least for the present, that they may expound freely the teachings set forth in the original statements from which the judicial case resulted.

The confused statements contained in the evidence, the Advisory Committee's confusing approval of the appeal despite their admissions that the statements are deficient, and the sustaining of the appeal by the General Assembly without comment upon or correction of those teachings, have proved to be confusing to many observers both within and outside the Orthodox Presbyterian Church. It is always incumbent on the Church to protect itself from misunderstandings or mistaken judgments and to clear its good name and its witness to the faith. That is especially so when the matter is such a basic doctrine as justification by faith alone.

The 70th (2003) General Assembly has sounded an unclear call regarding the doctrine of justification. The 71st (2004) General Assembly should state to the Church and the public clearly, in unmistakable language, its position that entrance into the Kingdom of Heaven is completely and solely on the basis of the substitutionary work of Jesus Christ, received by faith alone, works having no place in God's judicial act of justification. At the same time the Church should take steps to prevent recurrence of the error.

IV. CONCLUSION

Given the fact that confusion on the doctrine of justification has arisen in the Church, and given the fact that the doctrine of justification is one upon which the Church stands or falls, it is now the responsibility of this 71st General Assembly to both clarify the witness of the Church, and to comfort, protect, and edify the sheep of the flock, by adopting this overture.

Respectfully submitted (signed),

Chad E. Bond (except section IV.E.1.a.ii above)
Paul M. Elliott
John P. Galbraith
Carl W. Hayes
Joel C. Kershner
Arthur W. Kuschke
Jeffery A. Sheely
A. Craig Troxel (except section IV.E.1.a.ii above)
Brian T. Wingard

Scripture Index

Index

The Crisis of Our Time

HISTORIANS have christened the thirteenth century the Age of Faith and termed the eighteenth century the Age of Reason. The present age has been called many things: the Atomic Age, the Age of Inflation, the Age of the Tyrant, the Age of Aquarius; but it deserves one name more than the others: the Age of Irrationalism. Contemporary secular intellectuals are anti-intellectual. Contemporary philosophers are anti-philosophy. Contemporary theologians are anti-theology.

In past centuries, secular philosophers have generally believed that knowledge is possible to man. Consequently they expended a great deal of thought and effort trying to justify knowledge. In the twentieth century, however, the optimism of the secular philosophers all but disappeared. They despaired of knowledge.

Like their secular counterparts, the great theologians and doctors of the church taught that knowledge is possible to man. Yet the theologians of the present age also repudiated that belief. They too despaired of knowledge. This radical skepticism has penetrated our entire culture, from television to music to literature. *The Christian at the beginning of the twenty-first century is confronted with an overwhelming cultural consensus – sometimes stated explicitly but most often implicitly: Man does not and cannot know anything truly.*

What does this have to do with Christianity? Simply this: If man can know nothing truly, man can truly know nothing. We cannot know that the Bible is the Word of God, that Christ died for his people, or that Christ is alive today at the right hand of the Father. Unless knowledge is possible, Christianity is nonsensical, for it claims to be knowledge. What is at stake at the beginning of the twenty-first century is not simply a single doctrine, such as the virgin birth, or the existence of Hell as important as those doctrines may be, but the whole of Christianity itself. If knowledge is not possible to man, it is worse than silly to argue points of doctrine – it is insane.

The irrationalism of the present age is so thoroughgoing and pervasive that even the Remnant – the segment of the professing church that remains faithful – has accepted much of it, frequently without even being aware of what it is accepting. In some religious circles this irrationalism has become synonymous with piety and humility, and those who oppose it are denounced as rationalists, as though to be logical were a sin. Our contemporary anti-theologians make a contradiction and call it a Mystery. The faithful ask for truth and are given Paradox and Antinomy. If any balk at swallowing the absurdities of the anti-theologians who teach in the seminaries or have graduated from the seminaries, they are frequently marked as heretics or schismatics who seek to act independently of God.

There is no greater threat facing the church of Christ at this moment than the irrationalism that now controls our entire culture. Totalitarianism, guilty of tens of millions of murders – including those of millions of Christians – is to be feared, but not nearly so much as the idea that we do not and cannot know the literal truth. Hedonism, the popular philosophy of America, is not to be feared so much as the belief that logic – that "mere human logic," to use the religious irrationalists' own phrase – is futile. The attacks on truth, on knowledge, on propositional revelation, on the intellect, on words, and on logic are renewed daily. But note well: The misologists – the haters of logic – use logic to demonstrate the futility of using logic. The anti-intellectuals construct intricate intellectual arguments to prove the insufficiency of the intellect. Those who deny the competence of words to express thought use words to express their thoughts. The proponents of poetry, myth, metaphor, and analogy argue for their theories by using literal prose, whose competence – even whose possibility – they deny. The anti-theologians use the revealed Word of God to show that there can be no revealed Word of God – or that if there could, it would remain impenetrable darkness and Mystery to our finite minds.

Nonsense Has Come

Is it any wonder that the world is grasping at straws – the straws of experientialism, mysticism, and drugs? After all, if people are told that the Bible contains insoluble mysteries, then is not a flight into mysticism to be expected? On what grounds can it be condemned? Certainly not on logical grounds or Biblical grounds, if logic is futile and the Bible unknowable. Moreover, if it cannot be condemned on logical or Biblical grounds, it cannot be condemned at all. If people are going to have a religion of the mysterious, they will not adopt Christianity: They will have a genuine mystery religion. The popularity of mysticism, drugs, and religious experience is the logical consequence of the irrationalism of the present age. There can and will be no Christian reformation – and no restoration of a free society – unless and until the irrationalism of the age is totally repudiated by Christians.

The Church Defenseless

Yet how shall they do it? The official spokesmen for Christianity have been fatally infected with irrationalism. The seminaries, which annually train thousands of men to teach millions of Christians, are the finishing schools of irrationalism, completing the job begun by the government schools and colleges. Most of the pulpits of the conservative churches (we are not speaking of the obviously apostate churches) are occupied by graduates of the anti-theological schools. These products of modern anti-theological education, when asked to give a reason for the hope that is in them, can generally respond with only the intellectual analogue of a shrug – a mumble about Mystery. They have not grasped – and therefore cannot teach those for whom they are responsible – the first truth: "And you shall know the truth." Many, in fact, explicitly contradict Christ, saying that, at best, we possess only "pointers" to the truth, or something "similar" to the truth, a mere analogy. Is the impotence of the Christian church a puzzle? Is the fascination with Pentecostalism, faith healing, Eastern Orthodoxy, and Roman Catholicism – all sensate and anti-intellectual religions – among members of Christian churches an enigma? Not when one understands the pious nonsense that is purveyed in the name of God in the religious colleges and seminaries.

The Trinity Foundation

The creators of The Trinity Foundation firmly believe that theology is too important to be left to the licensed theologians – the graduates of the schools of theology. They have created The Trinity Foundation for the express purpose of teaching believers all that the Scriptures con-

CHRISTIANITY & NEO-LIBERALISM

tain – not warmed over, baptized, Antichristian philosophies. Each member of the board of directors of The Trinity
Foundation has signed this oath: "I believe that the Bible
alone and the Bible in its entirety is the Word of God and,
therefore, inerrant in the autographs. I believe that the
system of truth presented in the Bible is best summarized
in the *Westminster Confession of Faith*. So help me God."

The ministry of The Trinity Foundation is the presentation of the system of truth taught in Scripture as clearly
and as completely as possible. We do not regard obscurity
as a virtue, nor confusion as a sign of spirituality. Confusion, like all error, is sin, and teaching that confusion is all
that Christians can hope for is doubly sin.

The presentation of the truth of Scripture necessarily involves the rejection of error. The Foundation has exposed
and will continue to expose the irrationalism of the present
age, whether its current spokesman be an existentialist
philosopher or a professed Reformed theologian. We oppose anti-intellectualism, whether it be espoused by a Neo-
orthodox theologian or a fundamentalist evangelist. We
reject misology, whether it be on the lips of a Neo-evangelical or those of a Roman Catholic Charismatic. We repu-
diate agnosticism, whether it be secular or religious. To
each error we bring the brilliant light of Scripture, proving
all things, and holding fast to that which is true.

The Primacy of Theory

The ministry of The Trinity Foundation is not a "practical" ministry. If you are a pastor, we will not enlighten
you on how to organize an ecumenical prayer meeting in
your community or how to double church attendance in a
year. If you are a homemaker, you will have to read else-

where to find out how to become a total woman. If you are a businessman, we will not tell you how to develop a social conscience. The professing church is drowning in such "practical" advice.

The Trinity Foundation is unapologetically theoretical in its outlook, believing that theory without practice is dead, and that practice without theory is blind. The trouble with the professing church is not primarily in its practice, but in its theory. Churchgoers and teachers do not know, and many do not even care to know, the doctrines of Scripture. Doctrine is intellectual, and churchgoers and teachers are generally anti-intellectual. Doctrine is ivory tower philosophy, and they scorn ivory towers. The ivory tower, however, is the control tower of a civilization. It is a fundamental, theoretical mistake of the "practical" men to think that they can be merely practical, for practice is always the practice of some theory. The relationship between theory and practice is the relationship between cause and effect. If a person believes correct theory, his practice will tend to be correct. The practice of contemporary Christians is immoral because it is the practice of false theories. It is a major theoretical mistake of the "practical" men to think that they can ignore the ivory towers of the philosophers and theologians as irrelevant to their lives. Every action that "practical" men take is governed by the thinking that has occurred in some ivory tower – whether that tower be the British Museum; the Academy; a home in Basel, Switzerland; or a tent in Israel.

In Understanding Be Men

It is the first duty of the Christian to understand correct theory – correct doctrine – and thereby implement correct

459

practice. This order – first theory, then practice – is both logical and Biblical. It is, for example, exhibited in Paul's *Epistle to the Romans,* in which he spends the first eleven chapters expounding theory and the last five discussing practice. The contemporary teachers of Christians have not only reversed the Biblical order, they have inverted the Pauline emphasis on theory and practice. The virtually complete failure of the teachers of the professing church to instruct believers in correct doctrine is the cause of the misconduct and spiritual and cultural impotence of Christians. The church's lack of power is the result of its lack of truth. The *Gospel* is the power of God, not religious experiences or personal relationships. The church has no power because it has abandoned the Gospel, the good news, for a religion of experientialism. Twenty-first-century American churchgoers are children carried about by every wind of doctrine, not knowing what they believe, or even if they believe anything for certain.

The chief purpose of The Trinity Foundation is to counteract the irrationalism of the age and to expose the errors of the teachers of the church. Our emphasis – on the Bible as the sole source of knowledge, on the primacy of truth, on the supreme importance of correct doctrine, and on the necessity for systematic and logical thinking – is almost unique. To the extent that the church survives – and she will survive and flourish – it will be because of her increasing acceptance of these basic ideas and their logical implications.

We believe that The Trinity Foundation is filling a vacuum. We are saying that Christianity is intellectually defensible – that, in fact, it is the only intellectually defensible system of thought. We are saying that God has made the wisdom of this world – whether that wisdom be called science, religion, philosophy, or common sense – foolishness. We are appealing to all Christians who have not conceded defeat in the intellectual battle with the world to join us in our efforts to raise a standard to which all men of sound mind can repair.

The love of truth, of God's Word, has all but disappeared in our time. We are committed to and pray for a great instauration. But though we may not see this reformation in our lifetimes, we believe it is our duty to present the whole counsel of God, because Christ has commanded it. The results of our teaching are in God's hands, not ours. Whatever those results, his Word is never taught in vain, but always accomplishes the result that he intended it to accomplish. Professor Gordon H. Clark has stated our view well:

> There have been times in the history of God's people, for example, in the days of Jeremiah, when refreshing grace and widespread revival were not to be expected: The time was one of chastisement. If this twentieth century is of a similar nature, individual Christians here and there can find comfort and strength in a study of God's Word. But if God has decreed happier days for us, and if we may expect a world-shaking and genuine spiritual awakening, then it is the author's belief that a zeal for souls, however necessary, is not the sufficient condition. Have there not been devout saints in every age, numerous enough to carry on a revival? Twelve such persons are plenty. What distinguishes the arid ages from the period of the Reformation, when nations were moved as they had not been since Paul preached in Ephesus, Corinth, and Rome, is the latter's fullness of knowledge of God's Word. To echo an early Reformation thought,

when the ploughman and the garage attendant know the Bible as well as the theologian does, and know it better than some contemporary theologians, then the desired awakening shall have already occurred.

In addition to publishing books, The Trinity Foundation publishes a monthly newsletter, *The Trinity Review.* Subscriptions to *The Review* are free to U.S. addresses; please write to the address on the order form to become a subscriber. If you would like further information or would like to support us in our work, please let us know.

The Trinity Foundation is a non-profit foundation, tax exempt under section 501(c)(3) of the Internal Revenue Code of 1954. You can help us disseminate the Word of God through your tax-deductible contributions to the Foundation.

JOHN W. ROBBINS

Intellectual Ammunition

The Trinity Foundation is committed to bringing every philosophical and theological thought captive to Christ. The books listed below are designed to accomplish that goal. They are written with two subordinate purposes: (1) to demolish all non-Christian claims to knowledge; and (2) to build a system of truth based upon the Bible alone.

Philosophy

Ancient Philosophy

Gordon H. Clark   Trade paperback $24.95

This book covers the thousand years from the Pre-Socratics to Plotinus. It represents some of the early work of Dr. Clark – the work that made his academic reputation. It is an excellent college text.

Behaviorism and Christianity

Gordon H. Clark   Trade paperback $5.95

Behaviorism is a critique of both secular and religious behaviorists. It includes chapters on John Watson, Edgar S. Singer, Jr., Gilbert Ryle, B. F. Skinner, and Donald MacKay. Clark's refutation of behaviorism and his argument for a Christian doctrine of man are unanswerable.

Christ and Civilization

John W. Robbins   Trade paperback $3.95

Civilization as we know it is a result of the widespread proclamation and belief of the Gospel of justification by faith alone in the sixteenth century. Christ foretold this result in the Sermon on the Mount: "Seek first the Kingdom of God and his righteousness, and all these things will be added to you."

This brief overview of the history of western civilization makes it clear that our cultural debt is to the Gospel, not to Greece and Rome.

Christian Philosophy   Hardback $29.95
Gordon H. Clark   Trade paperback $21.95

This book, Volume 4 in *The Works of Gordon Haddon Clark*, combines three of his most important works in philosophy: *Three Types of Religious Philosophy*; *Religion, Reason and Revelation*; and *An Introduction to Christian Philosophy*. Together they constitute Dr. Clark's principal statement of his Christian philosophy.

A Christian Philosophy of Education   Hardback $18.95
Gordon H. Clark   Trade paperback $12.95

The first edition of this book was published in 1946. It sparked the contemporary interest in Christian schools. In the 1970s, Dr. Clark thoroughly revised and updated it, and it is needed now more than ever. Its chapters include: The Need for a World-View; The Christian World-View; The Alternative to Christian Theism; Neutrality; Ethics; The Christian Philosophy of Education; Academic Matters; and Kindergarten to University. Three appendices are included: The Relationship of Public Education to Christianity; A Protestant World-View; and Art and the Gospel. This is Volume 10 in *The Works of Gordon Haddon Clark*.

A Christian View of Men and Things   Hardback $29.95
Gordon H. Clark   Trade paperback $18.95
No other book achieves what *A Christian View* does: the presentation of Christianity as it applies to history, politics, ethics, science, religion, and epistemology. Dr. Clark's command of both worldly philosophy and Scripture is evident on every page, and the result is a breathtaking and invigorating challenge to the wisdom of this world. This is Volume 1 in *The Works of Gordon Haddon Clark*.

Clark Speaks from the Grave
Gordon H. Clark   Trade paperback $3.95
Dr. Clark chides some of his critics for their failure to defend Christianity competently. *Clark Speaks* is a stimulating and illuminating discussion of the errors of contemporary apologists.

Ecclesiastical Megalomania: The Economic and Political Thought of the Roman Catholic Church
John W. Robbins   Hardback $29.95
This detailed and thorough analysis and critique of the social teaching of the Roman Church-State is the only such book available by a Christian economist and political philosopher. The book's conclusions reveal the Roman Church-State to be an advocate of its own brand of faith-based fascism. *Ecclesiastical Megalomania* includes the complete text of the *Donation of Constantine* and Lorenzo Valla's exposé of the hoax.

Education, Christianity, and the State
J. Gresham Machen   Trade paperback $10.95
Machen was one of the foremost educators, theolo-

gians, and defenders of Christianity in the twentieth century. The author of several scholarly books, Machen saw clearly that if Christianity is to survive and flourish, a system of Christian schools must be established. This collection of essays and speeches captures his thoughts on education over nearly three decades.

Essays on Ethics and Politics
Gordon H. Clark   Trade paperback $10.95
   Dr. Clark's essays, written over the course of five decades, are a major statement of Christian ethics.

Gordon H. Clark: Personal Recollections
John W. Robbins, editor   Trade paperback $6.95
   Friends of Dr. Clark have written their recollections of the man. Contributors include family members, colleagues, students, and friends such as Harold Lindsell, Carl Henry, Ronald Nash, and Anna Marie Hager.

Historiography: Secular and Religious
Gordon H. Clark   Trade paperback $13.95
   In this masterful work, Dr. Clark applies his philosophy to the writing of history, examining all the major schools of historiography.

An Introduction to Christian Philosophy
Gordon H. Clark
   See *Christian Philosophy*.

Language and Theology
Gordon H. Clark   Trade paperback $9.95
   There were two main currents in twentieth-century philosophy – Language Philosophy and Existentialism.

Both were hostile to Christianity. Dr. Clark disposes of Language Philosophy in this brilliant critique of Bertrand Russell, Ludwig Wittgenstein, Rudolf Carnap, A. J. Ayer, Langdon Gilkey, and others.

Logic
Gordon H. Clark   Hardback $16.95
  Written as a textbook for Christian schools, *Logic* is another unique book from Dr. Clark's pen. His presentation of the laws of thought, which must be followed if Scripture is to be understood correctly, and which are found in Scripture itself, is both clear and thorough. *Logic* is an indispensable book for the thinking Christian.

Lord God of Truth, Concerning the Teacher
Gordon H. Clark and
Aurelius Augustine   Trade paperback $7.95
  This essay by Dr. Clark summarizes many of the most telling arguments against empiricism and defends the Biblical teaching that we know God and truth immediately. The dialogue by Augustine is a refutation of empirical language philosophy.

The Philosophy of Science and Belief in God
Gordon H. Clark   Trade paperback $8.95
  In opposing the contemporary idolatry of science, Dr. Clark analyzes three major aspects of science: the problem of motion, Newtonian science, and modern theories of physics. His conclusion is that science, while it may be useful, is always false; and he demonstrates its falsity in numerous ways. Since science is always false, it can offer no alternative to the Bible and Christianity.

Religion, Reason and Revelation
Gordon H. Clark   Trade paperback $10.95
   One of Dr. Clark's apologetical masterpieces, *Religion, Reason and Revelation* has been praised for the clarity of its thought and language. It includes these chapters: Is Christianity a Religion? Faith and Reason; Inspiration and Language; Revelation and Morality; and God and Evil. It is must reading for all serious Christians. Also see *Christian Philosophy.*

The Scripturalism of Gordon H. Clark
W. Gary Crampton   Trade paperback $9.95
   Dr. Crampton has written an introduction to the philosophy of Gordon H. Clark that is helpful to both beginners and advanced students of theology.

Thales to Dewey: A History of Philosophy   Hardback $29.95
Gordon H. Clark   Trade paperback $21.95
   This is the best one-volume history of philosophy in print. This is Volume 3 in *The Works of Gordon Haddon Clark.*

Three Types of Religious Philosophy
Gordon H. Clark
   See *Christian Philosophy.*

William James and John Dewey
Gordon H. Clark   Trade paperback $8.95
   William James and John Dewey are two of the most influential philosophers America has produced. Their philosophies of Instrumentalism and Pragmatism are hostile to Christianity, and Dr. Clark demolishes their arguments.

Without A Prayer: Ayn Rand and the Close of Her System
John W. Robbins   Hardback $27.95
  Ayn Rand has been a best-selling author since 1957.
Without A Prayer discusses Objectivism's epistemology,
theology, ethics, and politics in detail. Appendices include
analyses of books by Leonard Peikoff and David Kelley,
as well as several essays on Christianity and philosophy.

Theology

Against the Churches: The Trinity Review 1989-1998
John W. Robbins, editor   Oversize hardback $39.95
  This is the second volume of essays from *The Trinity
Review*, covering its second ten years, 1989-1998. This
volume, like the first, is fully indexed and is very useful
in research and in the classroom. Authors include: Gor-
don Clark, John Robbins, Charles Hodge, J. C. Ryle,
Horatius Bonar, and Robert L. Dabney.

Against the World: The Trinity Review 1978-1988
John W. Robbins, editor   Oversize hardback $34.95
  This is the first collection of essays published in *The
Trinity Review*, from 1978 to 1988, 70 in all. It is a valuable
source of information and arguments explaining and defending Christianity. Gordon Clark is the author of most
of the essays.

The Atonement
Gordon H. Clark   Trade paperback $8.95
  In *The Atonement,* Dr. Clark discusses the covenants,
the virgin birth and incarnation, federal headship and
representation, the relationship between God's sover-

eignty and justice, and much more. He analyzes traditional views of the atonement and criticizes them in the light of Scripture alone.

The Biblical Doctrine of Man
Gordon H. Clark   Trade paperback $6.95

Is man soul and body or soul, spirit, and body? What is the image of God? Is Adam's sin imputed to his children? Is evolution true? Are men totally depraved? What is the heart? These are some of the questions discussed and answered from Scripture in this book.

By Scripture Alone
W. Gary Crampton   Trade paperback $12.95

This is a clear and thorough explanation of the Scriptural doctrine of Scripture and a refutation of the recent Romanist attack on Scripture as the Word of God.

Can the Orthodox Presbyterian Church Be Saved?
John W. Robbins   Trade paperback $3.95

This small book, which demonstrates the central errors of OPC history and theology since the 1940s, is an alarm to awaken members of the OPC from their slumbers.

The Changing of the Guard
Mark W. Karlberg   Trade paperback $3.95

This essay is a critical discussion of Westminster Seminary's anti-Reformational and un-Biblical teaching on the doctrine of justification. Dr. Karlberg exposes the doctrine of justification by faith and works – not *sola fide* – taught at Westminster Seminary for the past

30 years, by Professors Norman Shepherd, Richard Gaffin, John Frame, and others.

Christianity and Neo-Liberalism: The Spiritual Crisis in the Orthodox Presbyterian Church and Beyond
Paul M. Elliott   Trade paperback $19.95
This massively-documented book details the influence Westminster Theological Seminary has had on the Orthodox Presbyterian Church and other churches and organizations. It is both a work of theological analysis and a call to action.

The Church Effeminate
John W. Robbins, editor   Hardback $29.95
This is a collection of 39 essays by the best theologians of the church on the doctrine of the church: Martin Luther, John Calvin, Benjamin Warfield, Gordon Clark, J. C. Ryle, and many more. The essays cover the structure, function, and purpose of the church.

The Clark-Van Til Controversy
Herman Hoeksema   Trade paperback $9.95
This collection of essays by the founder of the Protestant Reformed Churches – essays written at the time of the Clark-Van Til controversy in the 1940s – is one of the best commentaries on those events in print.

A Companion to The Current Justification Controversy
John W. Robbins   Trade paperback $9.95
This book includes documentary source material not available in *The Current Justification Controversy*, an essay tracing the origins and continuation of this controversy throughout American Presbyterian churches, and

an essay on the New Perspective on Paul by Robert L. Reymond.

Cornelius Van Til: The Man and The Myth
John W. Robbins   Trade paperback $2.45
   The actual teachings of this eminent Philadelphia theologian have been obscured by the myths that surround him. This book penetrates those myths and criticizes Van Til's surprisingly unorthodox views of God and the Bible.

The Current Justification Controversy
O. Palmer Robertson   Trade paperback $9.95
   From 1975 to 1982 a controversy over justification raged within Westminster Theological Seminary and the Philadelphia Presbytery of the Orthodox Presbyterian Church. As a member of the faculties of both Westminster and Covenant Seminaries during this period, O. Palmer Robertson was an important participant in this controversy. This is his account of the controversy, vital background for understanding the defection from the Gospel that is now widespread in Presbyterian churches.

The Everlasting Righteousness
Horatius Bonar   Trade paperback $8.95
   Originally published in 1874, the language of Bonar's masterpiece on justification by faith alone has been updated and Americanized for easy reading and clear understanding. This is one of the best books ever written on justification. See also *Not What My Hands Have Done*.

Faith and Saving Faith
Gordon H. Clark
   See *What Is Saving Faith?*

God and Evil: The Problem Solved
Gordon H. Clark   Trade paperback $5.95
   This volume is Chapter 5 of *Religion, Reason and Revelation*, in which Dr. Clark presents his solution to the problem of evil.

God-Breathed: The Divine Inspiration of the Bible
Louis Gaussen   Trade paperback $16.95
   Gaussen, a nineteenth-century Swiss Reformed pastor, comments on hundreds of passages in which the Bible claims to be the Word of God. This is a massive defense of the doctrine of the plenary and verbal inspiration of Scripture.

God's Hammer: The Bible and Its Critics
Gordon H. Clark   Trade paperback $10.95
   The starting point of Christianity, the doctrine on which all other doctrines depend, is "The Bible alone, and the Bible in its entirety, is the Word of God written, and, therefore, inerrant in the autographs." Over the centuries the opponents of Christianity, with Satanic shrewdness, have concentrated their attacks on the truthfulness and completeness of the Bible. In the twentieth century the attack was not so much in the fields of history and archaeology as in philosophy. Dr. Clark's brilliant defense of the complete truthfulness of the Bible is captured in this collection of eleven major essays.

The Holy Spirit
Gordon H. Clark   Trade paperback $8.95
   This discussion of the third person of the Trinity is both concise and exact. Dr. Clark includes chapters on the work of the Spirit, sanctification, and Pentecostalism.

The Incarnation

Gordon H. Clark   Trade paperback $8.95

Who is Christ? The attack on the doctrine of the Incarnation in the nineteenth and twentieth centuries was vigorous, but the orthodox response was lame. Dr. Clark reconstructs the doctrine of the Incarnation, building and improving upon the Chalcedonian definition.

The Johannine Logos

Gordon H. Clark   Trade paperback $5.95

Dr. Clark analyzes the relationship between Christ, who is the truth, and the Bible. He explains why John used the same word to refer to both Christ and his teaching. Chapters deal with the Prologue to John's Gospel; *Logos* and *Rheemata*; Truth; and Saving Faith. See also *What Is Saving Faith?*

Justification by Faith Alone

Charles Hodge   Trade paperback $10.95

Charles Hodge of Princeton Seminary was the best American theologian of the nineteenth century. Here, for the first time, are his two major essays on justification in one volume. This book is essential in defending the faith. See also *Not What My Hands Have Done.*

Karl Barth's Theological Method

Gordon H. Clark   Trade paperback $18.95

Karl Barth's Theological Method is perhaps the best critique of the Neo-orthodox theologian Karl Barth yet written. Dr. Clark discusses Barth's view of revelation, language, and Scripture, focusing on his method of writing theology, rather than presenting a comprehensive analysis of the details of Barth's theology.

Logical Criticisms of Textual Criticism
Gordon H. Clark   Trade paperback $3.25
    Dr. Clark's acute mind enables him to demonstrate the inconsistencies, assumptions, and flights of fancy that characterize the science of New Testament criticism. See also *Commentaries on Paul's Letters.*

Not Reformed at All
Medievalism in "Reformed" Churches
John Robbins and Sean Gerety   Trade paperback $9.95
    This book is a response to and refutation of Douglas Wilson's book *"Reformed" Is Not Enough: Recovering the Objectivity of the Covenant.* Wilson, one of the leading figures in the Neolegalist movement in Reformed and Presbyterian circles, attacked covenant theology and proposed a "visible, photographable" covenant which one enters by ritual baptism, making one a Christian. Salvation received in this way can be lost by one's own lack of performance or by action of authorized representatives of the church. This refutation of Wilson is a defense of the Biblical Covenant of Grace.

Not What My Hands Have Done
Charles Hodge, Horatius Bonar   Trade paperback $16.95
    This is the combined edition of *Justification by Faith Alone* (by Hodge) and *The Everlasting Righteousness* (by Bonar). Combined, these books offer both an introduction to and an in-depth discussion of the central doctrine of Christianity, justification by faith alone.

Predestination

Gordon H. Clark   Trade paperback $10.95

Dr. Clark thoroughly discusses one of the most controversial and pervasive doctrines of the Bible: that God is, quite literally, Almighty. Free will, the origin of evil, God's omniscience, creation, and the new birth are all presented within a Scriptural framework. The objections of those who do not believe in Almighty God are considered and refuted. This edition also contains the text of the booklet, *Predestination in the Old Testament.*

Sanctification

Gordon H. Clark   Trade paperback $8.95

In this book Dr. Clark discusses historical theories of sanctification, the sacraments, and the Biblical doctrine of sanctification.

Study Guide to the Westminster Confession

W. Gary Crampton   Oversize paperback $10.95

This *Study Guide* can be used by individuals or classes. It contains a paragraph-by-paragraph summary of the *Westminster Confession,* and questions for the student to answer. Space for answers is provided. The *Guide* will be most beneficial when used in conjunction with Dr. Clark's *What Do Presbyterians Believe?*

A Theology of the Holy Spirit

Frederick Dale Bruner   Trade paperback $16.95

First published in 1970, this book has been hailed by reviewers as "thorough," "fair," "comprehensive," "devastating," "the most significant book on the Holy Spirit," and "scholarly." Gordon Clark described this book in his own book *The Holy Spirit* as "a masterly and exceedingly well researched exposition of Pentecostalism. The documenttation is superb, as is also his penetrating analysis of their non-scriptural and sometimes contradictory conclusions." Unfortunately, the book is marred by the author's sacramentalism.

The Trinity
Gordon H. Clark   Trade paperback $8.95

Apart from the doctrine of Scripture, no teaching of the Bible is more fundamental than the doctrine of God. Dr. Clark's defense of the orthodox doctrine of the Trinity is a principal portion of his systematic theology. There are chapters on the Deity of Christ; Augustine; the Incomprehensibility of God; Bavinck and Van Til; and the Holy Spirit; among others.

What Calvin Says
W. Gary Crampton   Trade paperback $10.95

This is a clear, readable, and thorough introduction to the theology of John Calvin.

What Do Presbyterians Believe?
Gordon H. Clark   Trade paperback $10.95

This classic is the best commentary on the *Westminster Confession of Faith* yet written.

What Is Saving Faith?
Gordon H. Clark   Trade paperback $12.95

This is the combined edition of *Faith and Saving Faith* and *The Johannine Logos*. The views of the Roman Catholic Church, John Calvin, Thomas Manton, John Owen, Charles Hodge, and B. B. Warfield are discussed in this book. Is the object of faith a person or a proposition? Is faith more than belief? Is belief thinking with assent, as Augustine said? In a world chaotic with differing views of faith, Dr. Clark clearly explains the Biblical view of faith and saving faith.

In *The Johannine Logos*, Dr. Clark analyzes the relationship between Christ, who is the truth, and the Bible. He explains why John used the same word to refer to both Christ and his teaching. Chapters deal with the Prologue to John's Gospel; *Logos* and *Rheemata*; Truth; and Saving Faith.

Clark's Commentaries on the New Testament

Commentaries on Paul's Letters	Hardback	$29.95
(*Colossians, Ephesians, First and Second Thessalonians*)	Trade paperback	$21.95
First Corinthians	Trade paperback	$10.95
First John	Trade paperback	$10.95
New Heavens, New Earth (*First and Second Peter*)	Trade paperback	$10.95
The Pastoral Epistles	Hardback	$29.95
(1 and 2 *Timothy* and *Titus*)	Trade paperback	$14.95
Philippians	Trade paperback	$9.95

All of Clark's commentaries are expository, not technical, and are written for the Christian layman. His purpose is to explain the text clearly and accurately so that the Word of God will be thoroughly known by every Christian.

The Trinity Library

We will send you one copy of each of the books listed above for $500 (retail value $800), postpaid to any address in the U. S. You may also order the books you want individually on the order form on the next page. Because some of the books are in short supply, we must reserve the right to substitute others of equal or greater value in The Trinity Library. This special offer expires October 31, 2008.

Order Form

NAME _____

ADDRESS _____

_____

TELEPHONE _____

E-MAIL _____

Please:

❑ add my name to the mailing list for *The Trinity Review*. I understand that there is no charge for single copies of *The Review* sent to a U.S. address.

❑ accept my tax deductible contribution of $ _____ .

❑ send me ____ copies of *Christianity and Neo-Liberalism*. I enclose as payment U.S. $ _____.

❑ send me the Trinity Library. I enclose U.S. $500 as full payment.

❑ send me the following books. I enclose full payment in the amount of U.S. $ _____ for them.

_____

_____

_____

_____

The Trinity Foundation
Post Office Box 68
Unicoi, Tennessee 37692
Website: http://www.trinityfoundation.org/
United States of America

Shipping: Please add $6.00 for the first book, and 50 cents for each additional book. For foreign orders, please add $1.00 for each additional book.